BUSINESS RECORDS CONTROL

6th Edition

David G. Goodman, CRM

Professor, Business Education and
Office Administration
University of Wisconsin—Whitewater, Wisconsin

Joseph S. Fosegan

Department of Office and Reporting Technologies
School of Business Technologies
Alfred State College—Alfred, New York

Ernest D. Bassett

Analyst/Consultant, Records Systems
Santa Barbara, California

K14   *Published by*
SOUTH-WESTERN PUBLISHING CO.

CINCINNATI   WEST CHICAGO, IL   DALLAS   PELHAM MANOR, NY   LIVERMORE, CA

ISBN: 0-538-11140-2

Library of Congress Catalog Card Number: 85-61943

3 4 5 6 7 8 9 10 11 12 D 4 3 2 1 0 9 8

Printed in the United States of America

PREFACE

The 1980s have been referred to as the Information Age. Information management has moved high on the list of employment opportunities for people of all ages. The goal of BUSINESS RECORDS CONTROL, Sixth Edition, is to prepare students for an entry level position in records control, an important function in information management. Filing is a major element of records control. Upon completion of BUSINESS RECORDS CONTROL, Sixth Edition, students will be able to index, code, and file by four methods—alphabetic, subject, numeric, and geographic. Students will also be aware of recent technology advancements that apply to records control and will be able to apply records control procedures on the job.

In 1985, the Association of Records Managers and Administrators, Inc. (ARMA), published *Guidelines to Alphabetic Filing* to serve as the records management industry standard. The indexing rules in BUSINESS RECORDS CONTROL, Sixth Edition, are adaptations of ARMA's "Simplified Filing Standard Rules." Both teachers and students will be pleased with the consistency and directness of these rules and the ease with which they can be learned and applied.

The newest color-coded filing systems are illustrated and analyzed in the Sixth Edition. The latest advances in word processing and microcomputers and their impact on filing and retrieval are identified throughout the text. The methods used in indexing and storing magnetic media such as diskettes and tapes are described, as is the use of computers in maintaining indexes and in computer-assisted retrieval (CAR) systems. Micrographics, an increasingly used media for processing, storing, and retrieving information, is discussed as is the latest entrant in information processing—the optical data disk.

BUSINESS RECORDS CONTROL, Sixth Edition, is organized into six parts. Part 1—Introduction to Records Control, includes a dynamic overview of records control. Part 2—Alphabetic Indexing Rules and Procedures, supplies information needed to process business records in a controlled manner and includes the simplified indexing rules and procedures. Part 3—Alphabetic Filing Procedures and Controls, gives details of the structure of alphabetic filing systems and explains elements of control including requisitioning, charging, and following up; transfer, storage, and destruction; and the growing use of color in filing systems. Part 4—Other Filing Systems, describes filing systems and procedures for subject, numeric, and geographic filing. Part 5—Special Records Storage and Retrieval, explains storage and retrieval techniques for card and visible records and microcomputer, word processing, and micrographic records. Part 6—Records Control, gives an overview of the types of equipment used in business and industry. This part ends with specific practices and procedures necessary for maintaining and improving records control.

Each chapter opens with learning objectives that are correlated with the end-of-chapter activities. Important terms are printed in bold to emphasize their significance. At the end of each chapter, students have an opportunity to respond to Questions for Discussion, Applications, and Practice Set Jobs.

Two appendixes are included for additional information regarding the filing rules. Appendix A—Computer Indexing Considerations describes the changes that might be necessary for computer entry of the rules' examples presented in Chapters 2, 3, and 4. Appendix B—Alternate Indexing Rules contains frequently used alternate rules as reported in a survey of business offices conducted by the authors. The alternate rules are to be used as a reference only when confronted with business situations in which the simplified rules are not in use.

Accompanying BUSINESS RECORDS CONTROL, Sixth Edition, are two filing practice sets—OFFICE FILING PROCEDURES, Sixth Edition, and SIMPLIFILE, Third Edition. OFFICE FILING PROCEDURES, Sixth Edition, provides an indepth experience in records control. Students will work through jobs using alphabetic, subject, numeric, and geographic filing methods, as well as requisition, charge, and transfer procedures. SIMPLIFILE, Third Edition, gives students the opportunity to apply quickly the simplified filing rules using alphabetic, subject, numeric, and geographic filing methods. A Filing Placement Test and Final Examination are also available.

The first half of the Teacher's Manual for BUSINESS RECORDS CONTROL, Sixth Edition, contains teaching suggestions and answers to Questions for Discussion and Applications. The second half of the Teacher's Manual consists of the Manual for OFFICE FILING PROCEDURES, Sixth Edition, as well as the answers to the Filing Placement Test and Final Examination. Also, transparency masters, a valuable teaching aid, are provided at the back of the Teacher's Manual in this revised Sixth Edition. These transparency masters provide an opportunity to discuss various illustrations, the new simplified filing rules, and important records control procedures in detail.

BUSINESS RECORDS CONTROL, Sixth Edition, is a comprehensive records management text. It can be used, in part or totally, to satisfy a wide range of learning objectives. Nothing relevant in records control has been eliminated, and everything that is new has been added.

David G. Goodman
Joseph S. Fosegan
Ernest D. Bassett

CONTENTS

ACKNOWLEDGMENTS

For permission to reproduce the illustrations on the pages indicated, acknowledgment is made to the following:

Chapter 1

p. 4 (Illus. 1-1, upper left)	Permission from Supreme Equipment & Systems Corp.
p. 4 (Illus. 1-1, upper right)	Courtesy of Dennison National Co., Holyoke MA 01041
p. 4 (Illus. 1-1, lower left)	Photo courtesy of Fellowes Manufacturing Co.
p. 4 (Illus. 1-1, lower right)	Courtesy of Ring King Visibles, Inc.

Chapter 7

p. 90 (Illus. 7-5)	Photo courtesy of Fellowes Manufacturing Co.
p. 91 (Illus. 7-6)	Courtesy of Fellowes Manufacturing Co.

Chapter 8

p. 97	Jeter Systems Corporation
p. 99 (Illus. 8-1)	The Smead Manufacturing Company
p. 101 (Illus. 8-2)	Kardex Systems, Inc.
Color Illustration A	Jeter Systems Corporation
Color Illustration B	Photos courtesy of The Smead Manufacturing Company
Color Illustration C	Photos courtesy of Kardex Systems, Inc.
Color Illustration D	Shaw-Walker Co.

Chapter 10

p. 134 (Illus. 10-7)	USED WITH PERMISSION OF ESSELTE PENDEFLEX CORPORATION

Chapter 12

p. 164 (Illus. 12-6)	CENDEX® from Acme Visible Records
p. 165 (Illus. 12-7)	Kardex Systems, Inc.
p. 166 (Illus. 12-8)	Kardex Systems, Inc.
p. 167 (Illus. 12-9)	ACME VISIBLE RECORDS
p. 168 (Illus. 12-10)	Kardex Systems, Inc.
p. 171 (Illus. 12-13)	Delco Associates, Inc.

Chapter 13

p. 175 (Illus. 13-2)	Tab Products Co.
p. 177 (Illus. 13-3)	Sperry Univac Office Equipment Division
p. 179 (Illus. 13-4)	Spacesaver Corporation
p. 179 (Illus. 13-5)	Courtesy of Wright Line Inc., Worcester, Massachusetts
p. 183 (Illus. 13-8, upper left)	Photo courtesy of Fellowes Manufacturing Co.

p. 183 (Illus. 13-8, upper right) Photo courtesy of Fellowes Manufacturing Co.
p. 183 (Illus. 13-8, lower)   Courtesy of Dennison National Co., Holyoke MA 01041
p. 185 (Illus. 13-9)   CANON U.S.A., INC.
p. 185 (Illus. 13-10)   Minolta Corporation
p. 185 (Illus. 13-12)   Minolta Corporation
p. 190 (Illus. 13-17)   Photo courtesy of 3M Company

Chapter 14

p. 197 (Illus. 14-1)   Shaw-Walker Co.
p. 199 (Illus. 14-2)   Kardex Systems, Inc.
p. 200 (Illus. 14-3)   The HON Co., Division HON Industries
p. 202 (Illus. 14-5)   Rubbermaid® Commercial Products, Inc.
p. 203 (Illus. 14-6, 14-7)   Spacesaver Corporation
p. 203 (Illus. 14-8)   Spacesaver Corporation
p. 204 (Illus. 14-9)   ACME VISIBLE RECORDS
p. 205 (Illus. 14-10)   USED WITH PERMISSION OF ESSELTE PENDAFLEX
                                 CORPORATION
p. 207 (Illus. 14-11)   ACME VISIBLE RECORDS
p. 208 (Illus. 14-12)   Permission from Supreme Equipment & Systems Corp.
p. 209 (Illus. 14-13)   Kardex Systems, Inc.
p. 211 (Illus. 14-15)   Eastman Kodak Co., Business Imaging Systems Div.,
                                 Rochester NY
p. 212 (Illus. 14-16)   Eastman Kodak Co., Business Imaging Systems Div.,
                                 Rochester NY
p. 213 (Illus. 14-17)   Photo supplied by FileNet Corporation
p. 213 (Illus. 14-18)   Photo supplied by FileNet Corporation
p. 214 (Illus. 14-19)   Photo supplied by FileNet Corporation

For their cooperation and services, we would like to acknowledge Steve Jones and Robert Hight of Central Business Systems and Security Concepts, Cincinnati, OH.

PART 1

Introduction to Records Control

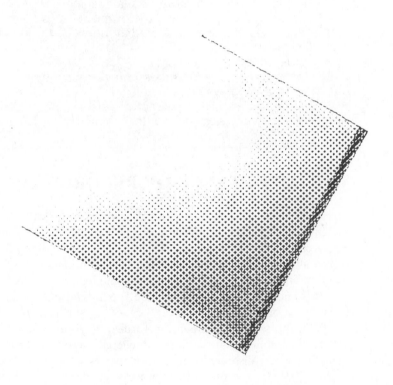

CHAPTER 1

A Preview of Records Control

Learning Objectives

After completing Chapter 1, you will be able to:

1. Explain the need for order in maintaining business information.
2. List the consequences of lost or misplaced records.
3. List the various records stored in the office for future reference.
4. Define filing.
5. Define records control.
6. Identify career opportunities in records control.
7. Define a filing system.
8. List three essential elements for establishing a filing system.
9. List the necessary controls for maintaining a filing system.

THE IMPORTANCE OF RECORDS CONTROL

I can't find it!

"I can't find it! I know it's here ... somewhere!" Who said that? A cook looking for a favorite recipe? A mechanic looking for a tool in the garage? A taxpayer looking for a receipt? Perhaps it is you looking for your favorite record album in a heap of records. Or is it a business executive looking for a letter, a report, or a statement of how much Georgina Andrews owes? "I can't find it! I know it's here ... somewhere!" Who said that? Just about *everybody* at one time or another.

At work, disorder is a CO$TLY matter.

Although we may tolerate a good deal of disorder in our personal lives, we are often annoyed at the time and energy wasted in looking for misplaced items. At work, disorder is another matter—a CO$TLY matter. A bank may handle 500,000 or more depositor cards. An airfreight line may generate 150,000 freight documents *a month*. An insurance company may handle over *a million* policies. Even a *small* hospital may maintain medical histories on 5,000 or more patient admissions a year. A staggering number of records, wouldn't you say? The offices in these organizations are responsible for maintaining and handling these important records so they are not lost, misplaced, or accidentally destroyed. Any disorder in handling these records is costly, if not disastrous. It is costly in terms of hours spent and stress created in search of a misplaced record. It is disastrous, perhaps, if the record is permanently lost or accidentally destroyed.

2

Many different kinds of records are kept.

Equally as amazing as the volume of records stored are the different kinds of records kept by various companies. Letters and memos, blueprints and maps, reports, inventory and price lists, purchase orders, shipping receipts, newspapers and catalogs, sales and personnel records, and computer printouts are just some familiar types of office records. New office techniques and equipment have created new kinds of office records—*paperless* records! Some of these paperless records include computer tapes, floppy disks, diskettes, cassette tapes, microforms (films on which a printed page is photographed in miniature), and X rays. Although these records are paperless, they must be held under control in filing systems. Illustration 1-1 shows how paperless records are stored in filing systems.

The variety and quantity of information and records handled in an office will vary from one organization to another. Common to all organizations, however, is the need to *store* and to *protect* these records and to *find* them when they are needed. **Filing** is defined as the process of storing many kinds of records for protection and for future reference. **Records control** is defined as the *systems and procedures* used to make filing a reliable and systematic process.

Filing is the process of storing records for protection and reference.

Filed information can be found quickly and easily because it is arranged in an orderly manner. Remember the last time you used the telephone directory? Without realizing it, perhaps, you made use of filing principles to find the information you needed. Telephone numbers are presented in an *alphabetic* listing of names. Businesses and services that advertise in the classified directory (Yellow Pages) are grouped *alphabetically* by occupation or subject. The area code numbers are listed in an *alphabetic* arrangement by state and city. So you see, you are already familiar with *alphabetic* indexing, the most frequently used filing arrangement in an office.

CAREER OPPORTUNITIES IN RECORDS CONTROL

The extent of records control work that is performed in business, industry, government, and professional offices is surprisingly great. In some organizations, records are controlled in a large *centralized* records department by a full-time records center supervisor and staff. The staff includes trained personnel with titles such as records analyst, records technician, records clerk, and administrative support worker. New records personnel must learn control procedures. The records manager is responsible for ensuring that established company control procedures are used by new employees (See Illustration 1-2).

In other organizations, *departmental* files staffed by records personnel are maintained in various offices and departments. Also, secretaries, bookkeepers, and general office workers all do some filing work and are a part of the overall records control system in the organization. Many office employees whose work is related to electronic data processing and microfilming are directly

Data Media Cabinets

Magnetic Tape Holder

Microfiche Holder

Diskette Rotary File

Illus. 1-1 Paperless Records Stored in Filing Systems

Illus. 1-2   A Records Manager Trains New Employees to Use Control Procedures

Over 90 percent of all office workers do some filing work.

involved in indexing and filing the records that are produced in their departments. In fact, studies show that filing and records control rank in the top 10 percent of all office activities and that over *90 percent of all office workers do some filing work.*

The field of records and information management is an expanding one. It involves the systematic control of all records and information in an organization. From their creation to their eventual disposition, records must be processed, distributed, organized, and retrieved. As more records are produced, more jobs are opened to qualified, well-trained people. The person who recognizes the importance of the filing function and chooses to study the field further may enjoy a variety of career opportunities in records management. The *Dictionary of Occupational Titles*, published by the U.S. Department of Labor, lists over 160 jobs that relate to records and records control.

There are a variety of career opportunities in records management.

The Association of Records Managers and Administrators, Inc. (ARMA), has published guidelines for a career path in the records and information management profession. Job descriptions range from records and information clerk to records and information manager. Your placement on the career ladder depends on your knowledge and experience in records and information management.

Although salaries for records managers may range from $20,000 to $45,000, those who seek records management positions must possess more than a desire for a good salary. Records managers are highly trained professionals who are familiar with all filing systems, equipment, and procedures. They keep up-to-date on all new developments in the field of records management and control. They are responsible for training records personnel to be accurate, neat, and orderly in their work. Records managers must convey enthusiasm and interest in this important office function. More than anything, they must appreciate and understand the need for order.

UNDERSTANDING RECORDS CONTROL

As a student of records control, you undoubtedly expect to do filing work someday. In order to establish or maintain a filing system, you will want to be familiar with the following aspects of records control:

Be familiar with the SECret of filing.

Systems of filing
Equipment and supplies
Controls for maintaining order in the filing system:
    Receiving, retrieving, releasing, and returning file materials
    Efficiency and economy controls
    Transfer and/or disposition of inactive materials

The SECret of filing lies in understanding each of these important areas. *Systems of filing* and *Equipment and supplies* are essential for establishing the file. *Controls* are necessary to maintain order in any filing system. Following is a preview of these three major topics that you will study in this course.

Systems of Filing

The term **filing system** refers to the orderly or systematic arrangement of office records in suitable containers so that information can be found quickly and easily. Office records are most commonly arranged by alphabet or by number. You will study alphabetic and numeric filing systems, as well as systems organized around geographic names and subject titles. You will learn how these filing systems contribute to the information storage and retrieval (finding) needs of an organization.

Equipment and Supplies

Filing equipment and supplies are many and varied.

The kinds of filing equipment and supplies that are needed to maintain a filing system are many and varied. This is true because business operations differ from one company to another. Filing systems must be geared to the needs of each company. Office layout and design, the kinds and volume of records kept, and an ever-increasing concern for reducing filing costs all affect the filing equipment and supplies to be used. You will want to become familiar with some of the equipment and supplies that support the filing system.

The vertical file cabinet is still the most common piece of filing equipment in the office. However, the traditional manila file folders in the familiar file drawers are making way to a new look: colored folders (sometimes plastic, reusable folders) on open shelves (See Illustration 1-3).

Available to protect and to hold the paperless records created by computers, text-editing typewriters, and microform printers are filing cabinets,

Vertical File   Open-Shelf File

Illus. 1-3   Types of Files

fan-styled albums, pocket binders, rotary stands, and divided tray files (See Illustration 1-1, page 4).

"Spin your files, not your heels," claim manufacturers of power files. Mechanical filing equipment comes in a variety of shapes and sizes: revolving tubs, wheel files, oval track rotating shelves, and movable aisle files (yes, movable aisles!). These mechanical files that have brightened and enlightened the lives of records personnel are illustrated in Chapter 14, "Equipment Used in Records Control."

Controlling the Filing System

Filers need to follow control procedures that make the best use of the filing system.

A filing system, no matter how carefully planned and set up, is only as good as the people who use it. The files need controls, and the filers need to follow the control procedures in order to make the best use of the filing system. The usefulness and completeness of the filing system are ensured when these controls are consistently and strictly applied. The three controls that you will study are:

1. how materials are processed as they enter, leave, and finally return to the system,
2. how efficiency/economy controls affect system changes, and
3. how inactive materials are removed from the system.

Receiving, Retrieving, Releasing, and Returning Records. Receiving and preparing records to be placed in the filing system is the first step in the control process. Once materials have been received for filing, the filer must determine *where* they are to be placed in the file. For example, the records department receives for filing a letter from Linda C. Horton, of Astroline of New York. The letter is inviting your company to participate in a business show sponsored by the Business and Commerce Association of Greater New York. Where would that communication be filed? Under H for Linda C. Horton? Under A for Astroline of New York? B for Business and Commerce Association of Greater New York? Or B for Business Show? It is much like looking in a cookbook for Applesauce Loaf. Will you find it under A for Applesauce? L for Loaf? Or C for Cake? Where to place materials in the file is the important beginning of the control process.

Where to place materials in the file is the important beginning of the control process.

Other procedures included in your study of controlling office records are (a) how filed materials will be retrieved from the file; (b) how records will be released (checked out) to the person or department requesting them; and (c) how the records will be returned to the file.

The filer must know where records are filed, where released records are, how long records have been out of the file, and if they have been returned. Rather like being a detective, isn't it? Or maybe more like being a guard, because the movement of information in and out of the files must be carefully *guarded.*

The movement of information in and out of the files must be carefully guarded.

Placing materials in the files, retrieving them for further use, and following up to ensure their safe return to storage are three closely related control functions. Each is dependent on the successful handling of the others. Neglect in any one of these control areas will soon break down a filing system, and the system will eventually become useless to the organization.

An Efficiency/ Economy ratio is a helpful tool.

Efficiency and Economy Controls. An Efficiency/Economy (E/E) ratio is a helpful tool when considering changes in a filing system. Basically, the ratio shows the benefits of a possible change divided by the cost of implementing the change. The outcome must be greater than 1. The formula looks like this:

$$\frac{\text{Efficiency (Benefits)}}{\text{Economy (Cost)}} = \text{Greater than 1}$$

For example, you may suggest the purchase of a simple desk wheel file that costs $50. If the wheel file saves you just 12 minutes throughout a day, the file will save you one hour each week. If you are paid $4 an hour, using the file for only one year can save your company $200 (50 hrs. × $4 per hour = $200). The formula looks like this:

$$\frac{\text{Benefits: Labor saved in using equipment}}{\text{Cost: Price of equipment}} = \frac{\$200}{\$50} = 4 \text{ (greater than 1)}$$

In the above example, the investment looks like a good one. The company saved $200, while spending only $50. The wheel file pays for itself in less than one year, and the company continues to benefit from its use long after it is paid for. The Efficiency/Economy ratio shows what a company receives in return for money it has spent. Who can argue with that? If a firm did not get back more money than it invested, it could not pay your salary.

A filing system becomes either more efficient or less efficient.

The filer who is aware of the benefit/cost factor appreciates the rapid changes taking place in filing and records control. Remember, a filing system becomes either *more* efficient or *less* efficient. The system cannot remain the same when change is taking place all around it. Wages and other operating expenses are soaring. New equipment is available. More information is needed to operate the business. And top speed is required in handling the information. "I need this information yesterday!" is a common exclamation from a busy executive. The filing system must meet the growing demands placed on it.

Increase efficiency! Reduce costs!

Increase efficiency! Reduce costs! If you understand these goals, you will be an adaptable and flexible office worker. You will be prepared for change. You will be able to explore, evaluate, and recommend to your employer ways to:

1. Minimize or eliminate the costly misfile.
2. Streamline the retrieval (finding) process.
3. Reduce time and fatigue throughout the entire filing process.
4. Minimize the use of valuable office storage space.
5. Utilize power files or mechanical retrieval systems, microform records, and computers.

A knowledge of the E/E ratio provides you with a realistic approach to your study of filing. You will not study *just* equipment and supplies, or *just* filing controls, or *just* space requirements for stored records. You will study each part in terms of how that part will increase the efficiency and reduce the cost of the total filing process. An awareness of the efficiency/economy control will make you a vital part of an information system in a rapidly changing environment.

Transfer and/or Disposal of Inactive Records. Records are classified as **vital**, **important**, or **useful**, according to their importance to the company. Records that are essential in order for the company to survive are the *vital* records. Vital records, such as patents, formulas, legal papers, corporate documents, and accounts receivable records, must be kept in fire-resistant and waterproof storage areas. The active accounts receivable records, showing how much customers owe, could not be replaced. If these vital records were destroyed, a company might not be able to survive the loss. Some organizations may store some of their vital records safely with commercial storage companies located in underground caves and abandoned salt mines.

Most office records are *important* and *useful* to an organization for only a certain period of time. Records such as letters, memos, invoices, and purchase orders are *important*, but not critical to the survival of a business. Sales catalogs, magazines, and price quotations are examples of records that are *useful*. An organization must determine for itself when records have outlived their

A retention schedule should be established for every type of record.

usefulness. In some instances, however, state or federal government regulations will determine how long records must be retained.

A **retention schedule** should be established for every type of record in a filing system. The retention schedule lists all kinds of records kept, where they should be kept, the length of time they must be saved, and when they should be destroyed. You will learn the methods of removing **inactive** (no longer used) materials and **semiactive** (sometimes used) materials from the **active** (frequently used) files. Too many offices ignore this transfer, or disposition, control. A file jammed with useless information costs a company time and money. Valuable office space is used to store useless records, and time is wasted plowing through these records to find what is needed. Attention to this "housekeeping" function will enable the other filing functions to operate at top efficiency.

"I can't find it! I know it's here . . . somewhere!" Who said that? When you complete your study of BUSINESS RECORDS CONTROL, that person won't be YOU!

Questions for Discussion

1. Why is order in handling records necessary? (1)

2. Why is disorder so costly? (2)

3. What are some kinds of records kept at home? at school? in business? (3)

4. Name three types of paperless records. (3)

5. Define filing. (4)

6. Define records control. (5)

7. What career opportunities can filing skills lead to? (6)

8. How can filing skills lead to a high-paying career choice? (6)

9. Define a filing system. (7)

10. Name three types of filing equipment that you have seen, read about, or used. (8)

11. What is the SECret of filing? (8,9)

12. What is the first task in controlling records? (9)

13. How is the Efficiency/Economy ratio used in records control? (9)

14. Why is transfer or disposition control a necessary and important control function? (9)

15. What is a retention schedule? (9)

PART 2

Alphabetic Indexing Rules and Procedures

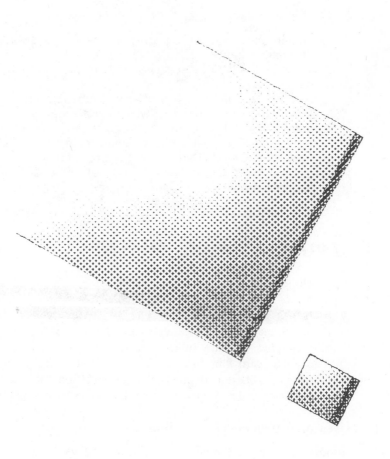

CHAPTER 2

Alphabetic Card Filing and Indexing

Learning Objectives

After completing Chapter 2, you will be able to:

1. Explain an alphabetic card filing system and describe types of information kept in the system.
2. Describe the various supplies used with an alphabetic card filing system.
3. Describe the organization of an alphabetic card filing system.
4. Explain indexing rules and why they are necessary.
5. Index and arrange in proper order common personal and business names, and names containing minor words, punctuation, possessives, single letters, and abbreviations.
6. Prepare cross-references for unusual personal names and for business names written as acronyms.

ALPHABETIC CARD FILING

Alphabetic card filing is the arranging of cards in alphabetic order and the placement of them in a container. An **alphabetic card filing system** consists of cards filed in alphabetic order in a file tray, box, or cabinet. The information on the cards may be names, addresses of persons or businesses, book titles, types of supplies, or many other items.

Alphabetic card filing has many personal and business uses.

Alphabetic card filing is one of the simplest filing systems. It has many uses in both business and personal filing situations. For these reasons, we shall begin our study of business records control with alphabetic card filing.

Uses of Alphabetic Card Filing

Almost all of us have used an alphabetic card file. For example, when you look for a book in a library, you can save time by using the card catalog. The card catalog is an alphabetic card file that tells you if the library has the book you want and where the book is stored. You can then quickly find the right book among the thousands of other books stored on the library shelves (See Illustration 2-1).

Illus. 2-1   The Library Card Catalog is an Alphabetic Filing System

Card files keep information available for quick and ready reference.

A card file may be based on an alphabetic, geographic, numeric, or subject system. Many people use card files to keep information available for quick and easy reference. A few of these users and some of the types of information they keep are included on the following list:

1. Secretaries: Names, addresses, and occupations of all frequent office callers. One card may contain the name of the caller, the name of the company represented, the time of the usual call, and the length of time spent in the office.
2. Office supervisors: Names of potential employees, their addresses, telephone numbers, and special abilities.
3. Word processing specialists: Names and addresses of frequent correspondents.
4. Typists: Names and addresses of persons who receive copies of company reports.
5. Club secretaries and treasurers: Name, address, and dues-payment status of each member of the organization.
6. People at home: Names and addresses on a holiday card list, dates of birthdays, an auto-repair tool list, and a household goods inventory.
7. Salespeople: Names and addresses of customers and potential customers.
8. Supply clerks: Names and addresses of suppliers of various office items, machine repairs, and other services.

Alphabetic Card Filing Systems

A study of alphabetic card filing requires an understanding of the cards, guides, tabs, and captions used in such files. The following paragraphs discuss these items as well as the organization of alphabetic card filing systems.

Cards. The **cards** in a card file are usually five inches wide by three inches high (5″ × 3″). Other standard sizes are 6″ × 4″ and 8″ × 5″. These cards are usually white, but many filers use different colors to help find the right one more rapidly. If the information to be placed on the card is to be handwritten, use ruled cards. It is easier to write in a straight line and in the same place on each card. If the information is to be typed on the cards, the typist may find it easier not to have to follow a ruled line, so unlined cards are often used. On unlined cards, the typist begins to type on the third line from the top of the card, three or four spaces from the left edge. This arrangement makes it easier to file as well as to find the desired card (See Illustration 2-2).

Cards may be ruled or blank.

Guides. **Guides** are special cards or partitions that divide the file drawer into convenient alphabetic sections. The guides are usually made of material heavier than that of the cards so that they will withstand long use (See Illustration 2-3).

Guides divide the file drawer.

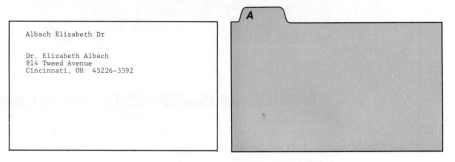

```
Albach Elizabeth Dr

Dr. Elizabeth Albach
814 Tweed Avenue
Cincinnati, OH  45226-3392
```

A

Illus. 2-2   File Card   **Illus. 2-3   Card Guide**

Tabs. A **tab** is a projection at the top of a guide (labeled A in Illustration 2-3). Tabs enable a person to see the guides above the other materials in the file. The tabs may be made of the same guide material, plastic, or metal with a plastic "window" through which information on the tabs can be read easily when the filer is looking down on the drawer.

A tab is a projection at the top of a guide.

Captions. **Captions** are titles or alphabetic divisions of the file that are written, typed, or printed on the tabs of guides. The label A in Illustration 2-3 is a caption. Illustration 2-4 shows a caption (A 1) on the tab. Numbers are sometimes included in the captions to indicate the order for placing guides in a file drawer. The illustration also shows the tabs on two other card guides to be used farther back in the file drawer. In this illustration, the tabs are cut one-third of the width of the guides with each tab the same size. Tabs of this width are called **third-cut tabs.** Tabs vary in position at the tops of guides so that they are staggered across the file drawer from left to right. In this way, three different positions are provided. This staggering of positions enables the filer to read the captions more easily.

Captions are written, typed, or printed on the tabs of guides.

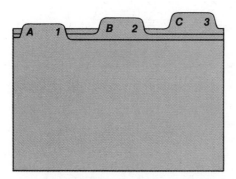

Illus. 2-4 Third-Cut Card Guides

Guides have tabs cut in different positions.

It is possible to obtain guides with tabs cut in different positions. The most common, in addition to third-cut, are **fifth-cut** (five tab positions), **half-cut** (two tab positions, each tab one-half the width of the guide), or **full-cut** (each tab covering the entire width of the guide).

Cards are arranged in order from front to back.

Organization. Cards are placed in a file tray, box, or drawer so that the names are arranged in alphabetic order from front to back. Illustration 2-5 shows a drawer from a card file cabinet. In studying the illustration, notice the use of the guides with third-cut tabs on which the captions are names and fifth-cut tabs on which the captions are letters of the alphabet.

The guides (Cas to Cu) that appear at the left are called **primary guides** and indicate the principal alphabetic sections into which the drawer is divided. The guides (Casper, Condon, and Cooper) that appear in a column at the center are called **auxiliary** or **secondary guides**. They divide the principal alphabetic sections into subsections according to frequently used last names.

The guides appearing at the right are **special auxiliary guides** that divide a single surname section into subsections according to the initial letters of the first names. In this system, an END or STOP guide is used to show the end of a subsection. Notice the alphabetic guides E, G, J, M, R, and W after Condon and the END guide following the last card after the special auxiliary guide W.

Cards are placed behind the guides.

The cards are placed behind the appropriate identifying guides. The captions on two consecutive guides indicate the alphabetic range of the names to be filed between the two guides. For example, in Illustration 2-5, the first guide is captioned *Cas* and the second, *Casper*. Thus, cards bearing names from *Cas* to *Casper* would be filed behind the first guide and cards with *Casper* would be filed behind the secondary guide. The special section for *Casper* would stop at the END guide. The *Cas* section would continue with a name such as *Castro*. A card bearing the name *Cintron* would be found between the guides labeled *Ci* and *Co*.

Provide one guide for every 20 cards.

For guides to be effective in an active file, one guide should be provided for about every 20 cards. For a less active file, one guide should be provided for about every half-inch or inch of cards.

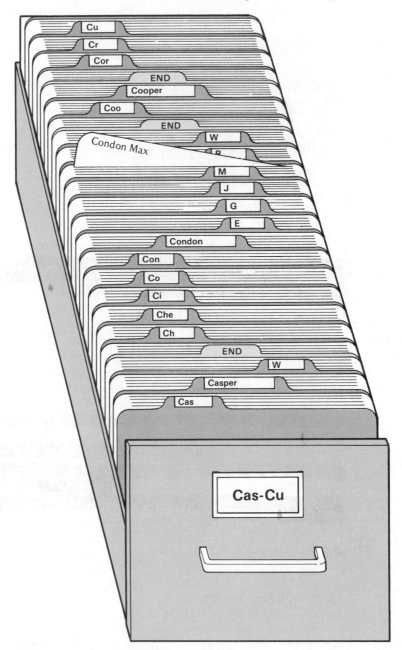

Illus. 2-5   Alphabetic Card File

A drawer label aids in locating the correct file drawer.

A **drawer label** is placed on the outside front of the drawer to aid in locating the correct file drawer. In Illustration 2-5, this label reads *Cas-Cu*, which tells the filer that the cards in this drawer range from those bearing last names beginning with *Cas* to those cards bearing names beginning with *Cu*.

ALPHABETIC INDEXING OF PERSONAL AND BUSINESS NAMES

Rules help file quickly and find easily.

Definite rules are necessary for determining the order in which cards are to be filed and located. These rules are known as **alphabetic indexing rules.** The same rules are used in filing correspondence or other materials in alphabetic files. Four of these rules are presented in this chapter. The remaining rules are given in Chapters 3 and 4.

Need for Procedures and Rules

The purpose of filing is to store your records so that they can be found immediately and easily whenever they are needed. Imagine, in an emergency, trying to find the telephone number of your family doctor in a telephone directory that has no logical arrangement of names. It would be almost impossible to locate the number unless the directory followed a consistent, planned system of listing that you knew how to use. Business and personal files would also be difficult to use unless materials were stored in a consistent, planned, and organized manner that was known and followed by everyone using them. In order to have a planned system of filing and finding records, it is necessary to use indexing rules.

Indexing Rules

Index means to point out. A *rule* is an established guide for action. **Indexing rules,** then, are established guides that point out the proper location of an item in a file. Therefore, each indexed name will have a special place in the file that will make it distinct from all other names in the filing system. By following indexing rules, you will be able to find any record immediately.

People find records because they follow rules.

The most consistent and commonly recommended indexing rules are presented in this chapter as well as in Chapters 3 and 4. These rules are followed by many businesses and are adapted from the rules developed by the Association of Records Managers and Administrators, Inc. (ARMA), as standards for records control systems. These rules have been designed by the Association for use with both manual and computerized filing systems.

Computer indexing may require some modifications of a few of the rules adopted for manual indexing. See Appendix A, "Computer Indexing Considerations," for changes in indexing for the microcomputer.

In addition, a number of businesses may modify some of these rules to fit their unique filing requirements. However, a good records control program requires that once indexing rules are written and adopted, they must be followed consistently by everyone using that organization's files.

Indexing Names for Filing Purposes

The process of indexing is made up of two steps: (1) dividing names into filing units and (2) numbering or writing the units in the sequence used for

Alphabetizing is placing names in alphabetic order.

filing. The names are then placed in alphabetic order (alphabetizing). Since a name must be divided into filing units before it can be alphabetized, we will consider this procedure first in the explanation of indexing practices.

Dividing Names into Units. Two steps must be taken before a name can be placed in alphabetic order in relation to other names. First, the filer must identify the units a name contains. Next, the filer must determine which of the several units is the most important one for filing purposes. A unit may be a word, a letter, a number, or any combination of these as stated in the indexing rule that applies to the name. For example, in the name *Karen A. Sanchez*, there are three units–Karen, A, and Sanchez. The total name (or subject or number) which is being used for filing purposes is called a **filing segment**.

A filing segment is a total name used for filing purposes.

As an example of the process, if the name *Karen A. Sanchez* is to be indexed for filing, the filer would first notice that the name has three units and that all three create a filing segment. Next, the filer must determine which of these three units is the **key unit**–the unit under which this name will be filed first. In this case, the key unit is the surname, Sanchez. The filer underlines *Sanchez* or rewrites it to point it out as the key unit.

The key unit is the unit under which a name will be filed first.

Numbering or Writing the Units. If the name is to be rewritten on an index card, the name is written in this order–Sanchez Karen A. The card on which the name appears is filed in the S section of the card filing system being used. If the name appears in a letter, on a printed or typed page, or as a signature, the name is not rewritten but is *coded* to show the key unit, the second unit, and the third unit of the filing segment. **Coding** (marking of the units in a filing segment) consists of (1) separating the units by diagonal lines, (2) underlining the key unit, and (3) writing numbers above the remaining units to indicate their rank in the filing order:

Coding is marking units in a filing segment.

$$\overset{\quad\quad\ 2\ \ \ 3\quad}{\text{Karen/A /\underline{Sanchez}}}$$

This coding indicates that the name is to be filed first under the key unit, *Sanchez*. The given name, *Karen*, is to be used next if needed to place the name in alphabetic order in relation to other names on cards or papers in the file. The middle initial, *A*, would be used as the third unit if there were another Karen Sanchez in the file in order to reach the proper location of Karen A. Sanchez.

Alphabetizing. If you wish to file alphabetically the two names Stacy Ames and Sean Burk, the procedure is as follows:

1. Notice that Stacy Ames is a two-unit name and determine that *Ames* is the key unit.
2. Notice that Sean Burk is a two-unit name and determine that *Burk* is the key unit.

3. Compare the key units in the two names.
4. File the name *Stacy Ames* before the name *Sean Burk* because A comes before B in the alphabet.

If both last names began with the same letter, the next letters would be compared and the letter coming first in the alphabet would be filed first. For example, Stacy Ames would be filed before Charlene Andrews because the *m* in Ames comes before the *n* in Andrews. This is referred to as "comparing equal units."

The following tabulation illustrates the indexing of the two names (filing segments):

Index Order of Units

Name	Key Unit	Unit 2
Stacy Ames	<u>A</u>mes	Stacy
Sean Burk	<u>B</u>urk	Sean

How to Study Indexing Rules

The way in which you study the indexing rules in Chapters 2, 3, and 4 is very important. First, read a rule twice to be sure that you understand it. Next, study all the names in the list below the rule. Finally, restudy the names in the list, comparing each name with the names above and below it. In this way, you will discover the unit or letter in a name that fixes its position above or below other names in the list. This last step is very important because the comparison of the names in the list shows how the rules are applied even when names vary from a standard pattern. *Names are sometimes so complex and varied that scores of rules could not cover every possible way of indexing all types of names.* Therefore, example names are sometimes presented in a manner designed to show many ways of applying a single rule.

As was explained earlier in this chapter, names indexed for computer filing and retrieval may require modification of a few of the rules. If a computer listing would be different from the listing contained in the examples of a rule, the computer listing is presented in Appendix A.

RULE 1: ORDER OF INDEXING UNITS

Personal Names

A. Personal Names. A personal name is indexed in this manner: (1) the surname (last name) is the key unit, (2) the given name (first name) or initial is the second unit, and (3) the middle name or initial is the third unit. Unusual or obscure (often foreign) names are indexed in the same manner. If it is not possible to determine the surname in a name, consider the last name as the surname. Cross-reference unusual or obscure names by using the first written name as the key unit (See Illustration 2-6).

```
┌─────────────────────────────────┐   ┌─────────────────────────────────┐
│ Soong Mai                       │   │ Mai Soong                       │
│                                 │   │                                 │
│ Mai Soong                       │   │ SEE Soong Mai                   │
│ 153 Flores Street               │   │                                 │
│ San Mateo, CA  94403-1033       │   │                                 │
│                                 │   │                                 │
│                                 │   │                                 │
│                                 │   │                                 │
│                                 │   │                                 │
└─────────────────────────────────┘   └─────────────────────────────────┘
```

Original Card   Cross-Reference Card

Illus. 2-6   Original and Cross-Reference Cards for an Unusual Personal Name

Why Rule 1A Is Needed. Personal names must be indexed by considering surnames as key units because last names are the ones commonly used first for identification. If surnames were not considered first, individual names would not be grouped under family names and would not be easy to locate.

Examples of Rule 1A

Index Order of Units in Names

Name	Key Unit	Unit 2	Unit 3
1. Antonia L. Cardona	Cardona	Antonia	L
2. Thomas J. Carlson	Carlson	Thomas	J
3. Thomas James Carlson	Carlson	Thomas	James
4. Marie T. Davison	Davison	Marie	T
5. Martin C. Davison	Davison	Martin	C

Note   In each example in the above list, the letter of the unit that determines the alphabetic sequence is underlined. This practice will be used in illustrations of each rule.

Business Names

B. Business Names. Business names are filed *as written** using letterheads or trademarks as guides. Business names containing personal names are indexed as written. Newspapers and periodicals are indexed as written. For newspapers and periodicals having identical names that do not include the city name, consider the city name as the last indexing unit. If necessary, the state name may follow the city name.

Why Rule 1B Is Needed. Names of businesses, institutions, organizations, newspapers, and periodicals usually are referred to by the first word in the name. This first word is the key unit. For consistency in following this rule and to avoid the difficult problem of identifying a personal name in a business name, personal names within a business name are also filed as written.

---

*Throughout the text, "as written" means the order of the words or names *as written or printed* on the person's, organization's, or publication's signature, letterhead, or title.

Examples of Rule 1B

Index Order of Units in Names

Name	Key Unit	Unit 2	Unit 3	Unit 4
1. Carl Johnson Construction	Carl	Johnson	Construction	
2. Chicago National Bank	Chicago	National	Bank	
3. Christian Church	Christian	Church		
4. Cleveland Discount Store	Cleveland	Discount	Store	
5. Cleveland News Magazine	Cleveland	News	Magazine	
6. Computer Dealer School	Computer	Dealer	School	
7. Connie Cintron Beauty Shop	Connie	Cintron	Beauty	Shop
8. Connie Shoe Factory	Connie	Shoe	Factory	
9. Credit Management Company	Credit	Management	Company	
10. Currier News (Cleveland)	Currier	News	Cleveland	
11. Currier News (Toledo)	Currier	News	Toledo	

RULE 2: MINOR WORDS IN BUSINESS NAMES

Symbols are indexed as spelled out.

Each complete English word in a business name is considered a separate indexing unit. Prepositions, conjunctions, symbols, and articles are included; symbols (&, ¢, $, #, %) are considered as spelled in full (and, Cent, Dollar, Number, Percent). All spelled-out symbols except "and" begin with a capital letter.

When the word "The" appears as the first word of a business name, it is considered the last indexing unit.

Why Rule 2 Is Needed. Unless this rule is used, when papers are being coded for filing purposes, papers bearing similar names might be coded in differing ways. For example, when coding the name *The Inside Lounge*, one person might use the word *The* as the key unit while another person might use the word *Inside*. In addition, the word *The* is used so frequently that too many names would be filed under *The.* The use of Rule 2 helps prevent this from happening and provides consistency in indexing.

Examples of Rule 2

Index Order of Units in Names

Name	Key Unit	Unit 2	Unit 3	Unit 4
1. The In Town Motel	In	Town	Motel	The
2. Inside & Outside Painters	Inside	and	Outside	Painters
3. The Inside Lounge	Inside	Lounge	The	
4. Intown Auto Repair	Intown	Auto	Repair	
5. Matsumi and Miranda Attorneys	Matsumi	and	Miranda	Attorneys
6. The Matsumi Music Hall	Matsumi	Music	Hall	The
7. Mechanics & Plumbers Shop	Mechanics	and	Plumbers	Shop
8. Monica Torres Cosmetics	Monica	Torres	Cosmetics	
9. Montana Bakeries	Montana	Bakeries		
10. Montana $ Savers	Montana	Dollar	Savers	

RULE 3: PUNCTUATION AND POSSESSIVES

All punctuation is disregarded when indexing personal and business names. Commas, periods, hyphens, and apostrophes are disregarded, and names are indexed as written. (For example, Smith's Playhouse would be filed after Smiths' Bakery.)

Why Rule 3 Is Needed. Sometimes names are written without the customary punctuation. Other times, the punctuation is included. By ignoring the punctuation when indexing, consistency is maintained.

Examples of Rule 3

Index Order of Units in Names

Name	Key Unit	Unit 2	Unit 3	Unit 4
1. Bank of Atlanta	Bank	of	Atlanta	
2. Sarah A. Bank	Bank	Sarah	A	
3. Banks & Georgi Foods	Banks	and	Georgi	Foods
4. Arnold M. Banks	Banks	Arnold	M	
5. Bank's Dump Trucks	Banks	Dump	Trucks	
6. George R. Banks	Banks	George	R	
7. Bank's Portable Coaches	Banks	Portable	Coaches	
8. Banks' Window Washing	Banks	Window	Washing	
9. Banktown Apple Cider	Banktown	Apple	Cider	
10. Bank-Town Credit Association	BankTown	Credit	Association	

RULE 4: SINGLE LETTERS AND ABBREVIATIONS

A. **Personal Names.** Initials in personal names are considered separate indexing units. Abbreviations of personal names (Wm., Jos., Thos.) and brief personal names or nicknames (Liz, Bill) are indexed as they are written.

B. **Business Names.** Single letters in business names are indexed as written. If there is a space between single letters, index each letter as a separate unit. An acronym (a word formed from the first, or first few, letters of several words) is indexed as one unit. Abbreviations are indexed as one unit regardless of punctuation or spacing (AAA, Y M C A, Y.W.C.A.). Radio and television station call letters are indexed as one word. Cross-reference spelled-out names to their acronyms or abbreviations if necessary. For example: American Automobile Association SEE AAA (See Illustration 2-7).

Why Rule 4 Is Needed. When a nickname or a brief personal name is to be coded for filing, the change to an assumed different form of the name should

```
┌─────────────────────────────────┐     ┌─────────────────────────────────┐
│ AAA                             │     │ American Automobile Association │
│                                 │     │                                 │
│ AAA                             │     │ SEE AAA                         │
│ 437 West Main Street            │     │                                 │
│ Madison, VA  22727-2513         │     │                                 │
│                                 │     │                                 │
│                                 │     │                                 │
│                                 │     │                                 │
│                                 │     │                                 │
└─────────────────────────────────┘     └─────────────────────────────────┘

        Original Card                          Cross-Reference Card
```

Illus. 2-7   Original and Cross-Reference Cards for an Abbreviation

not be made. For example, the name *Kate* may be a nickname for Katherine or Kathleen, or it may be the person's full name. To assume that it is Katherine may be incorrect, and the material filed could be misplaced. In the case of acronyms or abbreviations, very few are accepted as being universally known. For example, *AMA* could stand for American Medical Association, American Marketing Association, or merely be a convenient series of letters. By indexing all names as written, consistency is maintained for all names.

Examples of Rule 4

Index Order of Units in Names

Name	Key Unit	Unit 2	Unit 3	Unit 4
1. S. A. Ryder	Ryder	S	A	
2. S A Ryder Tavern	S	A	Ryder	Tavern
3. S. & R. Markets	S	and	R	Markets
4. SAR Motel	SAR	Motel		
5. Jos. Sumida	Sumida	Jos		
6. TacTight Glue Co.	TacTight	Glue	Co	
7. Tac-Tight Staples	TacTight	Staples		
8. U.S.A. Motors	USA	Motors		
9. WAR Radio Station	WAR	Radio	Station	
10. Word-Pro Services, Inc.	WordPro	Services	Inc	
11. Words Insurance Agency	Words	Insurance	Agency	
12. Word's Paint Bucket	Words	Paint	Bucket	
13. Jill Zell	Zell	Jill		

Typing Index Cards

The rules you have studied and those you will be studying are illustrated by lists of names; but in actual filing, names usually are typed on index cards or on folder labels. Since your first filing job in the practice set, OFFICE FILING PROCEDURES, Sixth Edition, will involve the use of index cards, the following explanation and illustration will show how index cards are prepared.

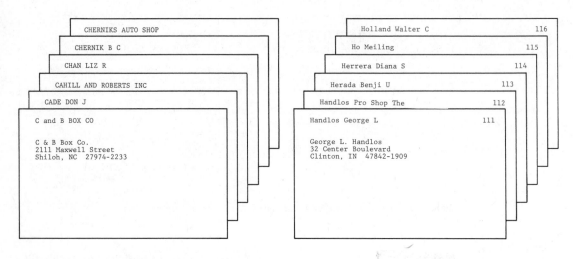

Illus. 2-8   File Cards Typed in Indexing Form

Filing segments are typed or written in indexed form.

As shown in Illustration 2-8, an index card includes (1) the filing segment typed or written in indexed form on the second or third line from the top edge of the card and three or four spaces from the left edge and (2) the name and address typed or written three or four lines below the filing segment. In Illustration 2-8, notice how names and titles are typed and spaced on cards. This format is neater and easier to read. It also makes filing, as well as finding, the desired card easier.

Either all capital letters or capital and lowercase letters may be used for a filing segment. Some records supervisors prefer to have the key indexing unit typed in all capital letters and the other indexing units typed in capital and lowercase letters. If *The* is the first word of a name, type it at the end of the filing segment.

If the card is to be filed according to a numeric system, the name is given a code number. The code number is then typed in the upper right corner of the file card (See Illustration 2-8).

Questions for Discussion

1. What is an alphabetic card filing system? (1)

2. What are some of the types of information kept in an alphabetic card file by (a) a secretary? (b) an office supervisor? (c) a word processing specialist? (d) a typist? (e) a club secretary? (f) a person at home? (g) a salesperson? (h) a supply clerk? (1)

3. What types of cards are usually used in a card file? (2)

4. What is a guide? a tab? a caption? (2)

5. What is a third-cut tab? What are the common cuts for tabs? (2)

6. In what order are cards placed in a file tray of an alphabetic card file? (3)

7. How close together should guides be placed in an alphabetic card file? (3)

8. What is a drawer label on an alphabetic card file? (3)

9. What are indexing rules? Why are they necessary? (4)

10. Why is it necessary to use a planned system of filing? (4)

11. What does the term *indexing* mean? (4)

12. What are the two steps in the indexing process? (5)

13. What is the key unit in your name? What is the filing segment in your name? (5)

14. If names are not rewritten in indexing form, how are the units marked (coded) for filing purposes? (5)

15. How is alphabetic order determined between two names? (5)

Applications

Use a separate sheet of paper to answer the following applications:

1. What is the *key unit* in each of the following names? What is the *second unit* in the same names? (5)

   a. John C. Samuels
   b. Computer Industries, Inc.
   c. George Mendosa Corporation
   d. Blanco and Bosak Accountants
   e. The Sunbelt Resorts
   f. Sandra Ann Casper
   g. Dick's Taxi Service
   h. At Home Window Washers
   i. PDQ Fried Chicken
   j. Wm. Saga Rugs

2. Indicate whether the alphabetic order of the two names in each of the following pairs is correct or incorrect. (5)

   a. Jane R. Wood
      Fire Wood Engineers
   b. Gerald D. Vendor
      G & A Vendors, Inc.
   c. Wilma J. Hands
      Wm. J. Hands
   d. B. Charlotte Hoye
      The Hoye Barber Supply Company
   e. Sims' Custom Bakers
      D. B. Sims
   f. Point of View Paints
      Point's View Cabins
   g. Jos. Saxe
      Joseph A. Sax
   h. Charles A. Barker
      Charlene J. Barker
   i. The Olson Realty Co.
      Olson's Real Cheese Pizzas
   j. One Hour Cleaners
      One Hour Muffler Service

3. What is the correct order in which each of the names within the following groups of three names would be arranged in an alphabetic file? Indicate

the order by writing the numbers representing the correct order. For example, the three names in item a. would be arranged with (2) first, then (1), then (3). Your answer sheet for question a. will be marked 2 1 3. (5)

a. (1) Melvin E. Meyer (2) Cathy J. Meyer (3) Meyer's Milk Bar
b. (1) Lang and Lang Builders (2) L. B. Lang (3) Alice Lange
c. (1) Enami Auto Imports (2) The Enami Photo Shop (3) Mary S. Enami
d. (1) Jos. Johnson (2) J. A. Johnson (3) Joe L. Johnsen
e. (1) The By Pass Motel (2) Theresa V. Bye (3) Byer's Dress Boutique
f. (1) Lifetime Fences (2) The Fence Builders (3) Marie A. Fence
g. (1) DEF Heating Co. (2) Def's Cleaners (3) D. E. Ford
h. (1) Donald M. Caine (2) Doris L. Cain (3) David J. Cane
i. (1) Turks' Auto Repair (2) Jos. P. Turks (3) Turk's Portrait Studio
j. (1) David's Writing Service (2) David C. Brown (3) David J. Brown

4. Indicate for each of the following names whether or not a cross-reference card would be helpful. Write the filing segment in indexing order as it would appear on the cross-reference card. For those names that, in your opinion, do not need a cross-reference card, write, "No cross-reference needed." (6)

a. David George
b. Cindi A. Brown
c. NBC Radio Station
d. Atsuko Akita
e. IBM Corporation
f. ARC Cleaners
g. Winston Paul
h. Samantha Johnson
i. Wm. T. Smythe
j. Jane Barker

Job 1   Alphabetic Indexing of Personal and Business Names (5,6)

At this time complete Job 1 in OFFICE FILING PROCEDURES, Sixth Edition. Instructions and supplies for this job and the following jobs are included in the practice set.

CHAPTER 3

Alphabetic Indexing of Names with Unique Characteristics

Learning Objectives

After completing Chapter 3, you will be able to:

1. Index and arrange in alphabetic order both personal and business names with titles.
2. Index, arrange in alphabetic order, and cross-reference a married woman's name.
3. Index and arrange in alphabetic order names containing articles and particles.
4. Index and arrange in alphabetic order identical personal and business names.
5. Index and arrange in alphabetic order business names containing numbers.

UNIQUE CHARACTERISTICS OF NAMES

In Chapter 2 you learned the order of indexing units in the filing segment for personal and business names. In addition, you learned standard rules for indexing minor words, punctuation, possessives, single letters, and abbreviations in personal and business names. In this chapter you will learn how to index names with titles (Doctor, Mr., Ms., Mayor, Reverend), and with seniority designations (II, III, Jr., Sr.). Names of married women and names with articles and particles will also be studied. In addition, you will learn how to determine the filing order of identical names and names containing numbers.

Complex names require definite indexing rules.

The more complex a name is, the more important it is to use definite indexing rules consistently. It would be impossible to locate important records quickly if indexing rules were not adhered to (See Illustration 3-1). Follow the same procedure in studying these rules as recommended in Chapter 2.

RULE 5: TITLES

Personal Names

A. Personal Names. A personal title (Miss, Mr., Mrs., Ms.) is considered the last indexing unit when it appears. If a seniority title is required for

Illus. 3-1   Hospitals Follow Indexing Rules in Retrieving Patients' Records

identification, it is considered the last indexing unit in abbreviated form, with numeric titles (II, III) filed before alphabetic titles (Jr., Sr.). When professional titles (D.D.S., M.D., CRM, Dr., Mayor) are required for identification, they are considered the last units and filed alphabetically as written. Royal and religious titles followed by either a given name or a surname only (Father Leo) are indexed and filed as written. When all units of identical names, *including titles,* have been compared and there are no differences, filing order is determined by the addresses.

Note   Titles are indexed as written without punctuation. For example: Jr., Dr., Maj., Major are indexed as Jr, Dr, Maj, Major.

Why Rule 5A Is Needed. A personal title is frequently used by correspondents to be sure they are identified properly. For example, seniority titles (II, III, Jr., Sr.) keep names of members of the same family from being confused with one another. Many people with the same name frequently add their professional title or degree (Dr., M.D., CRM) to aid in their identification. Consistent use of Rule 5 will ensure easy and accurate retrieval.

Examples of Rule 5A

Index Order of Units in Names

Name	Key Unit	Unit 2	Unit 3	Unit 4
1. Brother John	Brother	John		
2. A. Kenneth Brothers	Brothers	A	Kenneth	
3. A. Kenneth Brothers II	Brothers	A	Kenneth	II
4. A. Kenneth Brothers III	Brothers	A	Kenneth	III

Index Order of Units in Names

Name	Key Unit	Unit 2	Unit 3	Unit 4
5. A. Kenneth Brothers, Jr.	Brothers	A	Kenneth	Jr
6. A. Kenneth Brothers, Sr.	Brothers	A	Kenneth	Sr
7. Brother John M. Cain	Cain	John	M	Brother
8. John M. Cain, D.D.S.	Cain	John	M	DDS
9. Dr. John M. Cain	Cain	John	M	Dr
10. Miss Cindi A. Docter	Docter	Cindi	A	Miss
11. Ms. Cindi A. Docter	Docter	Cindi	A	Ms
12. Mrs. C. A. Doctor	Doctor	C	A	Mrs

Business Names

B. Business Names. Titles in business names are filed as written. See Rules 1 and 2.

Why Rule 5B Is Needed. Businesses use titles as part of their official names to make their business names unique. Consistently filing business names as they are written will ensure easy and accurate retrieval.

Titles in business names are filed as written.

Examples of Rule 5B

Index Order of Units in Names

Name	Key Unit	Unit 2	Unit 3	Unit 4
1. Doctor's Rest Home	Doctors	Rest	Home	
2. Dr. Pepper Bottling Co.	Dr	Pepper	Bottling	Co
3. Mister Huang Imports	Mister	Huang	Imports	
4. Mr. Anthony Stylist	Mr	Anthony	Stylist	
5. Mrs. Beall's Donuts	Mrs	Bealls	Donuts	
6. Ms. Colognes	Ms	Colognes		
7. Professor Carter Aspirin	Professor	Carter	Aspirin	
8. Professor's Book Sales, Inc.	Professors	Book	Sales	Inc
9. Senator Sacks Suits	Senator	Sacks	Suits	
10. Senators' Rental Units	Senators	Rental	Units	

RULE 6: MARRIED WOMEN

A married woman's name is filed as she writes it.

A married woman's name is filed as she writes it. It is indexed according to Rule 1. If more than one form of a name is known, the alternate name may be cross-referenced (See Illustration 3-2).

Note   A married woman's name in a business name is indexed as written and follows Rules 1B and 5B.

Why Rule 6 Is Needed. Some married women prefer to use their first name and their maiden surname with their husband's surname. Others use their first and middle names or initials with their husband's surname. Still others may prefer to use their husband's first name, initial, and surname. And some married women continue to use their maiden names after marriage for business or

```
Wegner Carol A Mrs

Mrs. Carol A. Wegner
2317 Mountain Road
Clearfield, UT  84015-3672
```

```
Wegner Richard C Mrs

SEE Wegner Carol A Mrs
```

Original Card   Cross-Reference Card

Illus. 3-2 Original and Cross-Reference Cards for the Name of a Married Woman

personal reasons. A woman's preference should be accepted. Cross-references keep all materials for the same person together.

Examples of Rule 6

Index Order of Units in Names

Name	Key Unit	Unit 2	Unit 3	Unit 4
1. Mrs. Jane Larkin Miller	Miller	Jane	Larkin	Mrs
*(Mrs. Kenneth T. Miller)				
2. Mrs. Janet Sue Miller	Miller	Janet	Sue	Mrs
3. Mrs. Jason C. Miller	Miller	Jason	C	Mrs
4. Mrs. Joan Wilson Miller	Miller	Joan	Wilson	Mrs
*(Ms. Joan Wilson)				
5. Ms. Judi Miller	Miller	Judi	Ms	
*(Mrs. Judi Miller Paxton)				
*(Mrs. Arthur Paxton)				
6. Mrs. Kenneth T. Miller	Miller	Kenneth	T	Mrs
7. Mrs. Jane Miller's Designs	Mrs	Jane	Millers	Designs
8. Mrs. Arthur Paxton	Paxton	Arthur	Mrs	
9. Mrs. Judi Miller Paxton	Paxton	Judi	Miller	Mrs
10. Ms. Joan Wilson	Wilson	Joan	Ms	

*These names are included as cross-references at their alphabetic locations.

RULE 7: ARTICLES AND PARTICLES

A foreign article or particle in a personal or business name is combined with the part of the name following it to form a single indexing unit. The indexing order is not affected by a space between a prefix and the rest of the name, and the space is disregarded when indexing. Examples of articles and particles are: a la, D', Da, De, Del, De la, Della, Den, Des, Di, Dos, Du, El, Fitz, Il, L', La, Las, Le, Les, Lo, Los, M', Mac, Mc, O', Per, Saint, San, Santa, Santo, St., Ste., Te, Ten, Ter, Van, Van de, Van der, Von, Von der.

Space in a prefixed name is disregarded.

Why Rule 7 Is Needed. Foreign articles and particles appear in many forms as prefixes to names. Sometimes there is a space in the prefix. Sometimes there is a space between the prefix and the rest of the word. Sometimes there are no spaces. In some cases, the first letter or one or more parts of the prefix is capitalized; sometimes not. Rule 7 is necessary to ensure that file materials concerning a certain name are all kept together regardless of how the article or particle is written.

Examples of Rule 7

Index Order of Units in Names

Name	Key Unit	Unit 2	Unit 3	Unit 4
1. Dr. August T. Damian	Damian	August	T	Dr
2. Professor Maria D'Amico	DAmico	Maria	Professor	
3. Damico Match Company	Damico	Match	Company	
4. Dana Maclean Art Supplies	Dana	Maclean	Art	Supplies
5. De La Camp Sports Wear	DeLaCamp	Sports	Wear	
6. Delano Meat Market	Delano	Meat	Market	
7. Miss Evelyn K. Della	Della	Evelyn	K	Miss
8. Brother Joseph E. Dell'Armi	DellArmi	Joseph	E	Brother
9. Henry H. Fitzgerald	Fitzgerald	Henry	H	
10. Rev. Loretta C. FitzGerald	FitzGerald	Loretta	C	Rev
11. LaSalle Interior Designers	LaSalle	Interior	Designers	
12. La Salle Mfg. Representatives	LaSalle	Mfg	Representatives	
13. Amanda D. Macks	Macks	Amanda	D	
14. Mack's Corner Market	Macks	Corner	Market	
15. Francis Q. Saint John	SaintJohn	Francis	Q	
16. San Francisco Cab Company	SanFrancisco	Cab	Company	
17. Gerald Q. Van Den Berg, Ph.D.	VanDenBerg	Gerald	Q	PhD
18. Vandenberg Hospital Supplies	Vandenberg	Hospital	Supplies	
19. Vanden Berg Moving & Storage	VandenBerg	Moving	and	Storage
20. Van den Berg Office Supplies	VandenBerg	Office	Supplies	

RULE 8: IDENTICAL NAMES

With identical names, addresses determine filing order.

When personal names and names of businesses, institutions, and organizations are identical, filing order is determined by the addresses. Cities are considered first, followed by states or provinces, street names, house numbers or building numbers in that order.

Note 1   When the first units of street names are written as figures, the names are considered in ascending numeric order and placed together before alphabetic street names.

Note 2   Street names with compass directions are considered as written. Numbers after compass directions are considered before alphabetic names (East 8th, East Main, Sandusky, SE Eighth, Southeast Eighth).

Note 3   House and building numbers written as figures are considered in ascending numeric order and placed together before spelled-out building names (The Charter

House). If a street address and a building name are included in an address, disregard the building name. ZIP Codes are not considered in determining filing order.

Note 4 Seniority titles are indexed according to Rule 5 and are considered *before* addresses.

Why Rule 8 Is Needed. Identical names occur frequently; therefore, a consistent method of indexing such names must be used to make sure that materials with identical names are properly filed. Since family members of different generations frequently live at the same address, seniority titles provide the proper identification and are therefore considered before addresses. Rule 8 provides the directions for consistent indexing of all types of identical names.

Examples of Rule 8

Index Order of Units in Names

Name	Key Unit	Unit 2	Unit 3	Unit 4	Address
(Names of Cities Used to Determine Filing Order)					
*1. Aaron Baker School Concord, Vermont	Aaron	Baker	School		Concord Vermont
2. Aaron Baker School Manchester, Vermont	Aaron	Baker	School		Manchester Vermont
(Names of States and Provinces Used to Determine Filing Order)					
3. Beechmont Hotel Freeport, Illinois	Beechmont	Hotel			Freeport Illinois
4. Beechmont Hotel Freeport, New York	Beechmont	Hotel			Freeport New York
5. Cranleys Bank Vancouver, British Columbia	Cranleys	Bank			Vancouver British Columbia
6. Cranleys Bank Vancouver, Washington	Cranleys	Bank			Vancouver Washington
(Names of Streets and Building Numbers Used to Determine Filing Order)					
7. Diamond Markets 43 - 12 Street Dayton, Ohio	Diamond	Markets			43 - 12 Street
8. Diamond Markets 12 - 23 Street Dayton, Ohio	Diamond	Markets			12 - 23 Street
9. Diamond Markets 213 Arch Street Dayton, Ohio	Diamond	Markets			213 Arch Street
10. Diamond Markets 944 Arch Street Dayton, Ohio	Diamond	Markets			944 Arch Street

*Notice that the key unit for this name is *Aaron*. The address is not the key unit; it is used only to determine the filing order of the two identical names.

Index Order of Units in Names

Name	Key Unit	Unit 2	Unit 3	Unit 4	Address
11. Diamond Markets 371 NE 13th Street Dayton, Ohio	Diamond	Markets			371 NE 13 Street
12. Diamond Markets 12 NE Eighth Street Dayton, Ohio	Diamond	Markets			12 NE Eighth Street
13. Diamond Markets 212 Park Avenue Dayton, Ohio	Diamond	Markets			212 Park Avenue

(Seniority Titles Used to Determine Filing Order Before Addresses)

Name	Key Unit	Unit 2	Unit 3	Unit 4	Address
14. George R. Edwards 358 Coleridge Easton, Pennsylvania	Edwards	George	R		
15. George R. Edwards II 126 Apple Drive Atlanta, Georgia	Edwards	George	R	II	
16. George R. Edwards III 111 Hermosa Drive Atlanta, Georgia	Edwards	George	R	III	
17. George R. Edwards, Jr. 111 Hermosa Drive Atlanta, Georgia	Edwards	George	R	Jr	Atlanta Georgia
18. George R. Edwards, Jr. 2210 Cypress Street San Mateo, California	Edwards	George	R	Jr	San Mateo California

RULE 9: NUMBERS IN BUSINESS NAMES

Digits are one unit.

Numbers spelled out in a business name are considered as written and filed alphabetically. Numbers written in digit form are considered one unit. Names with numbers written in digit form as the first unit are filed in ascending order before alphabetic names. Arabic numerals are filed before Roman numerals (2, 3; II, III). Names with inclusive numbers (33-37) are arranged by the first number only (33). Names with numbers appearing in other than the first position (Pier 36 Cafe) are filed alphabetically within the appropriate section and immediately before a similar name without a number (Pier and Port Cafe).

Note   In indexing numbers written in digit form which contain *st*, *d*, and *th* (1st, 2d, 3d, 4th), ignore the letter endings and consider the digits (1, 2, 3, 4).

Why Rule 9 Is Needed. If this rule were not followed, different filers would use different indexing patterns for the same types of names with numbers. For example, 2410 Photo Lab may be indexed and filed under "Twenty-four hundred ten," or "Two thousand four hundred ten," or "Twenty-four ten." Much time and effort would be wasted by searching through three possible locations. In large filing systems, the three locations are many drawers or shelves apart.

Examples of Rule 9

Index Order of Units in Names

Name	Key Unit	Unit 2	Unit 3	Unit 4
1. 8th & Indiana Exchange	8	and	Indiana	Exchange
2. 8th and Western Garage	8	and	Western	Garage
3. 8 Dollar Motel	8	Dollar	Motel	
4. 8 Track Recording Co.	8	Track	Recording	Co
5. 8th Ward Headquarters	8	Ward	Headquarters	
6. 800-812 Daniels Court	800	Daniels	Court	
7. The 800 Daniels Shop	800	Daniels	Shop	The
8. 1812 Records, Inc.	1812	Records	Inc	
9. The 18000 Apartments	18000	Apartments	The	
10. Eight Ball Restaurant	Eight	Ball	Restaurant	
11. The Eight Bells Room	Eight	Bells	Room	The
12. The Eighth Day, Inc.	Eighth	Day	Inc	The
13. Eight-Thousand Club	EightThousand	Club		
14. Route 18 Motel	Route	18	Motel	
15. Route 21 Hotel	Route	21	Hotel	
16. Route By-Pass Diner	Route	Bypass	Diner	

Questions for Discussion

1. Why is a title in a personal name considered the last unit of the filing segment while a title used in a business name is filed as written? (1)

2. Is a married woman's name filed differently than a single woman's name or a man's name? (2)

3. Why might a filer cross-reference a married woman's name? (2)

4. Why are articles and particles treated the same in indexing order regardless of the spacing between the prefix and the rest of the name? (3)

5. When two or more personal or business names are identical, is the state name or the city name considered first as the location unit for indexing purposes? (4)

6. When both a street address and a building name are included in an address, which unit(s) is used in indexing? (4)

7. In what order are house numbers considered when they are in figures? When they are written out? (4)

8. How are street names with compass directions considered in filing? (4)

9. How are seniority titles used in determining filing order? (4)

10. How are numbers written in digit form in a business name considered for filing? How are numbers spelled out in a business name considered? (5)

11. In what order do you file Arabic numerals when you also have the same numbers in Roman numerals? (5)

Applications

Use a separate sheet of paper to answer the following applications:

1. What is the *key unit* in each of the following names? What is the *second* indexing unit in the same names? (1,2,3,5)

   a. De la Salle Furniture Mart
   b. Dr. Shirley Samuelson
   c. 21st Century Builders
   d. Brother Paul
   e. Mr. Anthony Restaurant
   f. Ms. Debra Flores Ramos
   g. Rev. Charles TenBroek
   h. Brother Peter Garcia
   i. The Sixth Street Theater
   j. Doctor Sun's Lotion

2. Indicate whether the alphabetic order of the two names in each of the following pairs of names is correct or incorrect. (1,2,3,4,5)

   a. Ms. Sally A. Schwartz (Boston)
      Miss Sally A. Schwartz (Cleveland)
   b. Top's Radio Supplies (Boston)
      Top's Radio Supplies (Baltimore)
   c. Father & Son Plumbing
      Father Timothy Aiken
   d. H and D Specialties, Inc.
      Herbert D. MacDougal IV
   e. Dr. Michael A. Curtis, Jr. (St. Paul)
      Michael A. Curtis, Sr., M.D. (Minneapolis)
   f. Brother's Kitchen Ware
      Brother Louis Wade
   g. Susan M. Davies
      Susan L. Davis
   h. The Thos. Winter Shoe Shop
      Dr. Will S. Thomas
   i. 1018 River Road Ceramics
      10 Terrace Lane Inn
   j. Raymond D. Anzio
      D'Anzio Meat Wholesalers

3. What is the correct order in which each of the names within the following groups of three names would be arranged in an alphabetic file? Indicate the order by writing the numbers representing the correct order. (1,2,3,4,5)

   a. (1) Bill R. Kimura (2) William A. Kimura (3) Wm. Kimura and Sons
   b. (1) Miss Penny S. Canton (2) Ms. Canton's Bakery (3) Mrs. Charles A. Canton
   c. (1) Second Street Barber Shop (2) Secondhand Clothing, Inc. (3) Secure Zipper Company
   d. (1) O'Hare's Apple Cider (2) Fred C. Ohare (3) Janet O. Hare
   e. (1) Maj. Jack W. Edwards (2) Maj. Jack's Investment Service (3) Major Motor Repairs
   f. (1) Bert T. SanFelippo, Jr., 329 W. Poplar Street, Salem, Oregon
      (2) Bert T. SanFelippo, Sr., 197 W. Oak Street, Portland, Oregon
      (3) Bert T. SanFelippo, 26 W. Pine Street, Salem, Oregon
   g. (1) Lo Bue Studios (2) Greta M. Lo'Breglio (3) Gerry Lobus and Assoc.
   h. (1) 1263 Fourth Avenue Shop (2) 126 Fourth Avenue Dairy (3) 26 Fourth Avenue Cafe

4. Indicate for each of the following names whether or not a cross-reference card would be helpful. Write the filing segment in indexing order as it would appear on the cross-reference card. For those names that, in your

opinion, do not need a cross-reference, write "No cross-reference needed." (2)

a. Ms. Vicki L. Greene (Mrs. Charles J. Greene)
b. AAA (American Automobile Association)
c. Chi Chang
d. KL Motor Company
e. Mrs. Susan I. Casper
f. Mrs. Alberto L. Guerra (Ms. Louisa S. Guerra)

Job 2   Alphabetic Indexing of Names with Unique Characteristics   (1,2,3,4,5)

At this time complete Job 2 in OFFICE FILING PROCEDURES, Sixth Edition. Instructions and supplies for this job and the following jobs are included in the practice set.

CHAPTER 4

Alphabetic Indexing of Specialized Names

Learning Objectives

After completing Chapter 4, you will be able to:

1. Index and arrange in alphabetic order names of organizations and institutions.
2. Index, arrange in alphabetic order, and cross-reference single words separated into two or more parts.
3. Index, arrange in alphabetic order, and cross-reference hyphenated personal and business names.
4. Index and arrange in alphabetic order compound personal and business names.
5. Index and arrange in alphabetic order government names.
6. Explain how to determine when cross-referencing is helpful and list situations when cross-references are usually prepared.
7. Explain when subjects are used as primary titles.

ALPHABETIC INDEXING OF SPECIALIZED NAMES

The indexing order of the more common types of individual and business names was presented in Chapters 2 and 3. The rules in Chapter 2 covered the order of indexing units, as well as indexing minor words, punctuation, possessives, single letters, and abbreviations. The rules in Chapter 3 covered titles, names of married women, articles and particles, identical names, and numbers.

Chapter 4 now completes the indexing rules by presenting rules for indexing specialized names of organizations and institutions, separated single-word names, hyphenated names, compound names, and government names. Although deciding how to file some names is sometimes difficult, following specific indexing rules will ensure accuracy in filing and retrieving information (See Illustration 4-1). The importance of cross-referencing is also explained in this chapter.

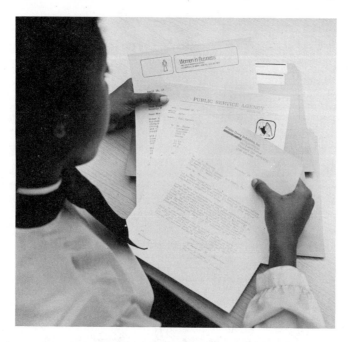

Illus. 4-1   Business Names are Indexed Using Letterheads as Guides

RULE 10: ORGANIZATIONS AND INSTITUTIONS

Use letterheads when indexing for filing.

Banks and other financial institutions, clubs, colleges, hospitals, hotels, lodges, motels, museums, religious institutions, schools, unions, universities, and other organizations and institutions are indexed and filed according to the names written on their letterheads. *The* used as the first word in these names is considered the last filing unit.

Why Rule 10 Is Needed. A consistent method of applying indexing rules is necessary in order to make filing and finding easy, quick, and accurate. Certain types of names of organizations and institutions sometimes present special indexing problems. Rule 10 will provide the safeguard that is needed for consistent indexing of such names.

Examples of Rule 10

	Index Order of Units in Names			
Name	**Key Unit**	**Unit 2**	**Unit 3**	**Unit 4**
1. The Association of Artists	Association	of	Artists	The
2. Atlanta Employees Union	Atlanta	Employees	Union	
3. Atlanta Savings Bank	Atlanta	Savings	Bank	
4. Baltimore Historical Museum	Baltimore	Historical	Museum	

Index Order of Units in Names

Name	Key Unit	Unit 2	Unit 3	Unit 4
5. Bank of Atlanta	Bank	of	Atlanta	
6. Bethel Lutheran Church	Bethel	Lutheran	Church	
7. Cape May High School	Cape	May	High	School
8. Church of Mental Science	Church	of	Mental	Science
9. The Committee for Justice	Committee	for	Justice	The
10. Council Community Hospital	Council	Community	Hospital	
11. Council on Human Relations	Council	on	Human	Relations
12. Eastern Association of Gardeners	Eastern	Association	of	Gardeners
13. Easton Hotel	Easton	Hotel		
14. Easton State University	Easton	State	University	
15. Foundation for the Blind	Foundation	for	the	Blind
16. Horace Mann Elementary School	Horace	Mann	Elementary	School
17. Hotel Victoria	Hotel	Victoria		
18. Local Order of Foresters	Local	Order	of	Foresters
19. Lutheran Church of Advent	Lutheran	Church	of	Advent
20. Motel Roberts	Motel	Roberts		
21. National Audubon Society	National	Audubon	Society	
22. National Federation for Gardeners	National	Federation	for	Gardeners
23. University of Texas	University	of	Texas	

RULE 11: SEPARATED SINGLE WORDS

Each part is a separate unit.

When a single word is separated into two or more parts in a business name, the parts are considered separate indexing units. If a name contains two compass directions separated by a space (South East Car Rental), each compass direction is a separate indexing unit. *Southeast* and *south-east* are considered single indexing units. Cross-reference if necessary. For example: South East SEE ALSO Southeast, South-East (See Illustration 4-2).

```
Good Will Copy Service


Good Will Copy Service
384 North Broad Street
Philadelphia, PA  19102-2386
```

```
Goodwill


SEE ALSO Good Will
```

Original Card   Cross-Reference Card

Illus. 4-2 Original and Cross-Reference Cards for a Name Using Separated Single Words

Why Rule 11 Is Needed. In order to follow Rule 1 consistently, business names must be indexed as they are written. This is done even though the local custom may be to combine words (especially compass terms) as one word or as hyphenated compound words. SEE ALSO cross-references will aid in referring the filer to the proper documents quickly.

Examples of Rule 11

Index Order of Units in Names

	Name	Key Unit	Unit 2	Unit 3	Unit 4
1.	Air Port Golf Range	Air	Port	Golf	Range
2.	Airport Florists	Airport	Florists		
3.	Good Will Copy Service	Good	Will	Copy	Service
4.	Wm. J. Good, DDS	Good	Wm	J	DDS
5.	Goodwill Industries	Goodwill	Industries		
6.	Goodwill Mfg. Co.	Goodwill	Mfg	Co	
7.	Ms.Natalie C. Goodwill	Goodwill	Natalie	C	Ms
8.	South East Veterans Cab	South	East	Veterans	Cab
9.	South Side Pharmacy, Inc.	South	Side	Pharmacy	Inc
10.	Miss Zelda P. South	South	Zelda	P	Miss
11.	Southeast Sales Corporation	Southeast	Sales	Corporation	

RULE 12: HYPHENATED NAMES

Personal Names

A. Personal Names. Hyphenated personal names are considered one indexing unit and the hyphen is ignored. *Jones-Bennett* is a single indexing unit—*JonesBennett.*

Business Names

B. Business Names. Hyphenated business and place names and coined business names are considered one indexing unit and the hyphen is ignored. *La-Z-Boy* is a single indexing unit—*LaZBoy.*

Why Rule 12 Is Necessary. Hyphenated personal surnames are becoming more common. Consistency is ensured in indexing these names according to Rule 3 by disregarding the hyphen. If a problem is expected in retrieving a document, a cross-reference could be made under the last word in the surname to refer the filer to the original name. Hyphenated business and place names also follow Rule 3 for consistency and could be cross-referenced, *if necessary.* (See Illustrations 4-3 and 4-4).

```
SnyderBaker Margaret Mrs


Mrs. Margaret Snyder-Baker
4136 Riverview Terrace
New York, NY  10022-1985
```

```
Baker Margaret Snyder Mrs


SEE SnyderBaker Margaret Mrs
```

Original Card   Cross-Reference Card

Illus. 4-3 Original and Cross-Reference Cards for a Hyphenated Personal Name

```
┌────────────────────────────────────┐   ┌────────────────────────────────────┐
│ BeckArnley Company                 │   │ ArnleyBeck Company                 │
│                                    │   │                                    │
│ Beck-Arnley Company                │   │ SEE BeckArnley Company             │
│ 842 Wabash Avenue                  │   │                                    │
│ Atlantic City, NJ  08401-1189      │   │                                    │
│                                    │   │                                    │
│                                    │   │                                    │
│                                    │   │                                    │
│                                    │   │                                    │
│                                    │   │                                    │
└────────────────────────────────────┘   └────────────────────────────────────┘
```

Original Card   Cross-Reference Card

Illus. 4-4 Original and Cross-Reference Cards for a Hyphenated Business Name

Examples of Rule 12

Index Order of Units in Names

Name	Key Unit	Unit 2	Unit 3	Unit 4
1. Dr. Rita F. Antic	Antic	Rita	F	Dr
2. Anti-Cruelty Society	AntiCruelty	Society		
3. Anti-Mite Termite Control	AntiMite	Termite	Control	
4. Antioch Insurance Agency	Antioch	Insurance	Agency	
5. Antonio's North-East Pizza	Antonios	NorthEast	Pizza	
6. Miss Mei-ling Niu	Niu	Meiling	Miss	
7. North Shore Boat Rentals	North	Shore	Boat	Rentals
8. North-East Tree Service	NorthEast	Tree	Service	
9. Dr. Sandra Northey-West	NortheyWest	Sandra	Dr	
10. North's Service Station	Norths	Service	Station	
11. Northshore Grocery Store	Northshore	Grocery	Store	
12. North-Shore Home Rentals	NorthShore	Home	Rentals	

RULE 13: COMPOUND NAMES

Personal Names

A. Personal Names. When separated by a space, compound personal names are considered separate indexing units. *Mary Lea Gerson* is three units.

   Note   Although *St. John* is a compound name, *St.* (Saint) is a prefix and follows Rule 7 which considers it a single indexing unit.

Business Names

B. Business Names. Compound business or place names with spaces between the parts of the name follow Rule 11, and the parts are considered separate units. New Jersey and Mid America are considered two indexing units each.

Why Rule 13 Is Needed. All compound names separated by spaces should be indexed according to Rule 1. Each word is filed as a separate unit each time it is indexed; otherwise, related documents would be filed in widely separated sections of the file.

Examples of Rule 13

Index Order of Units in Names

Name	Key Unit	Unit 2	Unit 3	Unit 4
1. Miss Mary Ann Mercado	Mercado	Mary	Ann	Miss
2. Miss Maryann Mercado	Mercado	Maryann	Miss	
3. Mid America Snow Blowers	Mid	America	Snow	Blowers
4. Mid-America Computer Sales	MidAmerica	Computer	Sales	
5. New Jersey Casualty Co.	New	Jersey	Casualty	Co
6. Sandra Lee Newhouse	Newhouse	Sandra	Lee	
7. Pan American Bus System	Pan	American	Bus	System
8. Pan-American Life Ins. Co.	PanAmerican	Life	Ins	Co
9. Panel-Fab, Inc.	PanelFab	Inc		
10. PanOhio Mortgage Co.	PanOhio	Mortgage	Co	
11. Sainte Marie Park	SainteMarie	Park		
12. Barbara Saint John	SaintJohn	Barbara		
13. San-Dee Chemical Products	SanDee	Chemical	Products	
14. San Jose Luxury Apartments	SanJose	Luxury	Apartments	
15. South Dakota Trucking Co.	South	Dakota	Trucking	Co

RULE 14: GOVERNMENT NAMES

Federal Government Names

Federal. The name of a federal government agency is indexed by the name of the government unit (United States Government) followed by the most distinctive name of the office, bureau, department, etc., as written (Internal Revenue Service). The words "Office of," "Department of," "Bureau of," etc., *if needed* for clarity and in the official name, are added and considered separate indexing units.

    Note If "of" is not a part of the official name as written, it is not added.

State and Local Government Names

State and Local. The names of state, province, county, parish, city, town, township, and village governments/political divisions are indexed by their distinctive names. The words "State of," "County of," "City of," "Department of," etc., are added only *if needed* for clarity and in the official name, and are considered separate indexing units (Wisconsin/Transportation/Department/of).

Foreign Government Names

Foreign. The distinctive English name is the first indexing unit for foreign government names. This is followed, *if needed* and in the official name, by the balance of the formal name of the government. Branches, departments, and divisions follow in order by their distinctive names. States, colonies, provinces, cities, and other divisions of foreign governments are followed by their distinctive or official names as spelled in English (Canada; Poland; France, Paris). Cross-reference the written foreign name to the English name, if necessary (See Illustrations 4-5 and 4-6).

Note The *United States Government Manual* and the *Congressional Directory*, published annually, report a current list of United States government agencies and offices. *Countries, Dependencies, Areas of Special Sovereignty, and Their Principal Administrative Divisions*, published by the U.S. Department of Commerce, National Bureau of Standards, provides a list of geographic and political entities of the world and associated standard codes. The *State Information Book* by Susan Lukowski provides an up-to-date list of state departments and their addresses. The *World Almanac and Book of Facts*, updated annually, includes facts and statistics on many foreign nations, and is helpful as a source which gives the English spellings of many foreign names.

```
Aluminum Corporation of Belgium The


The Aluminum Corporation of Belgium
Brussels, Belgium
```

```
LAluminum Beige Societe Anonyme


SEE Aluminum Corporation of Belgium The
```

Original Card   Cross-Reference Card

Illus. 4-5   Original and Cross-Reference Cards for a Foreign Business Name

```
Uruguay Republic of
    Public Education Secretary of

Secretary of Public Education
Montevideo, Uruguay
```

```
Republica Oriental del Uruguay
    Secretario de Educacion Publica

SEE Uruguay Republic of
    Public Education Secretary of
```

Original Card   Cross-Reference Card

Illus. 4-6   Original and Cross-Reference Cards for a Foreign Government Name

Why Rule 14 Is Needed. Most organizations correspond with several government offices. The trend toward multinational business has increased the correspondence with foreign government offices. The only way to retrieve documents to and from these offices properly is through consistent indexing as presented in Rule 14.

Examples of Rule 14

Name	Index Form of Name
1. Department of Commerce State of Alabama Montgomery, Alabama	Alabama State of Commerce Department of Montgomery Alabama
2. Department of Public Welfare State of Arkansas Little Rock, Arkansas	Arkansas State of Public Welfare Department of Little Rock Arkansas
3. State Protocol Hospitality and Conference Section Dominion of Canada Ottawa, Ontario Canada	Canada Dominion of Hospitality and Conference Section State Protocol Ottawa Ontario Canada
4. Department of Public Works Hartford, Connecticut	Hartford Public Works Department of Hartford Connecticut
5. Leon County Department of Public Welfare Tallahassee, Florida	Leon County Public Welfare Department of Tallahassee Florida
6. Department of Safety Tallahassee, Florida	Tallahassee Safety Department of Tallahassee Florida
7. Management Divisions Agricultural Research Service U.S. Department of Agriculture	United States Government Agriculture Department of Agricultural Research Service Management Divisions
8. Patent Office U.S. Department of Commerce	United States Government Commerce Department of Patent Office
9. Bureau of Enforcement Food and Drug Administration U.S. Department of Health and Human Services	United States Government Health and Human Services Department of Food and Drug Administration Enforcement Bureau of

CROSS-REFERENCING

When names are properly indexed and arranged alphabetically in a card file, there is usually little difficulty in locating a card bearing a particular name. In some cases, however, difficulties are encountered because (1) the unit in the name that was given second position or added to first position for filing purposes is not known to the person looking for the card or (2) the name that is thought of by the person looking for the card is not the name under which the card is filed, even though the two names may be related.

Cross-reference cards aid in finding names.

Business names, like individuals' names, sometimes present difficulties in filing because someone requesting information about a certain company may not remember the exact name of the company or may remember only part of it. Such difficulties are overcome in filing practice by using cross-reference cards. The index form of a name is used as the basis for filing the original card. Another form or arrangement of the name is used as the basis for the preparation of a second card, known as the **cross-reference card**.

Avoid unnecessary cross-referencing.

The extent of cross-referencing is determined primarily by the needs of the office or business the card file serves. If it is probable that more than one name will be associated with the same information or material, cross-reference cards should be used. Unnecessary cross-referencing should be avoided because it may create confusion and it is a time- and space-consuming operation.

Several examples of the use of cross-references have already been presented. In Chapter 2, Illustration 2-6 shows a cross-reference for an unusual personal name, and Illustration 2-7 shows a cross-reference for an organization using an acronym. In Chapter 3, Illustration 3-2 shows a cross-reference for a married woman's name.

In this chapter, Illustration 4-2 shows a SEE ALSO cross-reference for a name with separated single words. Illustration 4-3 shows a cross-reference for a hyphenated personal name, Illustration 4-4 presents a cross-reference for a hyphenated business name, Illustration 4-5 shows a cross-reference for a foreign business name, and Illustration 4-6 shows a cross-reference for a foreign government name. There are other instances where cross-references may be useful.

Compound Names

Compound Names

When a business name includes two or more individual surnames, it is often desirable to prepare a cross-reference card for each surname other than the first (See Rule 13). For example, if an original card is made out for Lorna Dorst & John Olsen Manufacturing, the original card and the cross-reference card should be made out to show the information in Illustration 4-7.

```
Lorna Dorst and John Olsen Manufacturing

Lorna Dorst & John Olsen Manufacturing
14 Industrial Park
Harrison, AR  72602-4531
```

```
John Olsen and Lorna Dorst Manufacturing

SEE Lorna Dorst and John Olsen
    Manufacturing
```

Original Card

Cross-Reference Card

Illus. 4-7 Original and Cross-Reference Cards for a Compound Name

If an original card is made out for O'Neill, Fletcher, and Buss Attorneys, two cross-reference cards may be needed and would look like those in Illustration 4-8.

Fletcher Buss and ONeill Attorneys SEE ONeill Fletcher and Buss Attorneys

Buss ONeill and Fletcher Attorneys SEE ONeill Fletcher and Buss Attorneys

First Cross-Reference Card   **Second Cross-Reference Card**

Illus. 4-8   Cross-Reference Cards for a Three-Name Firm

There are several circumstances under which a business may be known by more than one name:

1. A business operating under a long name may be popularly referred to by a shortened name, such as Rossing's for Rossing's Restaurant and Pizza Shop.
2. A business may have its own name, but it may actually be a subsidiary of another company. For example, a firm with the name of Alfonso Business Forms may be a subsidiary of the firm Southern Industries, Inc.
3. A store (for example, Aurora Distributors) may be a branch of a large organization (Mountain Wholesale Group) that gives to each branch the name of the city in which the branch is located.

Original Card	**Cross-Reference Card**
Rossings	Rossings Restaurant and Pizza Shop SEE Rossings
Alfonso Business Forms	Southern Industries Inc SEE Alfonso Business Forms
Aurora Distributors	Mountain Wholesale Group SEE Aurora Distributors

The name that is used on the original card is the name appearing on the letterhead.

Similar Names

Similar Names

When several surnames are identical or similar in pronunciation but different in spelling, permanent cross-references should be made to *each* of the various spellings of the name as shown below:

Meyer SEE ALSO Maier Mayer Mair   Maier SEE ALSO Meyer Mayer Mair
Mayr Meier Myer   Mayr Meier Myer

Mair SEE ALSO Meyer Maier Mayer   Mayer SEE ALSO Meyer Maier Mair
Mayr Meier Myer   Mayr Meier Myer

SUBJECTS AS PRIMARY TITLES

Subject titles may be preferred to names.

Sometimes the use of a certain subject title is preferable to the use of names as titles for indexing purposes. In such a case, a company's filing rules must authorize the specific subject title to be used. The subject title *then becomes the first part* of the filing segment, and personal or business names are used *as needed* for subsequent indexing units. If the subject title does not appear on material being coded, it should be written in the upper right corner of the document.

Applications for employment and bids on construction, as examples, are usually filed according to the subject titles rather than by correspondents' names. In such a subject breakdown, *use the subject title as the first unit(s) in the filing segment.* Names of correspondents are then arranged alphabetically within the subject classification.

Examples of Indexed Names When Subjects are Used as Key Units

		Index Order of Units in Names			
Key Unit	**Name**	**Unit 2**	**Unit 3**	**Unit 4**	**Unit 5**
Applications (for employment)	Sally A. Gregory	Gregory	Sally	A	
Applications (for employment)	George C. Hahn	Hahn	George	C	
Automobile Rental Service	Avis Rent A Car	Avis	Rent	A	Car
Automobile Rental Service	Budget Rent-A-Car	Budget	RentACar		
Insurance Agencies	Abbott & Adams, Inc.	Abbott	and	Adams	Inc
Insurance Agencies	Aetna Ins. Co.	Aetna	Ins	Co	

Questions for Discussion

1. In what order are the names of most organizations and institutions indexed? (1)

2. What is the difference between the indexing of two words separated by a hyphen and a single word separated into two parts? (2,3)

3. How would you determine if two or more words should be considered as one word or as a series of separate words? (2,3)

4. How are separate parts of compound personal names indexed? Compound place names? Compound business names? (4)

5. Give four examples of types of names that probably should be cross-referenced. (6)

6. Give two examples of subject titles that would probably be used as key units instead of names of businesses or of persons. (7)

Applications

Use a separate sheet of paper to answer the following applications.

1. What is the *key unit* in each of the following names? What is the *second indexing unit* in the same names? (1,2,3,4)

   a. The Minneapolis Bank
   b. New Jersey Milk Producers
   c. Crossroads Restaurant
   d. Julius V. Angus-Scott
   e. John St. Charles

   f. Chao-cheng Sun
   g. Biannual Flower Show
   h. Bay City Rotary Club
   i. Top-of-the-Rock Parking Co.
   j. Third Presbyterian Church

2. What is the *key unit* in each of the following names? What is the *second indexing unit* in the same names? (1,2,3,4)

   a. WCQU Radio Station
   b. The Motel Midway
   c. University of Nebraska, Lincoln
   d. Panama City Optimist Club
   e. Union Bank of Dayton, Ohio

   f. *The Daily Herald*, Kansas City, MO
   g. Northeast Bakery
   h. Association of Accounts
   i. St. Ann's Elementary School, Salem, MA
   j. North East Express Service

3. Is the order of the two names in each of the following pairs correct or incorrect? (1,2,3,4)

   a. Northeast Antique Shops
      Sally A. North
   b. B-4 Dinner Treats
      Arnold Q. Befour
   c. KVLY Radio Station
      KMTN Television Station
   d. Nonstop Power Generators
      Non-stop Water Softeners
   e. King George Hotel
      Hotel King Edward

   f. Kool-Lite Luminaries
      Kooling Coils, Inc.
   g. Peter L. St. Francis
      St. Francis Monastery
   h. First State Savings, Colby, KS
      First State Savings, Evansville, IN
   i. 2d Street Gas Station
      3d Street Arcade
   j. The Airport Restaurant
      The Air Port Hotel

4. What is the correct order in which each of the names in the following groups of three would be arranged in an alphabetic file? Indicate the order by writing the numbers representing the correct order. (1,3,4)

   a. (1) The In-Town Store (2) In and Out Cleaners (3) Introductions, Inc.
   b. (1) Sara M. De La Cotera (2) Sam's Delicatessen (3) Vinny C. Dela
   c. (1) Jos. Riteman, MD (2) The RTE Company (3) R-T-E Shops
   d. (1) Benj. F. Soga (2) Benjamin A. Soga (3) Soga Beauty Shoppe
   e. (1) Two-Brothers' Sandals (2) Brother Tom (3) Clara Brothers-Smith
   f. (1) University of Art (2) Artist's Hotel (3) Association of Artists
   g. (1) Mrs. Jane M. Carpenter (Charles E., Jr.) (2) Carpenter's Hoppy House (3) Charles E. Carpenter, Sr.
   h. (1) The Quick-Cote Paint Co. (2) The Quick House of Tools (3) C. H. Quick
   i. (1) San Francisco Appliances (2) Frank San (3) Bay High School, San Francisco
   j. (1) Hotel Miami (2) *The Miami Tribune* (3) Miami Beach Swim Suits

5. Write the following names in correct indexing order. If a name or address is incomplete, add the words required to complete it. (5)

   a. Research Division
      U.S. Department of Housing and
         Urban Development
      451 7th Street NW
      Washington, DC 20410-1177
   b. Thiel College
      Greenville, PA 16125-1292
   c. Peoples National Bank
      Dover, DE 19901-1080
   d. *The Clarion-Ledger*
      Jackson, MS 39210-1565
   e. Department of Public Safety
      Grand Forks, ND 58201-6321
   f. Martin Luther King High School
      Detroit, MI 48221-3147
   g. *Life Magazine*
      Time, Inc.
      New York, NY 10003-4590
   h. Butler County Sheriff's Department
      El Dorado, KS 67042-1330
   i. Department of Naturalization
      Republic of Ireland
      Dublin, Ireland
   j. Bureau of Dairy Industry
      Idaho Commissioner of Agriculture
      Boise, ID 83725-2559

6. Indicate for each of the following names whether a cross-reference card would be helpful by writing the filing segment in indexing order as it would appear on the cross-reference card. For those names that, in your opinion, do not need a cross-reference, write "No cross-reference needed." (6)

   a. C. M. Ames and T. L. Maxwell Medical Center
   b. Sportland Arena
   c. Mrs. Sara T. Greene (Mrs. Thomas C. Greene)
   d. The Clinton-Reed Company
   e. The Johnstown Inn
   f. Sackner, Marion, and Gordon Agency
   g. Mark S. Moeller (pronounced Miller)
   h. *The Philadelphia Inquirer*
   i. The American Plumbing Supply Company
   j. Explorers Association of Texas
   k. TAC Floor Coverings
   l. Northeast Paper Distributors, Inc.
   m. Johnson's Klear-Site Windows, Inc.

Job 3   Alphabetic Indexing of Specialized Names
(1,2,3,4,5,6,7)

At this time complete Job 3 in OFFICE FILING PROCEDURES, Sixth Edition. Instructions and supplies for this job are included in the practice set.

PART 3

Alphabetic Filing Procedures and Controls

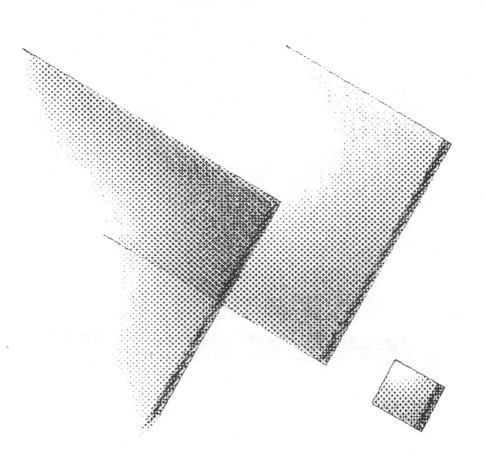

CHAPTER 5

Alphabetic Correspondence Filing

Learning Objectives

After completing Chapter 5, you will be able to:

1. Define an alphabetic correspondence file.
2. Describe the equipment necessary to establish the file.
3. List the supplies necessary to establish the file.
4. Describe the arrangement of guides and folders in the file.
5. Explain the use of guides and folders.
6. Explain the use of numbers and colors to code sections of an alphabetic correspondence file.
7. Prepare correspondence for an alphabetic correspondence file.
8. Prepare a cross-reference when necessary.
9. Sort correspondence for filing.
10. Place correspondence in the file.

DEFINING THE ALPHABETIC CORRESPONDENCE FILE

Alphabetic: an arrangement in the regular order of the alphabet.
Correspondence: the letters received or written.
File: a collection of related records treated as a unit.

An alphabetic correspondence file is . . .

An **alphabetic correspondence file** is a collection of letters and memos, received or written, arranged in alphabetic order. Correspondence may be classified by company or client name, by subject, or by geographic location. The classification of correspondence is determined by the special needs of the organization. If information is needed on a particular subject, idea, or geographic location, then the correspondence is organized in that way. If information is most likely to be requested by name, then that is how the correspondence should be classified.

A combination of name and subject classifications is possible.

Although the correspondence of an organization is *most commonly* arranged alphabetically by company or client name, a combination of name and subject arrangements is more realistic. An alphabetic correspondence *name* file may very well contain special *subject* sections for all correspondence related to one particular subject, such as Advertising Rates, Applications, or

Banks. The best classification of correspondence is the one that best serves the information needs of the organization.

EXAMINING THE FILE

The alphabetic correspondence file illustrated in this chapter classifies correspondence primarily by company or client name. The use of special subject classifications within the correspondence *name* file is also illustrated. First, you will examine the equipment necessary to establish the file; then you will examine the supplies and their arrangement in the alphabetic correspondence file.

Equipment

Naturally the first piece of equipment needed for a filing system is a container to protect and to store the business papers in an orderly manner. Both vertical and lateral files are used for this purpose.

The traditional filing cabinet is the vertical file.

Vertical File. The traditional **vertical filing cabinet**, like the one shown in Illustration 5-1, continues to be the most familiar housing for business papers. The cabinet has pull-out drawers which hold business papers in a front-to-back vertical arrangement. Vertical file cabinets are available in a variety of colors and in one- to six-drawer units. They may be water- and fire-resistant as well.

Illus. 5-1 Vertical Filing Cabinet

Lateral File. If you imagine a bookshelf with folders stacked upright in a side-by-side arrangement, you have a mental picture of a **lateral file.** An open-shelf lateral file may be enclosed with "front doors" that slide from side to side, lift up, or pull down. Lateral files are also available in single- or multiple-unit cabinets with pull-out drawers (See Illustration 5-2). Lateral filing cabinet drawers do not require as much pull-out space as vertical filing cabinet drawers. Because they require less floor space and provide easier access to records, lateral files are widely used.

Lateral files save floor space.

Illus. 5-2   Lateral Drawer File

Supplies

The important supplies from which the filing system is built include (1) **guides** to mark sections in the filing system, (2) **folders** to hold the papers, and (3) **labels** to affix to the folders. In Chapter 2 you studied guides, tabs, captions, and labels used in card filing. They are the same in a correspondence file, except they are larger.

Guides mark the location.

Guides. The **guides** used in a filing system can be compared to street signs. Guides show the names of areas within a filing system just as street signs show names of streets in a city. A file without guides would be like a city without street signs. It would take a door-to-door search to find anyone!

Guides mark and separate the major alphabetic sections of the filing system (A-Ac, Ad-Ag). Some special guides may point out the location of correspondence related to special subjects (Advertising Rates, Applications, Taxes) or correspondence that is frequently requested (Agatha Cosmetics, Bentley Electronics, Inc).

A guide such as the one shown in Illustration 5-3 is made from a single piece of heavy pressboard. The small piece that rises above the top of the guide is called a **tab.** Either a letter of the alphabet or a name appears on the guide tab. This letter, or name, on the tab is called a **caption.** Alphabetic guides are available with preprinted tabs for the letters in the alphabet. Some guides allow you to type your own captions and insert them into the tabs of the guides.

Folders. Papers are never filed loosely between the guides. Papers are placed in **folders** that protect them and keep them upright and accessible. Folders are made of a heavy paper known as manila or kraft paper. A sheet of this material is folded in a "V" shape, with the front panel about one-half inch shorter than the back. This fold forms the pocket into which papers can be placed. Generally several **score marks** (fold lines) are made at the bottom of the "V" so that the folder can be refolded in an expanded "U" shape. This permits the storage of more papers in the folder in an orderly manner.

Plastic folders are available.

Plastic folders in a variety of colors are also available. These folders are more expensive than manila folders, but they are more durable during excessive handling and, of course, can be used again and again.

File folders (See Illustration 5-4) have tabs similar to tabs on file guides. Folder tabs that protrude above the normal height of folders also require captions that show letters of the alphabet, names, subject, and/or numbers. Such captions tell which papers are stored in that particular folder.

Hanging Folders. As the name implies, hanging folders *hang* suspended in the file drawer (See Illustration 5-5). They do not touch the bottom of the file drawer. Rails can be installed down the sides of any file drawer. Metal or plastic hooks which extend beyond the edge of the folder simply rest on the rails. The hanging folders easily slide forward and back along the rails, and all folders remain in an upright position. A folder can be removed and replaced easily without disrupting other folders in the file.

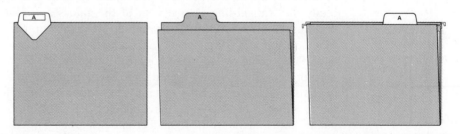

Illus. 5-3   Guide   **Illus. 5-4   Standard Folder**   **Illus. 5-5   Hanging Folder**

The Cut of Guide and Folder Tabs. Guides and folders are placed in file drawers or on shelves so that each guide and folder tab is easily visible when scanning the file. The more visible the guides and folders, the faster the search of a certain alphabetic section and the location of a needed folder. Manufacturers of guides and folders know this and have made provisions for it by cutting the tabs of both guides and folders at different positions across the top or side edges. Folders are manufactured in a variety of **cuts**, or positions. Illustration 5-6 shows fifth-, third-, half-, and full-cut folders. The fraction refers to the proportion of the total folder width that is used for the folder tab. A half-cut folder tab, for example, occupies one-half the total width of the folder.

Alternate tab positions allow guides and folders to be arranged in a number of ways in the vertical or lateral file. Tabs are on the side of the guides and folders in open-shelf lateral files. Generally tabs are at the top for the vertical and lateral *drawer* files.

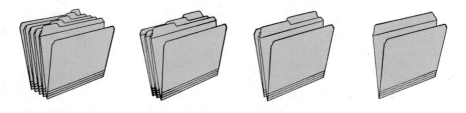

Illus. 5-6   Standard Tab Cuts on Folders

Labels. It is both difficult and inefficient to try to type directly on the folder tab. Captions for file folders are typed on **labels.** Labels are available in a variety of sizes and colors. The self-adhesive, pressure-sensitive (no lick!) labels on sheets or folded strips are the simplest to use. They are easy to insert into the typewriter and easy to apply to the folder tab.

Arrangement of Guides and Folders

A straight-line arrangement of guides and folders creates an orderly file.

Now you know about cabinets, guides, folders, tabs, and captions. Look next at how they all work together in the alphabetic correspondence filing system. Study the straight-line arrangement of the guides and folders, from front to back, in the file drawer in Illustration 5-7. The tabs on the guides and folders were selected and arranged to create a *straight-line* (front-to-back) file. Tabs and folders could be *staggered* horizontally across the file, but the addition or deletion of a folder would eventually create a jumbled arrangement of folders in the file. As you read the material that follows, study Illustration 5-7 and locate the parts of the system that are being described. Notice that the tabs on guides and folders are in four different positions. This is done to make the tabs as easy to see as possible. Each of the four positions is reserved for one

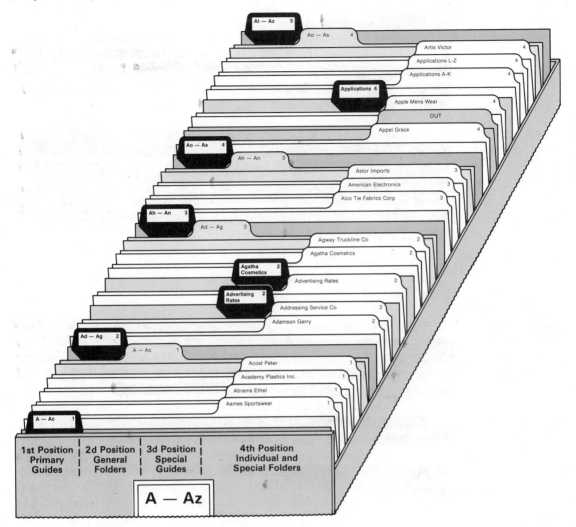

Illus. 5-7 Alphabetic Correspondence File

type of guide or folder and follows a straight line from the front to the back of the file drawer. In this system, the positions are used as follows:

1. *First position* (on the left side) is reserved for **primary guides**.
2. *Second position* (from the left side) is used for **general folders**.
3. *Third position* holds the **special guides**.
4. *Fourth position* is reserved for **individual folders** and **special folders**.

The positions of guides and folders may vary from one filing system to another. The names and functions of the guides and folders in a filing system, however, are more universally understood. Study them now.

Primary guides are in first position.

Primary Guides. The three primary guides in *first position* are the "street signs" referred to earlier in this chapter. They guide the eye to the main alphabetic sections of the filing system. They are placed in first position because they are seen first when the file drawer is opened. Sometimes primary guides are staggered between first and second positions, but this *first* position places them in a prominent visual location.

General folders are in second position.

General Folders. The tab on each of these *second-position* folders bears the same alphabetic caption as the one shown on the primary guide in each alphabetic section of the file. A primary guide opens an alphabetic section in the file; a general folder closes the section. These folders are given the name **general** (or **miscellaneous**) because each is used to hold papers from persons or companies with whom there is not enough correspondence to justify the use of an individual folder. For example, in Illustration 5-7 the A-Ac 1 general folder holds all papers from correspondents with names beginning with the letters A to Ac (Aames Tire Co., Abbott, and Acosta & Sons); the name Jane Adams would be placed in the next alphabetic section general folder, Ad-Ag 2.

Special guides are in third position.

Special Guides. In Illustration 5-7 special guides are located in *third position.* The guide for Agatha Cosmetics is an example of a special name guide. It pinpoints the location of a *fourth-position* individual folder for this company. This special guide was added to the filing system because of frequent requests for papers from the Agatha Cosmetics folder. With the aid of the special guide, this folder is more easily located.

Sometimes a special guide is used to mark the location of a single folder or a series of folders that relate to a particular subject. Notice the guides labeled Advertising Rates and Applications in the illustration. These special guides show the location of special subject folders that contain correspondence related to a specific subject. Obviously it is more efficient in the organization to keep all correspondence related to these topics in one location in the file.

Individual folders are in fourth position.

Individual and Special Folders. When correspondence or other material relating to persons or companies increases in volume, individual folders are prepared for those persons or companies. Generally when five pieces of correspondence relate to the same person or organization, the filer prepares an individual folder for that correspondent. Sometimes the anticipated activity of a particular company or client will prompt the preparation of an individual folder. The use of individual folders speeds up the retrieval of active correspondence and also helps to relieve the overcrowded conditions that may exist in the general folder.

Folders for Agatha Cosmetics and Applications (in fourth position in Illustration 5-7) are examples of individual folders. Notice that the tabs on these individual folders are double the width of the tabs on the guides and general folders. This extra width provides the space required for labeling long personal or company names.

Coding by Number and/or Color

Number Coding

Study Illustration 5-7 again and notice that there are four complete alphabetic sections in the illustration. Each section is opened by a primary guide and is closed by a general folder. Also, note that every item in a particular alphabetic section is assigned the same number. This is a form of **alpha-numeric** coding: all guides and folders within an **alpha**betic section of the file are identified as belonging to a particular **numeric** group. Numeric coding makes it easier to return borrowed folders to their correct file locations.

Color Coding

Colored folders and labels are used effectively also to code sections of the file. A color in the wrong section of a file is even more noticeable than a number out of sequence. Numeric and color coding help to locate specific sections of the file more quickly, as well as to reduce the number of misfiled records.

USING THE FILE

The alphabetic correspondence file is now established. Its primary function is to locate information quickly. The value of a filing system as an information center is determined by how the correspondence has been placed in it. If the file is to continue to be a valuable resource center, then procedures for preparing correspondence and placing it into the files must be followed systematically and consistently by ALL file users.

Preparing the Correspondence

Filing correspondence should never be a question of "Where shall I file it?" but always "How will I most likely ask for it?" Filing *to find* is relatively simple if you master and apply the skills and procedures that follow:

Apply indexing rules and procedures consistently.

1. Know and use consistently an acceptable set of indexing rules. You learned these in Chapters 2, 3, and 4.
2. Learn to select the one name in a letter that is to be used for the filing segment.
3. Know how to code the filing segment. You learned this in Chapter 2 and in Jobs 1, 2, and 3. More about coding names in letters is given in this chapter.
4. Use the same procedures every time you receive and prepare letters or other materials for filing. You will learn these procedures now.

Using a Time Stamp. In many companies a mail room clerk opens the mail and marks each letter with a dated rubber stamp or a time-stamp machine. This mark is called a **time stamp.** The stamp records the date, and sometimes the time, of the receipt of each piece of mail. (See Illustration 5-8 for an example of a time-stamp mark.)

Making a Release Mark. After mail is time stamped, it is sorted according to names of individuals or departments and is delivered to them. After a letter has been read and answered, both the original letter and a copy of the reply to it are *released* to the records department for filing.

The **release mark** is made on the letter by a secretary or by the person who originally received the letter. The initials of either person are written in the upper left part of the original letter. (See Illustration 5-8 for an example of a release mark.) A copy of an answering letter does not need a release mark. Assume that such a copy would not have reached the records department without the knowledge and approval of the person who wrote it.

Preparing letters for the file.

Inspecting Papers for Filing. When the records department receives material for filing, a filer *inspects* it to see that it has been released in the proper manner. The filer also determines whether or not the paper has been *precoded*. Precoding is explained later.

Making Filing Segment Decisions. The name by which a piece of correspondence is filed is called the **filing segment.** Sometimes it appears that more than one name in a letter might be used as the filing segment. In this case, the filer must decide which of several names is to be used as the filing segment for filing purposes.

In making such decisions, the filer must know and use consistently a set of coding rules. If the rules are not known or used consistently, filing segments might not be the same from one time to another or between one filer and another. This would make the finding of papers in a filing system more difficult and, because of wasted time, more costly.

Rules for Selecting Filing Segments. In general, correspondence is filed under the most important name in it. That name must be the one by which the letter is most likely to be requested. When selecting a name as the filing segment, use the following rules:

1. Use either the *name of the company that appears on the letterhead* or the *name of the person who signs the incoming letter* as the filing segment.
2. Use the *company name* that appears in the letter address of an outgoing letter for the filing segment; if no company name appears in the letter address, then use the *name of an individual* in the letter address as the filing segment.
3. If a *subject* or a *name* written *in the body of a letter* is considered to be of greatest importance to filing and finding, use that subject or that name as the filing segment. Write the filing segment on the top right side of the letter.
4. When *special sections* with *special titles* occur in a filing system, use them as filing segments. Write the filing segment in exact form on the tops of letters or other materials being coded for filing in special sections. For example, if there is a special section in the filing system for Advertising Rates, code the letter by writing the title, Advertising Rates, at the top of the letter.

Coding and Rating Filing Units. Once the filing segment is selected, code and rate the filing units to show the proper filing order. Marking the filing segment is called **coding.** Marking the *order* in which the various parts of the filing segment are to be considered for filing purposes is called **rating.**

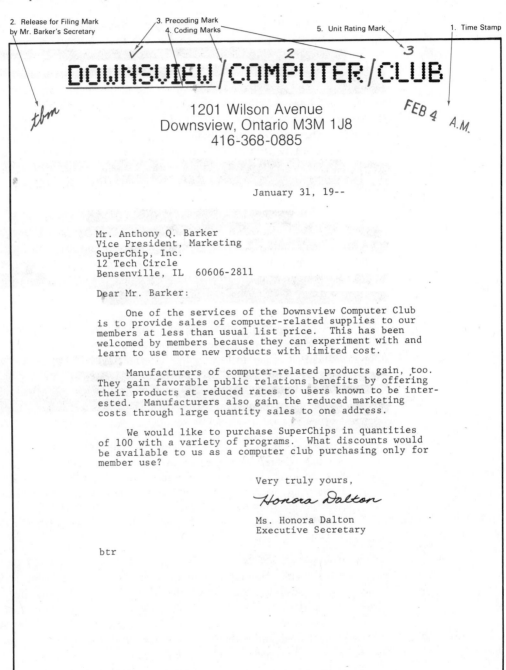

2. Release for Filing Mark
by Mr. Barker's Secretary

3. Precoding Mark
4. Coding Marks

5. Unit Rating Mark

1. Time Stamp

DOWNSVIEW/COMPUTER/CLUB

1201 Wilson Avenue
Downsview, Ontario M3M 1J8
416-368-0885

FEB 4   A.M.

January 31, 19--

Mr. Anthony Q. Barker
Vice President, Marketing
SuperChip, Inc.
12 Tech Circle
Bensenville, IL 60606-2811

Dear Mr. Barker:

    One of the services of the Downsview Computer Club
is to provide sales of computer-related supplies to our
members at less than usual list price. This has been
welcomed by members because they can experiment with and
learn to use more new products with limited cost.

    Manufacturers of computer-related products gain, too.
They gain favorable public relations benefits by offering
their products at reduced rates to users known to be interested. Manufacturers also gain the reduced marketing
costs through large quantity sales to one address.

    We would like to purchase SuperChips in quantities
of 100 with a variety of programs. What discounts would
be available to us as a computer club purchasing only for
member use?

                    Very truly yours,

                    Honora Dalton

                    Ms. Honora Dalton
                    Executive Secretary

     btr

Illus. 5-8   Incoming Letter Time Stamped, Released, Precoded, Coded, and Rated

Underline the key unit.

When you write a note to someone, you probably automatically underline the most important part in order to be sure that the person "gets the message." Do the same when coding papers for filing: Underline the most important filing unit in the filing segment. This underlined unit is the **key** (first) **unit** under which a name will be filed. Any other units in the name are separated by diagonal lines. Each of these filing units is given a rating number that shows its place in the indexing order of the name in relation to other names in the filing system. For example, when the name *Chicago Art Center* is selected as the filing segment, it is coded and rated as Chicago/Art/Center. The underlined word, *Chicago*, is the *key unit* under which the name will be filed. Art is the second unit. Center is the third filing unit in this name.

Precoding. Sometimes a secretary or the person to whom a letter is addressed in the organization will release and **precode** a letter by checking or underlining a name in the letter that should be used as the filing segment. Such a check mark is shown in the letter in Illustration 5-8. If there is no indication of a checked name, then the filer must scan the letter and select the name in it that is to be used as the filing segment.

Cross-Referencing. Sometimes the filing segment of a letter may have an alternate name under which the correspondence may be requested. A cross-reference makes it easier to locate such a letter. A **cross-reference** is an entry made by the filer to direct attention to an alternate location for a particular filed document. When there is a possibility that a letter may be called for by a name other than the one selected as the filing segment, prepare a cross-reference in this way:

File the letter by the filing segment; cross-reference the alternate name.

1. Draw a wavy line under the cross-reference name if it appears in the letter, or write the cross-reference name in the margin of the letter.
2. Mark the name to be cross-referenced with an "X" in the margin either opposite the name with the wavy underscore or next to the name written in the margin as the cross-reference.
3. Prepare a *cross-reference sheet* and file it under the name selected as the cross-reference.

An example of the need for a cross-reference is a company name composed of two personal names. Either of these names might be used when someone is requesting papers from the files. For example, in the company name Long & Richter, the correspondence would be filed under *Long*, but it might be desirable to cross-reference the name under *Richter*. A cross-reference sheet filed under the name *Richter* alerts a filer looking for Long & Richter papers that these are filed under *Long*.

An example of the need for a cross-reference when a letter contains another important name is shown in Illustrations 5-9 and 5-10. Benjamin Diaz Development Co. is the filing segment and Berman, Duncan & Archer, Attorneys, P.C., is the name to cross-reference. Illustration 5-9 shows a copy of the outgoing letter with the filing segment coded and rated and the cross-reference marked. Illustration 5-10 shows the cross-reference sheet prepared for this letter.

CROSS-REFERENCE SHEET

Name or Subject _Administration_
Financial and Legal Berman
Duncan and Archer Attorneys PC

Date of Item _3/28/--_

Regarding _Franchise_
Application

SEE

Name or Subject _Production_
Benjamin Diaz
Development Co

Authorized by _MD._ Date _3/31/--_

Illus. 5-10 Cross-Reference Sheet

March 28, 19--

Mr. Benjamin Diaz, President
Benjamin Diaz Development Co.
4700 Atlantic Avenue
Margate, NJ 08402-3212

Dear Mr. Diaz

Congratulations on the production and marketing success
of your small boat powered by a SuperChip-supported computer. We are pleased with your achievement.

We would be very happy to consider your application for
a franchise to program SuperChips at your manufacturing
facility. All franchise agreements and their details are
handled by our attorneys. Please contact Mr. Charles
Duncan, of Berman, Duncan & Archer, Attorneys, P.C., 216
State Street, Chicago, IL 60606-9303. Mr. Duncan will
send you the list of requirements for a franchise, the
application forms, and other details I am sure you will
want to review.

We are looking forward to receiving your application
through Mr. Duncan.

Sincerely

Ms. Karen L. DeCarlo
Vice President, Production

md

cc Mr. Charles Duncan

Illus. 5-9 Coded Copy of Letter

Sorting the Correspondence

After filing segments have been coded and necessary cross-references made, materials for the files are sorted. **Sorting** is the process of placing papers in alphabetic order before they are taken to the files and placed in folders.

Sorting serves two purposes: (1) It saves time. If materials were not sorted, you would have to move back and forth from one cabinet or shelf section to another in a random manner. If it doesn't give you a headache, this random movement wastes time; and since "time is money," money is wasted. (2) It makes finding easier. If papers are needed before they are filed, they can be found more easily if they are held in a sorted order rather than in a random stack.

Papers may be sorted by using specialized equipment such as sorting trays (See Illustration 5-11). Equipment such as this is composed of a series of alphabetically labeled guides that are held together in either a vertical or horizontal position.

If special sorting equipment is not available, papers can be sorted into alphabetic units in the following manner:

1. Divide materials into alphabetic stacks according to the first letters of the key units in the filing segments. For example, use five alphabetic stacks: A-D, E-H, I-M, N-S, T-Z.
2. Sort each of the five stacks into single alphabetic units. For example, the A-D stack may be sorted into separate stacks for A, B, C, and D.
3. Finally, sort each alphabetic section.

Steps 1 and 2 are known as **rough sorting**. Step 3 is **fine sorting**.

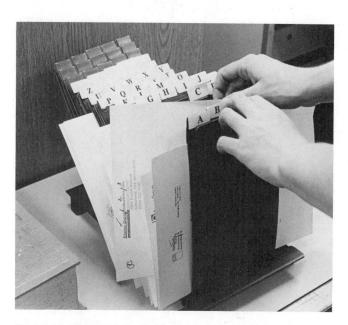

Illus. 5-11 Correspondence Sorter

Placing Correspondence in File Folders

All correspondence is placed in folders with the letterhead or the letter address at the left side and with the writing facing forward.

In *individual folders*, arrange letters according to the date of writing, with the most recently dated letter *at the front.*

In *general folders* and in single *special section folders*, place correspondence in alphabetic order according to the filing units in the filing segments. Then within each group of letters from and to the same person or company, place correspondence according to the date of writing. The letter with the most recent date is placed in front of all others in the group. For example, in a general folder captioned E-Em, letters would be filed as follows (reading from the front of the folder to the back):

	Order of Letters	Correspondents' Names	Dates on Letters
(Back)	6	2 El Rancho/Brands	October 28, 19–
	5	2 El Rancho/Brands	November 1, 19–
	4	2 El Rancho/Brands	November 6, 19–
	3	2 Ralph/Ekdahl	July 10, 19–
	2	3 2 The/Eiko/Corp.	September 26, 19–
(Front)	1	3 2 The/Eiko/Corp.	October 5, 19–

Questions for Discussion

1. Define an alphabetic correspondence file. (1)

2. What two kinds of equipment are commonly used to store and protect business papers? (2)

3. List the supplies necessary to establish the alphabetic correspondence file. (3)

4. Describe the arrangement of guides and folders in the alphabetic correspondence file. (4)

5. Why are guides and folders cut to various positions? (5)

6. How are primary guides used in an alphabetic correspondence filing system? (5)

7. How are general folders used in an alphabetic correspondence filing system? (5)

8. Are individual folders needed in an alphabetic correspondence filing system? Why or why not? (5)

9. Why are special sections useful in an alphabetic correspondence filing system? (5)

10. How are numbers and colors used to code sections of an alphabetic correspondence file? (6)

Job 4   Alphabetic Correspondence Filing   (7,8,9,10)

At this time, complete Job 4 in OFFICE FILING PROCEDURES, Sixth Edition. Instructions and supplies for this job are included in the practice set.

CHAPTER 6

Requisition, Charge, and Follow-Up Controls

Learning Objectives

After completing Chapter 6, you will be able to:

1. List the five procedures that are required for controlling the use of filed materials.
2. List the information required on a requisition form.
3. Explain the use of a requisition form (card or sheet).
4. Explain the use of an OUT guide and an OUT folder.
5. List two advantages of using a carrier folder.
6. Explain how to cancel the charges when borrowed materials are returned to the files.
7. List and explain the three methods for following up, or tracing, papers not returned to the file when expected.
8. List the four steps included in the procedures for using a follow-up file in a records department.
9. Describe procedures for providing needed information to users without removing valuable papers from the records department.
10. Explain how file materials to be used at a future time are reserved for a potential borrower.
11. List at least three uses of a follow-up file *other than* to retrieve papers that are not returned when expected.

In *Hamlet*, Act 1, Scene 3, part of the advice given by Polonius to his son Laertes is, "Neither a borrower nor a lender be. . . ." This might still be good advice for *personal behavior*, but not so good if you are working in a bank OR trying to control business records. In these operations, borrowing and lending are vital. Records departments exist in order to lend papers to those who need to borrow them (See Illustration 6-1).

Lending must be strictly controlled.

However, lending must be strictly controlled because some who borrow materials have the habit of not returning them. Left unchecked, the results of unreturned file materials are lost papers, frustrated borrowers, and unhappy records personnel. Avoid headaches such as these by following a systematic method of charging borrowers for materials removed from the files.

Illus. 6-1   Records Departments Control the Movement of File Materials

A complete system for controlling borrowed papers must include the following procedures:

1. *Requisitioning*: a well-known and accepted way for borrowers to request materials from the filing system.
2. *Charging*: a check-out system of charging borrowers (holding them responsible) for papers they have borrowed from the files.
3. *Canceling*: a method for canceling charges held against the borrower when papers are returned.
4. *Following up*: a way to follow up, or trace, and locate papers not returned on time.
5. *Reserving*: a reliable means of reserving papers that will be needed at some future time.

Each of these parts of a complete check-out system will be considered in this chapter.

REQUISITIONING

The form used to request records is known as a **requisition**. Illustration 6-2 shows one style of requisition form that is widely used—a **requisition card**.

Usually requisition cards are 5″ × 3″ in size and are printed to show (1) the name of the company or person whose papers are needed, (2) the name of the person and department making the request, (3) the date of the papers being borrowed, (4) the date the papers are taken, and (5) the date the papers are to be returned to the records department.

Name or Subject	Date Wanted
Johnson Pearl	*10/26/--*
Re	Date of Letter
Employment	*10/5/--*
Taken by	Date Taken
Mark Brown	*10/26/--*
Signed	Dept.
M B	*Personnel*

REQUISITION

Return Date *11/2/--*

Illus. 6-2   Requisition Card

Another style of requisition form commonly used is shown in Illustration 6-3—a **requisition sheet**. Requisition cards or requisition sheets are prepared in duplicate by the borrower or the records personnel.

O U T

To Records Dept.

REQUEST FOR PAPERS

Papers Wanted on *6/21/--*
(date)

Description of Papers

Date *1/18/--*

Name *M R Conrad*

Address *Phoenix, AZ*

Subject *Matter concerning Bancroft + Serrano*

Wanted by *Rose Toshiba*

Department *Administration*

For Records Dept. Use

Return Date *6/25/--*

Illus. 6-3   Requisition Sheet

CHARGING

Requests for information from the files may be for a single paper, an entire folder, a series of papers, or several folders. Whatever the request, the filer must provide a check-out system that will account for the absence of materials from the files. Several commonly used methods that show what file records have been charged out include (1) the OUT guide method, (2) the requisition sheet method, (3) the OUT folder method, and (4) the carrier folder method.

OUT Guide Method

There are two styles of OUT guides.

When a requisition card is used for borrowing selected papers from a particular folder, the marker that is put in that folder in place of the borrowed papers is called an **OUT guide**. The two main styles of OUT guides—an OUT guide with a pocket and an OUT guide with printed lines—are discussed below.

OUT Guide with Pocket. When an OUT guide with a pocket is used, a copy of the requisition card is placed in the pocket (See Illustration 6-4). The filer then places the OUT guide in the file folder in the exact place from which the letter or other papers have been taken—it substitutes for the borrowed papers. The OUT guide is a sturdy, visible marker showing what papers have been removed and to whom they have been charged. A duplicate copy of the requisition card is placed in a follow-up file. The follow-up file is explained later.

OUT Guide with Printed Lines. When an OUT guide with printed lines is used (See Illustration 6-5), information from the requisition is written on the ruled form of the OUT guide. The filer then places the OUT guide in the file folder to replace the papers that were removed and to indicate who borrowed them. The requisition card is placed in the follow-up file.

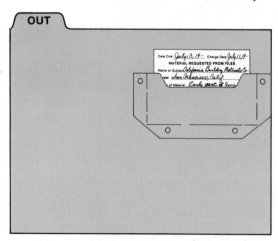

Illus. 6-4   OUT Guide with Pocket

OUT			
NUMBER, NAME, OR SUBJECT	DATES OF LETTERS	ISSUED TO	DATE ISSUED
C.R. Cramer	May 6, 19--	K. Jones	June 1, 19--
Brooks + Co.	July 9, 19--	D. Towns	Aug. 6, 19--
Huber + Son	Sept. 7, 19--	Ray Smith	Oct. 1, 19--

Illus. 6-5   OUT Guide with Printed Lines

Illustrations 6-6 and 6-7 on page 71 show the use of OUT guides in a shelf file and a drawer file. Notice that the prominence of these OUT guides

Illus. 6-6   OUT Guides in a Shelf File

Illus. 6-7   OUT Guide in a Drawer File

makes it easy to find the correct location of borrowed papers when they are to be refiled.

Requisition Sheet Method

When requisition sheets like the one shown in Illustration 6-3 are used to charge out borrowed papers, the requisition sheets are used as markers in file folders. Two copies of the requisition sheet are prepared. One copy is placed in the file folder from which papers have been removed; the other copy is filed in the departmental follow-up file.

OUT Folder Method

There are two types of OUT folders.

When an entire folder is requisitioned and removed from the filing system, an OUT folder is used to replace it. OUT folders are of two types: (1) a folder with a ruled form printed on the front (See Illustration 6-8) or (2) a folder with a visible pocket attached to the inside back flap (See Illustration 6-9). This pocket is used to hold a requisition card.

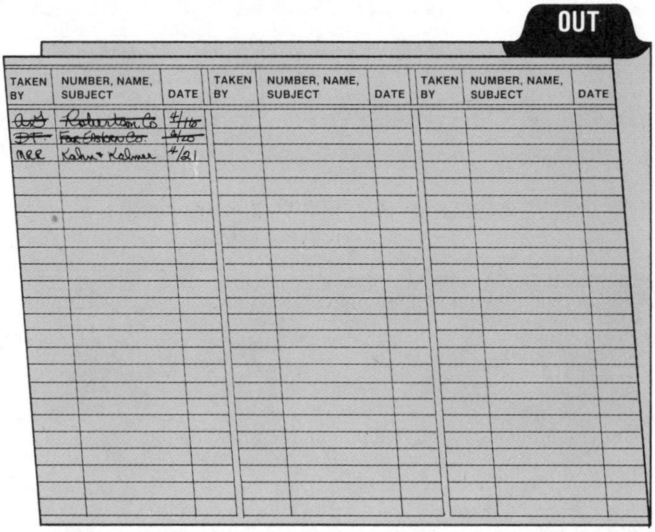

Illus. 6-8   OUT Folder with Printed Sections

When the ruled-line OUT folder is used, information from a requisition card is written on the printed ruled form on the outer face of the OUT folder. The requisition card is then placed in a follow-up file.

When the pocket-type OUT folder is used, the requisition card is prepared in duplicate. One copy is placed in the pocket of the OUT folder; the other copy is placed in a follow-up file.

Regardless of its type, the OUT folder is used as a substitute for the folder that has been borrowed. While the original folder is out, all materials that are received for filing are held in this OUT folder. When the original folder is returned, all materials accumulated in the OUT folder are transferred in proper order to the regular folder. The charge information on the OUT folder is crossed out (or the requisition card is removed from the pocket), and the OUT folder is now available for reuse.

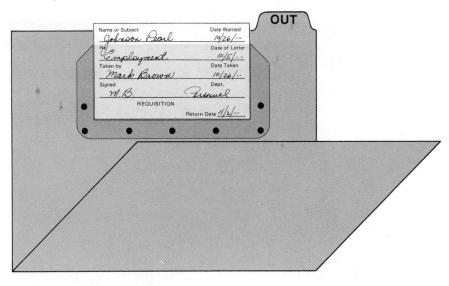

Illus. 6-9   OUT Folder with Pocket

Carrier Folder Method

When the entire contents of a folder are requested, consider transferring the contents of the folder to a **carrier folder**. The carrier folder "carries" the contents to the borrower.

Advantages of using carrier folders.

Using carrier folders has several advantages over removing and sending regular file folders to borrowers: (1) carrier folders are made of heavy manila stock and are more durable than the standard file folders; (2) carrier folders usually are of a color different from that of regular manila file folders; they are marked with phrases such as "Return to Files." These distinguishing characteristics make it easier to remember to return them to the records department; and (3) since regular file folders are not taken from the files, incoming papers are filed in the regular folders. Filing goes on as usual. Remember, however, to use an OUT guide or a requisition sheet to show that the folder contents have been borrowed!

CANCELING

Charges are canceled when the borrowed papers are returned.

As you probably suspect, charges against a borrower must be canceled when papers are returned to the records department. The way charges are canceled depends on the method used in the charge-out system. When requisition cards are used, remove the cards from the pockets of OUT guides or OUT folders and destroy them. Remove the requisition cards from the follow-up file and save them. They are used later to check on the activity of the filing system.

When requisition sheets are placed in regular file folders and used as OUT sheets (See Illustration 6-3), remove these sheets from the file folder and destroy them when the borrowed papers are returned. Remove copies of OUT sheets held in the follow-up file and save them for checking on the activity of

*Save requisitions to
identify records
activity.*

the files. These copies are helpful at transfer time to identify active records that should remain in the files and to report to management the activity of the filing system.

When lined and printed OUT guides or OUT folders are used, cross out the charges written on them when papers are returned. These OUT guides and folders are returned to the filer's desk and reused. Remove copies of requisition cards held in the follow-up file so that the charge against the borrower is canceled. As usual, save them in order to determine the activity of the filing system.

FOLLOWING UP

When you rent a car, you arrange to keep it for a certain number of days. You return it on the due date unless you have asked for, and received, an extension of time. The car rental company keeps an accurate record of all this and starts a tracing procedure (a follow-up) if a car is not returned on time. A similar procedure is used by a records department in order to control the return of borrowed papers and folders.

Setting Time Limits

Control over the return of file materials is achieved by establishing time limits for the return of borrowed items. Such limits vary from one firm to another, largely because of differences in the value of items being held in different filing systems or the demand from other borrowers for the same material.

*Allow a short time
for the return of
papers.*

Some records held in files are very valuable or they are needed often by other members of the organization. Company rules usually determine that these records may not be borrowed for a period of time greater than one day, or less. Other less valuable papers may be borrowed over a period of a week, ten days, or two weeks. In general, it is better to allow relatively short periods of time for the return of papers. The longer the time permitted, the less chance there is of having materials returned on time. However, it is necessary to extend a set time for returning borrowed papers when it is evident that the borrower still needs them. This can be done either by rewriting the due date on the original requisition or by preparing a new requisition and noting a change of date on all OUT forms held in the files.

Follow-Up Methods

If all borrowed materials were returned on time, there would be no need for following up, or tracing, overdue papers. Since this is not the case, however, the records department must have a system for checking on out-of-file materials.

To check on the due dates for the return of borrowed papers and folders, any one of three basic procedures may be used: (1) the main files may be scanned, (2) a master control sheet may be maintained, or (3) a follow-up filing system may be used.

Scanning the Files. A simple way to check the due dates of borrowed materials is to scan the files and read the due dates written on requisition sheets, requisition cards, OUT guides, and OUT folders. This method works if the records department is relatively small; for example, when the filing area consists of approximately five cabinets or sections.

Maintaining a Master Control Sheet. If the records department has 6 to 15 cabinets or sections, follow-up work can be handled by using a master control sheet, a simple follow-up method. A **master control sheet** is a running record of borrowed file materials kept at the filer's desk. As requisitions are written or received in the department, data from these are posted to the master control sheet. When borrowed materials are returned, the corresponding charges written on the master control sheet are crossed out.

Using a Follow-Up File. In a large records department, a **follow-up file** simplifies charging for papers and folders taken from the department. A follow-up file, like the one shown in Illustration 6-10, is a convenient method of tracing papers that are overdue; it is also useful in keeping a variety of time-related routines up-to-date and under control.

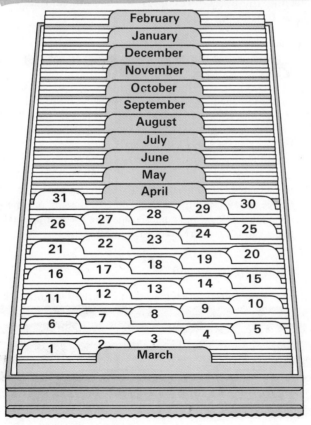

Illus. 6-10   Follow-Up File

A follow-up file is a "vertical calendar."

You will recall that requisition cards are filled out when papers are borrowed from the main files. These cards serve as a charge against a borrower. At least two copies of each card usually are prepared. One goes into the main files; the other goes into a follow-up file similar to the one shown in Illustration 6-10. It looks like a vertical calendar, doesn't it? This follow-up file consists of 12 monthly guides in central position and 31 secondary guides captioned for days in the month. Normally only one set of daily guides is needed for a follow-up file. After the filer checks and processes the requisitions held behind the date guide for the current day, the date guide is moved from the current-month section to the next-month section. Thus, the daily guides keep advancing. Unless a large volume of requisitions must be handled, a single set of daily guides is sufficient.

If requisition sheets are used instead of requisition cards, the follow-up file consists of 12 monthly guides and 31 folders captioned for each day in the month. The follow-up file is sometimes called a **tickler follow-up file** because it "tickles" the mind to remember to follow up!

Follow-Up File Procedures

Review the following procedures when using a follow-up file of the type shown in Illustration 6-10:

1. Place only requisition cards in the file.
2. Place the requisition cards in the follow-up file according to the anticipated return date of the borrowed papers.

Check the follow-up file daily.

3. Check daily to see which borrowed materials are due and notify the borrowers; extend the due date to a later one if materials are still needed by the borrower; change the requisition to conform to the new date and refile it accordingly. Enter the new due date on the face of a lined and printed OUT guide or OUT folder, if either is used in the main files.
4. Cancel the charge against the borrower when papers are returned by (a) removing the requisition from the follow-up file and saving it; it will help to assess the activity of the file later on; (b) removing and destroying a requisition card that is in the OUT folder or guide OR crossing out the notations entered on ruled OUT folders and guides, if they are used; and (c) returning all guides and folders to a centralized workstation for reuse.

No Follow-Up Required

Send an exact copy of the record.

No matter how careful the filer is in charge-out and follow-up procedures, important papers may be lost in transit or may be accidentally destroyed. To guard against such possibilities, use the office copier and send an exact copy of the record requested instead. With this method, the requested paper is removed from the folder only long enough to be copied. Refile the original and send the copy to the borrower with instructions to destroy it after use. This method is used most frequently when only a single letter or a few related pieces are requisitioned.

RESERVING

The records department frequently receives requests to reserve files materials that are desired at a future date. A follow-up procedure is needed to ensure the delivery of the requested papers on the date that they are needed.

Requests for the future delivery of papers can reach the records department in any of three ways: (1) by a written notation on a letter that has been released to the records department. The note might read, "Wanted by S.A.R. on 11/18/--"; (2) by a telephone call or intercom system; or (3) by a requisition card or requisition sheet with an advanced date written on the form, "Papers needed by 11/18/--." However the request is made, a requisition sheet or card placed behind the appropriate date in the follow-up file will ensure the delivery of the materials when they are needed. The placement in the main file folder of an OUT guide or requisition sheet showing the date the materials are needed is a good idea; this additional step will keep others from borrowing the records at a time when they have been reserved for someone else.

The same reserving procedure may be used when requests are made for records already checked out. A requisition form with a notation to send the materials to the next person as soon as the materials are returned helps to control the materials and still serves the users.

A VERTICAL MEMORY

The follow-up file is a useful memory aid.

The follow-up file is your "vertical memory." It is a memory aid used to avoid overlooking important matters at a future date. A follow-up file consisting of dated folders with movable signals (See Illustration 6-11) is a useful file in other departments in the organization as well. For example, purchasing, accounting, shipping, production, and sales departments are all concerned with matters that require future attention.

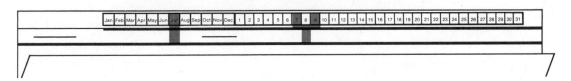

Illus. 6-11   Dated Follow-Up Folder with Two Movable Signals

When materials, supplies, or equipment are purchased for a company, the purchasing department watches delivery dates closely. Supplies not received when expected could slow down, or even stop, production in some companies. A copy of a purchase order placed in a follow-up folder similar to the one in Illustration 6-12 is one way to follow up on expected delivery dates. The vendor's name is shown on the tab of the follow-up folder (A and I Inc). The folder holds a copy of the purchase order, a copy of the original purchase requisition, and any correspondence related to the order. The movable signal is set for October 15, the expected delivery date.

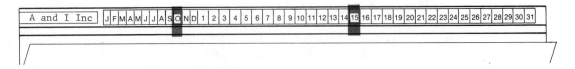

| A and I Inc | J | F | M | A | M | J | J | A | S | O | N | D | 1 | 2 | 3 | 4 | 5 | 6 | 7 | 8 | 9 | 10 | 11 | 12 | 13 | 14 | 15 | 16 | 17 | 18 | 19 | 20 | 21 | 22 | 23 | 24 | 25 | 26 | 27 | 28 | 29 | 30 | 31 |

Illus. 6-12   Dated Follow-Up Folder Used in a Purchasing Department

Similar follow-up files are used in a credit and collection department to note dates when action is to be taken on overdue accounts. A sales department may set tabs for the next date to call on a particular customer. The sales manager will welcome a reminder that it is time to begin preparing for quarterly sales reports, the next sales conference, or the annual stockholders' meeting.

In your personal life a follow-up file can help you to remember important dates: social functions, friends' birthdays, payments due . . . and your next dental appointment!

In order to use any follow-up file effectively, be sure to enter all future events that you want to remember *and* check the file every day to see what needs to be done that day.

Questions for Discussion

1. What are the five procedures required to control the use of filed materials? (1)

2. What information is required on a requisition form (card or sheet)? (2)

3. Why are requisition forms usually made in duplicate by records personnel? (3)

4. How is an OUT folder similar to an OUT guide? How is it different? (4)

5. When entire folders are requested, would you release regular manila folders from the files or would you remove papers from file folders and send them in carrier folders? Why? (5)

6. Once borrowed papers have been returned and placed in file folders, is that the end of the action taken by records department personnel? If not, why? (6)

7. Name three ways to check on the due date of borrowed papers. (7)

8. When would you use each of the ways in No. 7 to check on the due date of borrowed papers? Why? (7)

9. Why does a records department need to keep a follow-up file? (7)

10. Explain the procedures for managing a follow-up file in a records department. (8)

11. When it is not possible to release a valuable paper from the files, how can the need for information best be met by the records department? (9)

12. When dated follow-up folders with signals are used in a follow-up file, describe the procedure for handling a request such as "Papers needed by Bronson on 11/22/--." (10)

13. How are follow-up files used in ways other than tracing and reserving papers in a records office? (11)

Job 5   Requisition and Charge Procedures   (2,3,6,8)

At this time complete Job 5 in OFFICE FILING PROCEDURES, Sixth Edition. Instructions and supplies for this job are included in the practice set.

CHAPTER 7

Records Transfer, Storage, and Disposition Controls

Learning Objectives

After completing Chapter 7, you will be able to:

1. Define active, semiactive, and inactive records.
2. Define vital, important, useful, and nonessential records.
3. Define a retention schedule.
4. Describe perpetual and periodic record transfers.
5. Describe the three methods of periodic transfer: one-period, two-period, and maximum-minimum.
6. Describe the transfer containers used in a records storage center.
7. Explain the use of labels, guides, and record control cards in the records storage center.
8. Explain four types of control files used in a storage center.
9. Transfer records from an active file.
10. Describe the cycle of records control.

An experience common to many people is the tendency to save almost everything. Then when the drawer or the closet door will not close, comes the "time of reckoning." Which things to keep permanently? Which to store close at hand? Which to "file" in the closet, attic, or basement? Which things to destroy?

Birth certificates and deeds to property are records that are kept *permanently* in a safe place; they are records showing identity and ownership. A driver's license and insurance identification are records that must be kept *close at hand* in order to drive a car. A variety of financial, medical, academic, and household appliance records are "filed" in various locations around the house, depending on availability of space, tolerance for disorder, and the importance of reproducing or referring to these records when necessary. Although duplicate copies of most records can be obtained, most people will agree that the process is a costly, time-consuming inconvenience.

Then there are the newspapers, magazines, and junk mail received by every household. Although these records may alter the quality of one's life

To keep ... or not to keep.

somewhat, they have a low retention value in most homes and eventually find their way to the "circular file," or trash!

If you are familiar with the high and low retention value of records in your personal life, you can more easily understand the problems business and industrial organizations face as they try to control the volume of records that builds up from day to day. If all papers that accumulate each day were kept in the office, there would soon be no room left in which to work.

How quickly the volume of records can grow when you consider the many sources from which they enter the filing system. For example, records of one sort or another come from departments such as accounting, advertising, auditing, executive, insurance, purchasing, personnel, production, sales, and shipping. Don't forget about the records generated through building maintenance and security.

An additional concern to the variety of records maintained is the retention period of these records: how long to keep them. Depending on both the information needs of the organization and federal and state record retention requirements, different records are retained for various periods of time.

The conclusion is this:

Record volume, accessibility, and retention are concerns of records control.

1. A considerable number of records must be processed in a records control department.
2. Records that provide necessary information for operating the business must be readily available.
3. Records that cease to be of value to an organization must be moved out or destroyed.

The "housekeeping" functions of records control—transfer, storage, and disposition—are the topics of this chapter.

THE ACCESSIBILITY OF RECORDS

Records are maintained, transferred, stored, and ultimately destroyed according to the information that they provide to the organization. Records that are referred to most frequently are maintained differently from those records that require infrequent or no reference. Active, semiactive, and inactive are the terms used to describe the activity of records and, subsequently, their degree of accessibility.

Active Records

Active records are those records that require frequent reference. These records relate to the day-to-day activities and important matters of the organization. Because of their value as active sources for needed information, the active files are located in areas that are the most accessible (within easy reach) to office personnel (See Illustration 7-1).

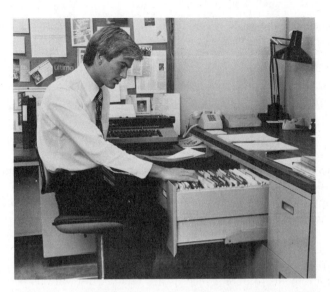

Illus. 7-1   **Active Records are Located in Easily Accessed Areas**

Semiactive Records

Semiactive records are those records with limited reference value. Semiactive record files are generally accessible to office personnel and located within or near the active files (See Illustration 7-2). For example, they may occupy the upper and/or lower drawers of filing cabinets in some offices. If open shelves are used, semiactive records occupy the top and bottom shelves. An alternative is to store semiactive records in less expensive storage locations somewhere in the building where access is still possible.

Illus. 7-2   **Semiactive Records are Found Near the Active Files**

Inactive Records

Inactive records are those that may be kept for either legal or historical purposes, but they need not be readily accessible for reference. Because the inactive records are rarely needed for reference, they are located in an area where floor space is less costly than that of the area where active files must be located. Inactive records are packed in storage boxes or cases and sent to a storage center (See Illustration 7-3). Boxes can be stacked eight or more high in the storage center, and aisles can be relatively narrow—about 30 inches across.

Illus. 7-3   Inactive Records are Kept in the Storage Center

THE RETENTION VALUE OF RECORDS

Office records—whether they are paper, tapes, diskettes, or microforms—may have *high* to *low* to *no* retention value to an organization. The importance of records depends on how seriously the loss of the records would impair the operation or continuation of the organization. To indicate their value to business operations, records are classified as vital, important, useful, or nonessential.

Vital Records

Vital records are those valuable documents and papers kept under strict security and protection. These vital records are essential to:

1. the legal and financial status of the organization,
2. the rights and responsibilities of those involved in the organization, and
3. the resumption and continuation of operations within the organization.

These vital reference documents and correspondence come from many sources. A partial list of the kinds of papers in this category includes the following:

Accounts receivable	Incorporation records
Annual reports	Leases
Audit reports	Patents and related correspondence
Copyrights and related correspondence	Permits
	Stock records and reports
Government contracts	Tax records and reports

These and other similar documents and papers may be kept in departmental files, in central filing systems, or in underground storage centers. Such materials are frequently protected in fire-resistant cabinets or vaults and are not readily available for reference.

Important Records

Important records are those records that relate to the day-to-day activities and important matters of the organization: customer accounts and correspondence, sales and marketing records, manufacturing records, inventory, purchasing records, and other in-process activities. Active files can consist of information on floppy disks, cassette tapes, microforms, or papers. These working files are the "brain" or "memory" center of any records control system. These important records must be well protected and be the most accessible records in the system.

Useful Records

The **useful records** are those of limited, but helpful, reference value. They may have entered the system with limited reference value or have been reduced to this level of value over time. Although the loss of useful records might be an inconvenience, they can be replaced and their loss would not seriously impair operations. These records are likely to be placed in a semiactive filing system or sent to a storage area; their location would depend on both the frequency of reference to them and the availability of filing space in the office.

Nonessential Records

Nonessential records are of two varieties: (1) those records that never had a retention value in the first place and (2) those records that have ceased to be of value to the organization.

Some memos, notices and announcements, once scanned and noted, can and should be destroyed immediately. Those who are afraid to destroy anything for fear of "needing it someday" should try this: Keep nonessential records in a folder or binder chronologically with the last received nonessential record in front or on top. When finally convinced that some of these records have no future reference value, destroy the back half of records in the binder or folder. This simple procedure satisfies the office "pack rat," clears the tops of desks for work, and keeps nonessential records out of the working files. Records of doubtful value in an active filing system add needlessly to the cost of keeping records. More supplies, equipment, and space are needed, and time is wasted searching through useless papers to locate needed information.

Keep all nonessential records out of the active files.

Records that have become nonessential through time should be either sent to a storage center for a period of time specified by the established retention schedule or destroyed.

Retention Schedule

A **retention schedule** is a comprehensive list of all records in the organization (papers, disks, tapes, microforms) to which retention periods have been assigned. The retention period might be one month, two years, seven years, or ten years. Each organization must develop a retention schedule that suits its operational needs. Destruction dates are established for records only after careful consideration has been given to the future usefulness of each type of record in the company. Consultation with various department heads and file users is necessary to determine the life cycle of a particular record. Federal and state governments set retention periods for some documents also. So, from a legal, as well as an operational, standpoint, the development of a retention schedule is a serious, complicated, and time-consuming task. Once the retention schedule is established, it must have the approval of the executive and legal branches of the organization. A primary concern in a records office or a storage center, however, is that retention periods *have been* established and that the destruction of nonessential records is carried out as scheduled.

Consider future usefulness of all records.

THE TRANSFER OF RECORDS: METHODS AND PROCEDURES

In records departments, active files occupy the most accessible drawers in the filing cabinets or the most reachable shelves in a shelf area. This "first-class" treatment of active records is not likely to continue indefinitely, however. New material for the files keeps coming in, and folders become more and more crowded. As active records become less useful, they must be moved out, or transferred, to allow efficient access to the more active records.

Because of the variations in the kinds of work performed in different offices, two major methods of transferring records are possible: perpetual transfer and periodic transfer.

Perpetual Transfer

The **perpetual transfer method** is a *continuous* process of transferring records. Contractors' offices and law offices, where work is completed in units, are likely to transfer all records relating to a *completed* job or case.

When a task is completed, transfer all records related to that task to either a semiactive file or a storage center. If the active and semiactive files are held in the same area, check the active file frequently for "dead" materials—records no longer being requested for reference. Such a check is made by saving requisition forms like the ones shown in Illustrations 6-2 and 6-3 on page 69. These requisitions identify which materials are in demand and which are not. Remove the "dead" ones and file them in the semiactive file.

An alternate method of checking the activity of records is to make a tally mark on the upper part of the face of a folder each time materials or folders are requested. A tally mark on the right side of a paper requisitioned from a general folder identifies a paper or group of papers that are still active.

Periodic Transfer

Periodic transfer refers to the method of transfer and not the time when transfer is to take place. There are three methods of periodic transfer: one-period, two-period, and maximum-minimum transfer.

One-period transfer method. As the name implies in the **one-period transfer method**, *one* entire *period* of records is transferred at one time. A new active file is then established.

At the established transfer time, remove all folders from the active files and transfer them to a storage center. Do not transfer the guides. Captions on the folders' tabs serve as guides for stored records. Then prepare new folders for the active files. Although it is a simple way to transfer files, materials received just prior to transfer are immediately sent to storage where they are less available for reference. This objectional practice can be partly remedied if records that continue to be active are held for a short time in an auxiliary file near the filer's desk. Such a file is sometimes called a "hot file." As the need for the papers in the hot file becomes less critical—in a month or so—the records can then be transferred to the storage center. If records are *infrequently* accessed *and* the storage area is accessible, the one-period transfer method is the quickest and simplest way to transfer records.

Two-period transfer method. In the **two-period transfer method** two periods of records are transferred at one time. The two-period method requires duplicate files: an active file and a semiactive file. A storage center is needed also. The storage center is often located in an area that is removed from the active and semiactive files in a business office. At a set date, remove all folders that have been held in the existing semiactive file drawers. Box, and transfer them to the storage center. Next, transfer folders from the existing active file to the drawers formerly occupied by the semiactive file. Leave all guides in the active file drawers but prepare new general folders for the newly formed active file.

Use the most convenient drawers or shelves—the upper two drawers in a four-drawer cabinet or the middle three shelves in a shelf unit—for the active files. Use the lower two drawers of a four-drawer cabinet or the upper and lower shelves in a shelf unit for the semiactive files. In five-drawer cabinets use the top and bottom drawers for the semiactive records (See Illustration 7-4).

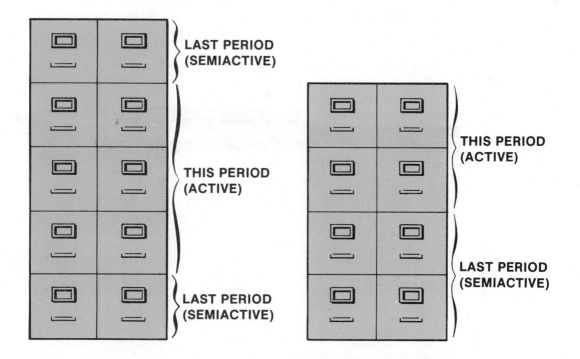

Illus. 7-4   Two-Period Transfer Method Using Five- and Four-Drawer Cabinets

Maximum-minimum transfer method. With the **maximum-minimum transfer method** all records are retained for a specified maximum and minimum period of time. If transfer day is December 31 and the **minimum** period of record retention is six months, then all folders with papers dated July 1 to December 31 of the current year remain in the active file: minimum period—six months. If transfer is done the following year (12 months later), then the **maximum** time records are in the file is 18 months (12 months since the last transfer added to the six-month-old records). Records dated July of the previous year to July of the current year are transferred to a semiactive file; the records in the semiactive file are transferred to a storage center. The maximum-minimum transfer method is similar to the two-period transfer

Selected records are maintained.

method except that *selected* records are transferred at transfer time. The method is illustrated in this way:

Transfer   Transfer
Time   Time

JUL AUG SEP OCT NOV DEC JAN FEB MAR APR MAY JUN JUL AUG SEP OCT NOV DEC

⊢——— 6 months ———⊣
⊢————————————————— 18 months —————————————————⊣
⊢————————— 12 months ——————————————— 6 months ———⊣
(Move to semiactive file)   (Remain in active file)

The process repeats itself every transfer period: The active files hold the last six months of records. The following year at transfer time, twelve months of records are transferred to the semiactive files, again leaving only the last six months of the current year. The advantage of this method is the retention of current records in the active files while transferring out the old. The disadvantage is the time needed to select by date the records for transfer.

Here are detailed procedures to accomplish the maximum-minimum periodic transfer using the above dates: *Before* transfer day—

Prepare for the transfer of records.

1. Inspect each individual and special folder in the *active file* to find the latest dated paper in it. This is relatively simple because the last record received is the first paper in the folder. The *date* on this *letter* determines how this *folder* is to be processed at transfer time.
2. Mark *only* the individual and special folders holding papers dated *before* July 1 of the current year with a *T* on the upper right edge. These folders will be transferred to the semiactive file on transfer day. Folders with papers dated July 1 of the current year and later remain in the active file.
3. Prepare a new set of general folders to be used in the new active file that will be established on transfer day.*

On transfer day, follow these procedures—

1. Transfer *all* folders from the current *semiactive file* to the *storage center*. To do this, remove the folders from the semiactive file and place them in prelabeled transfer boxes. Then send the transfer boxes to the storage center.
2. Remove the general folders from the *active file*. Select from them all papers to be kept in the new active file (dated *after* July 1). Place these papers in the new general folders previously prepared for that section.* Transfer the "old" general folders and the papers left in them to the recently cleared semiactive file. Since all guides were left in the active file, the general folders now serve as guides in the semiactive file.
3. Remove all the individual and special folders marked with a *T* from the first primary section of the current active file. Put them in the appropriate places *behind* the general folder for that section in the semiactive file.
4. Repeat Steps 2 and 3 for each section in the current active file.

In the method presented above, entire individual and special folders are transferred, depending upon the date of their contents. Folders containing correspondence dated *after* the cutoff date (July 1) are retained. Folders containing correspondence dated *before* the cutoff date are transferred to the semiactive file on transfer day, December 31.

Only selected papers remain in active files.

The maximum-minimum transfer procedures may be applied only to *papers* in the folders rather than to the entire folders. When folders contain numerous papers dated both before and after the cutoff date, transfer only papers dated *before* the cutoff date to the semiactive file. In such a case prepare new general, individual, and special folders for the current active materials beforehand. On transfer day, transfer the current active materials to the new folders and place the folders in the new active file; leave the older correspondence in the old folders and transfer these folders to the semiactive file.

THE CONTROL OF STORED RECORDS

All the elements needed for records control in the active files are also needed to maintain order in the storage center. There is little point in transferring papers to storage unless adequate controls are used for locating and releasing stored records. Such control requires that storage locations be identified, that boxes or drawers be labeled, and that central records of these matters be maintained.

In large storage areas, the aisles, shelf sections, and boxes or cases are all assigned numbers. These numbers are written on the box labels, as well as on record control forms or cards held at the control desk. Thus, the location of a particular box might be marked "Aisle:4/Section:12/Box:325." In smaller storage areas, the boxes or cases are given consecutive numbers. These numbers are written on labels affixed to the box fronts or on tags inserted into drawer fronts.

Equipment and Supplies

File materials in the storage center are held in either of two types of containers specially made for this kind of storage filing area: (1) transfer cases or (2) transfer boxes.

Transfer Cases. Transfer cases are made of heavy corrugated fiberboard. They are box-shaped units that are equipped with sliding drawers and plastic handles. This sliding drawer feature permits relatively easy reference to the materials within the case. They are, therefore, ideal containers for records that are occasionally needed for reference.

Transfer Boxes. Transfer boxes do not have sliding drawers but are equipped with lift-up tops, lift-off tops, or lift-out sides. Lift-up tops or lift-out sides are held down with a fastener of one kind or another. In Illustration 7-5, notice that string fasteners are used and that tops of boxes have overlapping sections. These features are used to prevent dust from entering the boxes. Transfer boxes are most suitable for transferred records with a relatively low degree of reference value.

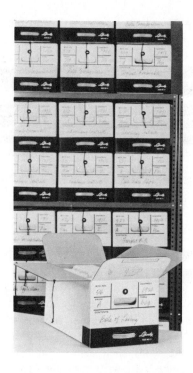

Illus. 7-5   Transfer Boxes

Labels. In order to locate requisitioned papers quickly in the storage center, each case or box must be labeled so that it is distinguishable from all others. This is done in either of two ways: (1) by making identifying marks directly on the case or box or (2) by filling out a label that is then affixed to the case or box.

In Illustration 7-5, the transfer box on the table bears several identifying marks. It is Box No. 516, and it holds bills of lading bearing titles ranging from A through Dag. The boxes on the shelves have labels such as *Accounts Receivable*, *Cash Sales Slips*, and *Freight Bills*.

Guides and folders. Guides used in the active file are not moved with other materials at transfer time. When active files are transferred, the general folders serve adequately as guides for locating folders.

Plastic folders and folders with plastic tabs and other refinements stay in the active files. They are too expensive to be included in a transfer file. In such a case, less expensive manila folders are prepared in advance and used in the transfer file.

Record control cards. Record control cards are also called catalog cards, transfer control cards, or records storage index and destruction control cards. This card or form lists the holdings of the storage center. Whatever the name used, these cards or forms make up the master directory held at a control center (or desk) and are the most useful records in the storage center.

Record control card: Who, what, where, and when.

The record storage index and destruction control card shown in Illustration 7-6 shows when the records were received, by whom they were sent, the contents of the storage box, the exact location of the box, and the date set for the destruction of the contents of the box.

RECORD TITLE												
				Correspondence, Purchasing				RECEIVED FROM *Purchasing Department*				
DATE RECEIVED	FILE OR BOX NO.	CONTENTS				LOCATION			DATE TO DESTROY	DATE DES-TROYED	CERTIFIED BY	
		ALPHABETIC NUMERIC		DATE		BLDG. OR ROOM	AISLE	SECTION				
		FROM	TO	FROM	TO							
1/5/81	231	A	Az	1/1/80	12/31/80	Basement	9	4	1985			
"	232	B	Bi	"	"	"	"	4	"			
"	233	Bj	Bo	"	"	"	"	"	"			
"	234	Bp	Bz	"	"	"	"	"	"			

RECORDS STORAGE INDEX AND DESTRUCTION CONTROL CARD

BANKERS BOX record storage systems
DIVISION OF FELLOWES MANUFACTURING COMPANY

FORM 1607

Illus. 7-6   Storage Record Card

Record control cards are generally prepared by storage center personnel. One control card is prepared for every transfer box or drawer representing a single transfer period. If a cumulative record control form like that shown in Illustration 7-6 is used, then a one-line entry is made for every box or case in the storage center. If a box contains more than one type of material, a record control entry is made for each kind of record to be found in that box.

One of the primary advantages of using a record control card is the flexibility allowed in the placement of boxes and cases in the storage center. Information posted on the cards tells exact locations in the center of carefully described materials. In large records storage centers, the information normally placed on the record control card is entered on a computer for rapid, automatic reference.

The Control Files in Storage Center Operations

Four types of records are required for maintaining order in storage operations: (1) a master control file (retrieval control file) for locating and retrieving stored records, (2) a charge-out and follow-up file, (3) a tickler file for destruction dates, and (4) a destruction file.

The "Master" is in
control of the storage
center!

Master Control File. The master control file is kept at the control desk in the storage center. It is composed entirely of record control cards of the type shown in Illustration 7-6. These cards are held in a system that is primarily alphabetic. Primary guides show names of departments from which file materials have been transferred. Secondary guides show names of types of records being held for particular departments, for example, "Correspondence," "Purchase Orders," or "Accounts Receivable." Finally, a series of date guides are used to show specific locations of dated records within a departmental group.

When a reference request is received from the Sales Department for correspondence material of a given date, the filer scans the master control file to locate (1) a primary guide for "Sales," (2) a secondary guide for "Correspondence," and finally, (3) a date guide corresponding to the date shown on the reference request form. Behind the date guide is the storage record card bearing the location of the papers needed. Location data are transcribed from the card to a routing slip, which is taken to the storage section indicated. There, the storage box or case is opened and the needed papers withdrawn and sent to the requester.

Generally three copies of a reference request form are prepared: One is placed in the storage container on an OUT guide to show that records were removed from the storage box; one accompanies the borrowed records; and a third is placed in the charge-out and follow-up file.

Charge-Out and Follow-Up File. The use of a charge-out and follow-up file in a storage center is the same as that previously described for use in a filing department. A type of follow-up file similar to that shown in Chapter 6, Illustration 6-11, is used for tracing as well as for charging borrowed materials that have been removed from the storage center.

Reference request cards or sheets are filed in the tickler follow-up file by the "due date." The tickler follow-up file is checked daily to trace due and overdue materials that should be returned to storage (See Illustration 7-7).

Tickler File for Destruction Dates. A tickler or reminder file is the same type of tickler follow-up file shown in Chapter 6. It is used to follow a predetermined time schedule for the destruction of various types of records. The file is checked periodically to determine when destruction dates are scheduled. The tickler file for destruction dates is also known as a *destruction tickler* or a *destruction follow-up*. The file holds only the second copies of the record control cards that are prepared in duplicate when transfer materials are received. These cards are filed according to the destruction date assigned them.

At the time indicated for disposition of a particular group of records, the department head whose papers are to be destroyed is contacted to approve

Illus. 7-7   Tickler File in a Records Storage Center

the disposition. Unless complications arise, the records are destroyed by shredding or burning, selling for recycling, or other approved means.

Destruction File. When materials are destroyed, there must be witnessed or certified proof of this action. A record of the disposition is prepared and retained for an indefinite period of time. Destruction of records is a matter of vital importance, and legally acceptable records must be kept in a **destruction file**.

The primary records held in a destruction file are completed copies of the record control cards that were held in the tickler file for destruction dates. These cards are pulled from the tickler file when destruction dates arrive. When destruction and certification have been completed and recorded, these record control cards are filed according to the name of the department and by the date of destruction.

SUMMARY OF THE RECORDS CONTROL CYCLE

A cycle of records control is completed with the destruction of records. This cycle includes all the procedures used in maintaining order during the useful life of those records. Review these procedures now:

1. Code released papers for filing according to indexing rules and cross-reference when necessary.
2. Place records in a filing system according to the predetermined coding.

3. Release papers under a charge-out plan and use a follow-up system to be sure they are returned.
4. Transfer inactive records to semiactive files or to storage centers according to a suitable transfer method.
5. Continue to apply retrieval, charge-out, and follow-up controls to transferred materials in the storage center.
6. Finally, destroy papers according to a predetermined retention schedule and make the necessary documentation of this action. Obviously this step represents the final phase of records control.

Questions for Discussion

1. Define active, semiactive, and inactive records. (1)

2. How do the terms active, semiactive, and inactive relate to the accessibility of records? (1)

3. Name the four classifications of records and explain their retention value to an organization. (2)

4. What is a retention schedule? What does a retention schedule tell the filer? (3)

5. Explain the basic difference between the perpetual and periodic transfer methods. (4)

6. Describe what records are actually being transferred in the three types of periodic transfer: one-period, two-period, and maximum-minimum. (5)

7. Are transfer cases better than transfer boxes for holding semiactive records? Why or why not? (6)

8. Are guides usually transferred from active files to storage files? Why or why not? (7)

9. What is a record control card and how is it used? (7)

10. How are record control cards and labels on storage containers used together to locate stored records? (7)

11. Name the four types of control files used in a storage center and explain how these files are used. (8)

12. Outline briefly the six procedures in the records control cycle. (10)

Job 6   Transfer Procedures   (9)

At this time, complete Job 6 in OFFICE FILING PROCEDURES, Sixth Edition. Instructions and supplies for this job are included in the practice set.

CHAPTER 8

Use of Color in Alphabetic Filing Systems

Learning Objectives

After completing Chapter 8, you will be able to:

1. List the advantages of using color in filing systems.
2. Define color coding and color accenting.
3. Describe the system layout and guide plan for the following color-coded filing systems:
   a. Jeter Top Coder by Jeter Systems Corporation
   b. Alpha-Z® alphabetic system by The Smead Manufacturing Company
   c. Colorscan by Kardex Systems, Inc.
   d. Accu-Find by The Shaw-Walker Company
4. Color code personal and company names for the following color-coded filing systems:
   a. Jeter Top Coder
   b. Alpha-Z®
   c. Colorscan
   d. Accu-Find

In this chapter you will study filing systems that are constructed around an element that is both beautiful and useful: color. Before you read further, look at each of the four color illustrations in this chapter. They are colorful and attractive, aren't they?

WHY COLOR IS USED IN FILING SYSTEMS

While color in filing systems improves the appearance of the file, the main purpose of color is to increase the accuracy and the speed of filing and retrieving office records. On the highway, streetlights are more visible than street signs; in the office, color-coded folders are more visible than the names printed on them. Because color attracts the eye from longer distances than words, filers are directed to the needed information long before they are able to read the folder caption. As you study the color-coded systems in this chapter, you will learn not only that records are stored and retrieved quickly and efficiently with color-coded systems, but also that misfiled records are more easily detected.

Color attracts the eye.

HOW COLOR IS USED IN ALPHABETIC FILING SYSTEMS

Color can be used in any system.

How color is used in alphabetic filing systems is the main topic of this chapter. The use of color in filing systems is not restricted to alphabetic systems, however. Color is also used in numeric systems and other systems that you will study in Chapters 9, 10, 11, and 12. In general, color is used either for color coding or for color accenting filing systems.

Color Coding

Color is used in a precise color scheme.

Color coding is a process of using different color schemes to divide file drawers, or shelves, into alphabetic or numeric sections. Color folders, guides, and labels are used in a very precise color scheme. One color is always associated with the same alphabetic unit or digit in the system. The use of color becomes a code—a systematic pattern of identification.

Color Accenting

Each part of a system may be a different color.

Another way of using color is to mark each part (guides, folders, labels) of a system with a different color. Primary, secondary, and special guides; individual and general folders; OUT guides; and labels *may* carry contrasting colors simply to make parts of the system stand out. For example, primary guides may be red and general folders may be blue. This use of color is referred to as **color accenting** a filing system.

COLOR-CODED ALPHABETIC FILING SYSTEMS

Each of the four filing systems illustrated in this chapter is widely publicized and used throughout the country. It is very possible that you have seen one of these systems in a current records management periodical. It is likely that one of these systems will be used in the office where you will work. It is useful, therefore, for you to understand how color-coded systems are constructed and how colors are used to make filing easier, faster, and more reliable.

Each of the filing systems is presented first according to its design and guide arrangement. This discussion includes the manner or style of arranging the various sections in the system, the types of notations used on guides and folders, and any special features that make the system unique. Then the color schemes used in the system are explained and illustrated.

Jeter Top Coder

The Jeter Top Coder, manufactured by Jeter Systems Corporation in Akron, Ohio, is shown in Color Illustration A. The illustration is of a lateral file with top coding, but the system can be converted to side coding for shelf filing as well. In fact, OUT guides and folders that have been side coded for a shelf file are displayed in the Color Illustration A inset. The inset also displays numeric, date, alphabetic, and solid color labels used to color code a variety of useful information. Notice in the file illustration that the labels create a straight-line (in-line) arrangement of color blocks that help to detect and prevent misfiles.

System Design and Guide Arrangement. Refer to Color Illustration A as you study the guide arrangement of the Jeter Top Coder outlined below. The eight tab positions are described from left to right.

1. Solid color, date, numeric, or alphabetic labels form bands of colors in the first four positions. These labels color code a variety of helpful information. A label might code (a) a particular doctor in a medical clinic to whom a patient has been assigned, (b) an attorney in a law firm to whom a client has been assigned, (c) a specific geographic region or district, (d) a particular department in an organization, or (e) the date the file was opened or the date the folder was last active (helpful at transfer time!). Noticeably lacking in first position are primary guides. Although the file drawers may be labeled to show the range (AA-AW) of records in them, the alphabetic labels on each folder make separate primary guides unnecessary.
2. Name labels occupy the fifth (slightly off center) position in the file drawer.
3. Alphabetic labels to color code the first and second letters of the key unit are next in the sixth and seventh positions. The highly visible color block created by these labels facilitates fast and accurate storage and retrieval of the individual folders and eliminates misfiles.
4. OUT guide tabs are clearly visible in the extreme right (eighth position) of the file drawer. The OUT guides indicate what records have been borrowed and mark the location for the return of borrowed records.

Color Scheme. Thirteen different colors are used to code letters of the alphabet. Because there are 26 letters in the alphabet, two different label patterns are used. Solid color labels are used for letters A through M. The same colors are used for letters N through Z, but a solid white vertical line separates the label into a two-part color label.

 The label patterns and the 13 colors used to represent the letters of the alphabet in the Jeter Top Coder:

Solid Label Letter	*Color*	*Two-Part Label* Letter
A	Red	N
B	Brown	O
C	White	P
D	Gray	Q
E	Orange	R
F	Beige	S

G	Yellow	T
H	Dark Blue	U
I	Light Blue	V
J	Light Green	W
K	Black	X
L	Dark Green	Y
M	Magenta	Z

The long, straight-line block of red in the file illustration represents names beginning with A. The second letters of the key units are color coded to yellow (G), black (K), and then dark green (L). Names like Richard Agate, Connie Agent, Dino Agosta, and Agway Inc., are all coded in the same way: A solid red label (A) and a solid yellow label (G) represent the first and second letters of the key unit in the name. The straight-line color blocks help to keep together all filing segments with key units beginning with the same two letters (Ag, Ak, Al, for example).

Alpha-Z® System

The Alpha-Z® system is shown in Color Illustration B. It is produced by The Smead Manufacturing Company of Hastings, Minnesota. Guides and folders are available for use in vertical, lateral, and shelf filing equipment. The pull-out shelf file in Color Illustration B shows guides and folders tabbed in a vertical arrangement for an open-shelf file. In such an arrangement, the uppermost position is the *first* position. Second position is the next lower cut. Third position and beyond are in successively lower positions.

System Design and Guide Arrangement. The equivalent of seven positions (from top to bottom) are used in the design of the Alpha-Z® system shown in Color Illustration B. Refer to the illustration as you study the guide arrangement described below.

1. Primary guides are in first position (the top position).
2. A unique name label consisting of a color band, name, and alphabetic letter color codes the *first* letter of the key unit. The color band, name, and alphabetic letter form the second, third, and fourth positions when the name label is applied to the folder tab. The design, the preparation, and the application of the name label are shown in Illustration 8-1.

   The Alpha-Z® color-coded name labels provide for all 26 letters of the alphabet on 13 distinctively colored, self-adhesive labels. A-M are color-on-white; N-Z are white-on-color. Each label may be used for either of two alphabetic characters by simply stripping away the one character not needed. These labels are scored to fold for easy application and are available in a complete alphabetic package or in individual letter packages. A single label is designed to represent two different letters and to be attached in either a top tab or an end tab arrangement.

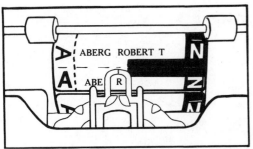 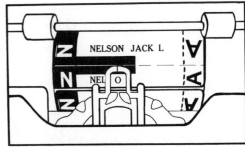

1. Insert strip of labels with letter to be used at left

 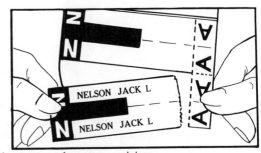

2. Remove label from backing and separate from unused letter

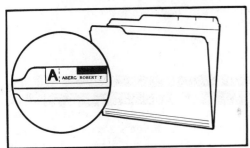 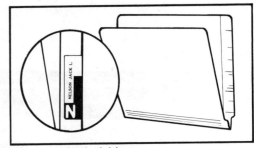

3. Labels may be used on top tab or end tab folders

Illus. 8-1   Name Label Application

3. Alphabetic labels, next in fifth position, color code the *second* letter of the key unit.
4. A second alphabetic label is next in sixth position and color codes the *third* letter of the key unit in large systems. The small system shown in Color Illustration B does not make use of this additional coding option, however.
5. OUT guides are last in seventh position.

Color Scheme. The color scheme (plan) for the Alpha-Z® system consists of 13 colors in a solid and three-part label pattern. The colors and patterns code letters of the alphabet as shown on page 100.

Solid Label Letter	*Color*	*Three-Part Label Letter*
A	Red	N
B	Dark Blue	O
C	Green	P
D	Light Blue	Q
E	Purple	R
F	Orange	S
G	Gray	T
H	Dark Brown	U
I	Pink	V
J	Yellow	W
K	Light Brown	X
L	Violet	Y
M	Light Green	Z

Alpha-Z® name labels and alphabetic labels appear as insets in Color Illustration B. The insets clearly show the 13 colors used to code A to Z. Note particularly the *solid* color labels used for A to M and the *three-part* label pattern used for N to Z. Although the colors are repeated once throughout the system, hash marks (=) create a distinct three-part color pattern for labels N-Z. It is not necessary to memorize these color codes. Wall charts are always available for reference until the color designations are learned.

Colorscan

Colorscan by Kardex Systems, Inc., is a color-coded alphabetic system that focuses more on alphabetic guides and color folders than on a strict alphabetic arrangement of records. See Color Illustration C and notice that the names are not in STRICT alphabetic sequence. Folders are filed first behind appropriate primary alphabetic sections (A to Z) of the file according to the first letter of the key unit. Then according to the first letter of the second indexing unit, the folders are placed at the beginning of one of ten sections which subdivide each primary guide section. The ten subsections are color coded and divided alphabetically as follows: (1) AB, (2) C, (3) DEF, (4) GHI, (5) J, (6) KL, (7) MNO, (8) PQR, (9) ST, (10) U-Z. This means that all names with key units beginning with A and second indexing units beginning with D, E, or F would be returned to the beginning of the DEF subsection of the file. This form of random filing keeps the more active records in the front of appropriate alphabetic sections for faster and easier retrieval of information. Random filing procedures will become more evident as you study the system design and guide arrangement that follows.

System Design and Guide Arrangement. Illustration 8-2 is a diagram of the Colorscan file shown in Color Illustration C. The diagram shows (1) primary guides, (2) straight-line blocks designating the primary alphabetic

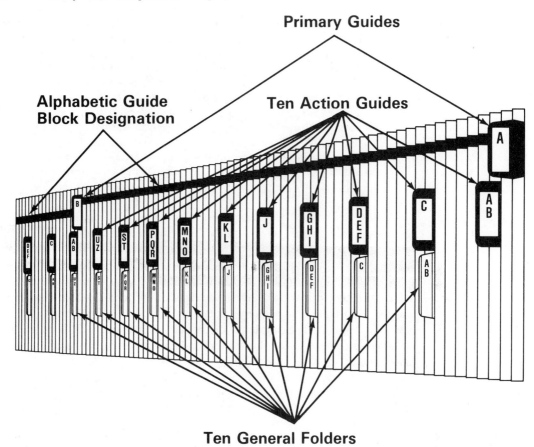

Illus. 8-2 Colorscan Arrangement

guide sections, (3) color-coded action guides separating each color subsection, and (4) general folders ending each color subsection.

A careful study of the diagram will help to distinguish and identify the Colorscan file shown in the inset in Color Illustration C.

1. Primary guides are clearly marked and visible in first position. Primary guide block designations for the A and B sections of the file are shown in Illustration 8-2. These straight-line blocks are created by a black pressure-sensitive label applied to the A box on the preprinted folder. See Color Illustration C again for a closer look at the preprinted folders. Notice that the letter A has been blocked out on all the folders—all key units begin with A. Illustration 8-2 shows the primary guide B block designation as well. These black blocks appear at subsequently lower positions as the alphabet progresses, so it is impossible to assign them a single position in the file.

2. Color-coded alphabetic action guides appear in the next lower position. These action guides, which subdivide each primary alphabetic section of the file, code the *first letter of the second indexing unit*. Folders are always returned to the

front of the alphabetic subsection to which they belong. This is one feature of Colorscan which inhibits a strict alphabetic sequence of names. All active records stay in the front of each subsection for easy access. For example, when the folder for Howard Anderson is returned to the file, it is placed behind primary guide A (Anderson) and Action Guide GHI (Howard). At this moment, Howard Anderson's folder is *first* in the GHI section.

3. General folders are in third position. The Colorscan system provides storage for correspondence that is not active enough to warrant an individual folder. Each color, or alphabetic subdivision, ends with a general folder. Alphabetic sequence should be observed in the general folders or it becomes difficult to determine when sufficient records have accumulated for a client and an individual folder should be prepared.

Color Scheme. The effective use of color in this random filing system becomes more apparent as you study the system more carefully. All you need to know to use Colorscan is the first letter of the key unit and the first letter of the second indexing unit. Because other letters in the name are ignored, names will not appear in strict alphabetic order. The first letter of the key unit determines the primary alphabetic guide section behind which the folder is placed. Then color immediately takes over to code the first letter of the second indexing unit. The first letter of the second indexing unit is coded to one of ten color folders. Color Illustration C shows the ten colors used to code the first letter of the second indexing units. A color wheel inset shows the alphabetic breakdown and the colors used. Since there are only ten colors and 26 letters of the alphabet, alphabetic subsections are divided and color coded in this way:

Letters	*Color*
AB	Red
C	Yellow
DEF	Pink
GHI	Green
J	White
KL	Brown
MNO	Blue
PQR	Orange
ST	Violet
U-Z	Tan

Study the eight folders in Color Illustration C. The folders are labeled and ready for filing in a Colorscan system. Notice that all the filing segments have key units that begin with A. These folders will appear behind the primary guide A. Then folders would be placed in one of ten alphabetic subsections according to the first letter of the second indexing unit in the name.

Anacombs Language Center is filed before Adams Michael because Language comes before Michael. Anacombs Language Center is placed in the KL subsection of primary guide A, and Michael Adams in the MNO subsection of primary guide A. These subsections are color coded and clearly distinguished by *action guides*. Review the following retrieval procedures that make this random filing system unique:

1. Locate alphabetic guides for the first letter of the name you are looking for.
2. Locate the appropriate COLOR of folder for the first letter of the second name. Refer to a color wheel like the one in the inset of Color Illustration C.
3. SCAN folders for the specific name. Active records will be toward the front of the section, less active records toward the back of the section.

Accu-Find

Color Illustration D of Accu-Find by The Shaw-Walker Company, Muskegon, Michigan, includes (1) a shelf-file inset, (2) an assortment of color-coded alphabetic labels, (3) a file sample showing names color coded to folders and labels, and (4) a complete set of color-coded alphabetic folders. All the supplies necessary to establish the system and a sample file arrangement are shown.

System Design and Guide Arrangement. Study the shelf-file inset in Color Illustration D. Notice the following:

1. An alphabetic letter preprinted on a color folder codes the first letter of the surname, or key unit. A folder tab up to the placement of the first label creates a four-inch band of color which codes that particular letter of the alphabet.
2. A two-inch pressure-sensitive label codes the second letter of the surname or key unit. The color scheme for these alphabetic labels is the same as that used for the alphabetic folders.
3. A one-inch pressure-sensitive alphabetic label may be used to code the first letter of the second indexing unit in larger systems.

Study the sample file section of the Accu-Find color system in Color Illustration D. Study the color folders and labels used to code the names. Can you spot the misfiled record? It is quite obvious, isn't it?

Color Scheme. The generous use of color folders in the Accu-Find system makes a misfiled record stand out. Thirteen different colors are used to distinguish the alphabetic folders. Folders A through L are colored differently and are preprinted with a black alphabetic letter. The color scheme is repeated for folders Mc to W, except the letters appear with hash marks to distinguish them from the first half of the alphabet. The X, Y, and Z folders, generally the smallest sections in an alphabetic system, are all coded in the same buff color. The color scheme used on both folders and labels in the Accu-Find system is shown on the following page.

Labeled Solid	*Color*	*Labeled With Hash Marks*
A	Pink	Mc
B	Red	M
C	Orange	N
D	Gold	O
E	Yellow	P
F	Light Green	Q
G	Dark Green	R
H	Gray	S
I	Light Blue	T
J	Dark Blue	U
K	Violet	V
L	Purple	W
	Buff	X,Y,Z

Even though you may have studied the four different color-coded filing systems carefully, memorizing the design of the systems in one sitting is impossible. The following table will help you to review what you have just learned. It is not necessary to memorize the colors. Use color charts until you become familiar with the color schemes. The method of coding filing segments and special features of each system are reviewed in Illustration 8-3.

Color-Coded Filing System	1st Letter of Key Unit	2d Letter of Key Unit	1st Letter of 2d Indexing Unit	Additional Features
Jeter Top Coder	Alphabetic color-coded label	Alphabetic color-coded label	None	Date, numeric, or solid color labels to code a variety of helpful information
Alpha-Z®	Color-coded alphabetic NAME label	Color-coded alphabetic label		
Colorscan	The primary alphabetic guide	None	One of ten color-coded folders behind an alphabetic action guide	(1) Action guides for each section of ten color-coded folders; (2) alphabetic boxes preprinted at folder edge to designate primary alphabetic blocks; (3) random filing
Accu-Find	Color-coded, preprinted alphabetic folders	Two-inch color-coded alphabetic label	One-inch color-coded alphabetic label (optional)	

Illus. 8-3   Methods of Color Coding Indexing Units

Jeter Top Coder Color - Coded System
and Supplies

Jeter Systems Corporation

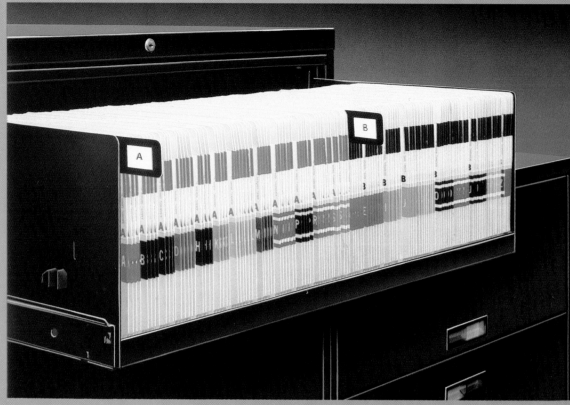

ALPHA - Z® SYSTEM
The Smead Manufacturing Company

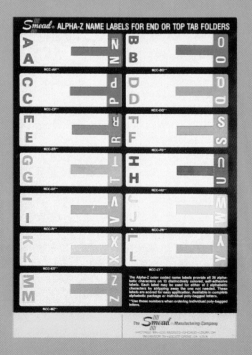

Alpha - Z color-coded name labels

Alpha - Z color-coded alphabetic labels

ILLUSTRATION C

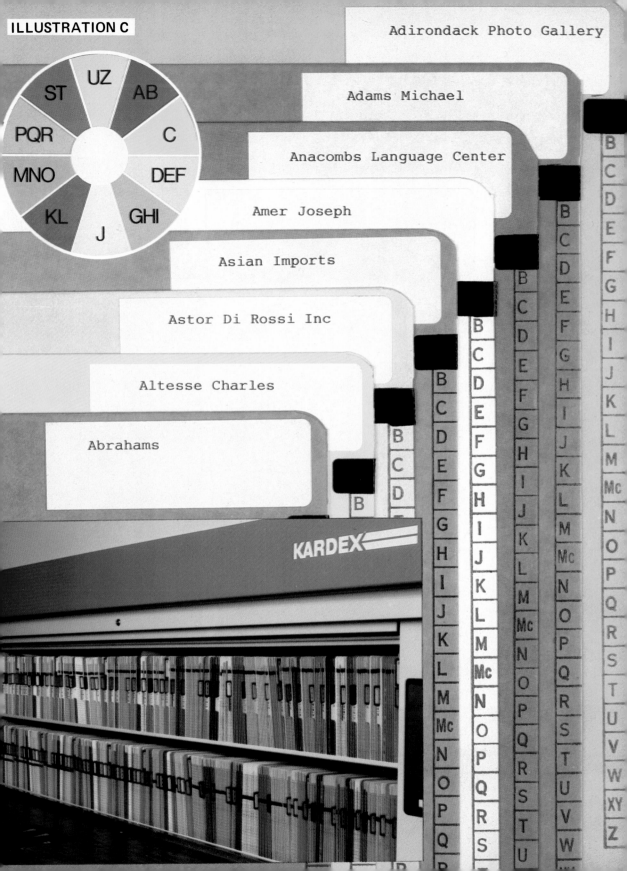

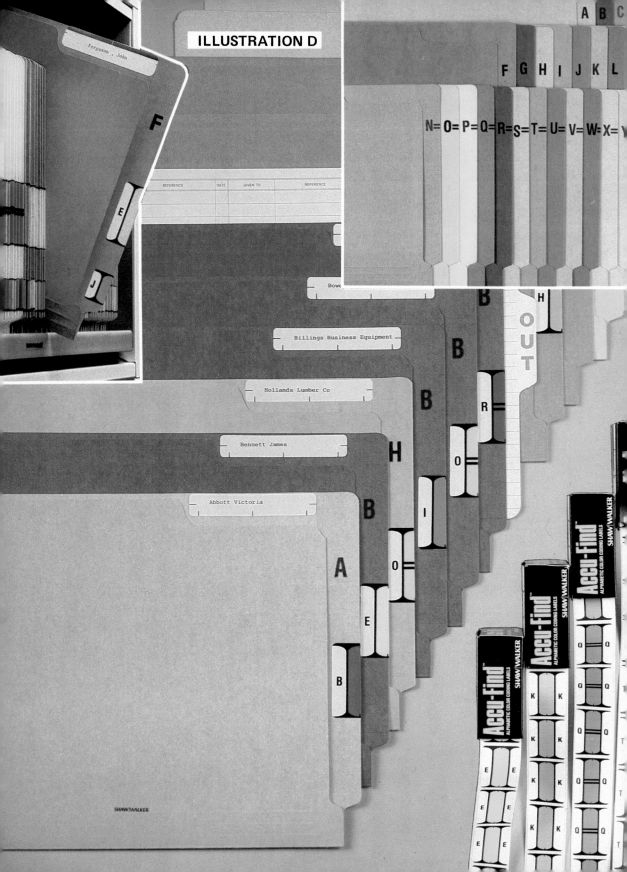

Questions for Discussion

1. What are the important advantages of using color in a filing system? (1)

2. What is the difference between color coding and color accenting a filing system? (2)

3. What use is made of a straight-line (in-line) arrangement of color blocks in the Jeter Top Coder? (3a)

4. What additional color-coded features distinguish the Jeter Top Coder from the other three systems illustrated in this chapter? (3a)

5. What is unique about the name labels used in the Alpha-Z® color-coded system? (3b)

6. What is the method for coding names in the Alpha-Z® system? (3b)

7. Describe the use of guides and folders in the Colorscan system. (3c)

8. Why is the Colorscan filing system considered a random filing system? (3c)

9. How does the use of color folders in the Accu-Find system differ from the use of color folders in the Colorscan system? (3d)

10. Explain the use of the two-inch and the one-inch color-coded alphabetic labels used in the Accu-Find system. (3d)

Applications

Prepare a table like those shown in the following examples. Then color code each of the listed names according to the four color-coded alphabetic systems. Be sure to indicate when necessary whether the color is solid, two-part, three-part, or includes hash marks (=).

Jeter Top Coder. (4a) Prepare a table similar to the example. In the space provided, write the color of the first label and the second label used to code names in the Jeter Top Coder. Be sure to indicate that the color label is a solid (S) or a two-part (2) label.

Name	1st Color Label	2d Color Label
First City National Bank		
Robert Lubbock Manufacturing Co.		
Electrical Repair Service Co.		
The Battone Sisters		

Alpha-Z®. (4b) Prepare a table similar to the example. In the spaces provided, indicate the color of the name label and the color of the second label to be used for each of the names listed. Be sure to indicate whether the color label is a solid (S) label or a three-part (3) label.

Name	Name Label Color	2d Color Label
Houston Chronicle		
Schrafft Bakery, Inc.		
Van Chevrolet Co.		
Maria Lisse		
Jason Peterson		

Colorscan. (4c) Prepare a table similar to the following sample. In the columns provided, indicate the primary guide behind which each of the following names is placed. Then in the Action Guide column, specify the alphabetic subdivision for each name. Finally, indicate the color to which the name is coded.

Name	Primary Guide	Action Guide	Color Folder
Dale Campbell			
Kelly Imports			
Beverly Sing			
Chita Valero			
Retson Electronics			

Accu-Find. (4d) Prepare a table similar to the example. Specify the color of the alphabetic folder, the color of the two-inch label, and the color of the one-inch label used to color code each of the listed names. Be sure to indicate whether the color is solid (S) or has hash marks (=).

Name	Color-Coded Alphabetic Folder	Two-inch Label Color	One-inch Label Color
R & R Industries, Inc.			
Viacom Livestock Marketing			
Casey Alvarez			
Wayne Granger			
Morris Underhill			

PART 4

Other Filing Systems

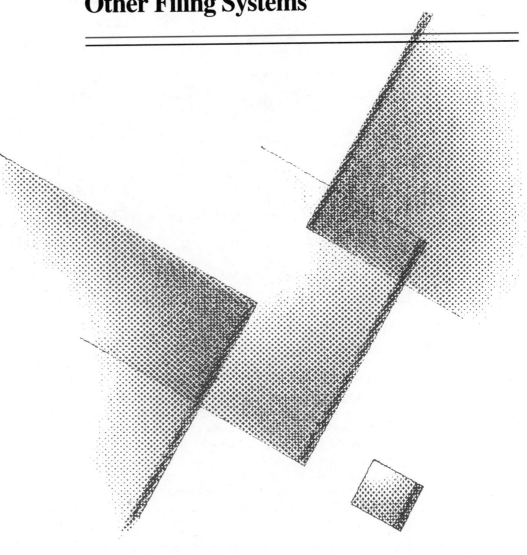

CHAPTER 9

Subject Filing

Learning Objectives

After completing Chapter 9, you will be able to:

1. Describe a subject filing system.
2. Recommend when to develop a subject file. .
3. List the advantages and disadvantages of filing by subject.
4. Arrange a subject file.
5. Describe the steps to follow in preparing and storing material in a subject file.
6. Prepare a master record of subject captions used in the records department.
7. Understand why an index is helpful in subject filing.

We have learned how to file correspondence and other materials in alphabetic order by individual or company name. Thus, a letter from Clara Burgos is located in front of letters from Juan Cruz because Burgos comes before Cruz alphabetically. But what if Clara's name is not our major concern? It may be more important to us that Clara, an accountant, has written about the solution of an important tax accounting question. How can we locate the answer to this accounting question if we do not remember that it was written by Clara Burgos? Many letters from other accountants relating to the same tax question may be in our files. If we are using an alphabetic filing system, we would have to remember the names of all these correspondents before we could locate all the correspondence on the same question. This chapter discusses subject filing—one way to solve this problem.

SUBJECT FILING SYSTEMS

When most of the materials in a file may be requested by subject titles rather than by names of persons or companies, using a filing system in which subject titles are used as captions is wise. A system in which information is filed primarily under subject titles is called a *subject filing system*.

Nature of Subject Filing

In a subject filing system information is filed primarily under subject titles.

In a subject filing system, the captions on the guides and folders are generally based on subject titles rather than on names of people or companies. In the case of Clara Burgos' letter concerning the tax accounting question, the letter can be filed under a subject title such as "Accounting–Tax." All other materials concerning this topic will be placed in the same folder or file section with Clara Burgos' letter, regardless of who wrote the material. When someone wants information on this question, all the related materials, including Clara Burgos' letter, will be located in the same folder or section of the system. Remembering Clara Burgos' name in order to locate the material will not be necessary. If, on the other hand, there is a lot of correspondence from Clara Burgos on this same topic, a separate folder with the caption "Accounting–Tax–Burgos Clara" may be placed after the subject folder "Accounting–Tax." This individual correspondence folder is a part of the subject file and is located with all folders on the same subject.

The arrangement of a subject file looks like an outline.

Frequently the arrangement of a subject file looks like an outline of the activities of the business. This is true because the titles used as captions on guides are very similar to those that describe the activities, the departments, or the problems of a business or an office. For example, titles used in a subject filing system might be based on the following alphabetic list of activities or departments in a particular company:

Accounting	Manufacturing
Administration	Marketing
Construction	Office
Engineering	Personnel
Insurance	Public Relations
Legal	Purchasing

Each of the main subject headings listed above would probably be separated into subdivisions. These subdivisions, in turn, could be broken down further into smaller subject areas. For example, a more complete subject breakdown of "Accounting," such as the following one, might be developed.

ACCOUNTING

Audits

    Cash Payments
    Cash Receipts
    Management Statements
    Payroll

Costs

    Administrative
    Manufacturing
    Office

Budgets

    Branch
    Corporate

Credit

    Secured
    Unsecured

Expense	Financial
Administrative	Bonds
Executive	Investments
Office	Stocks
Marketing	
Advertising	
Research	Taxes
Sales	
	Federal
	Local
	State

Uses of Subject Filing

Subject filing groups all materials on one subject in one place.

Subject filing can be used to advantage whenever it is desirable to have all materials on one subject grouped in one place in the files rather than separated under many different names. This is especially important when all the records related to one product or one activity are needed at the same time. Such a situation is generally more typical of single departments in a business than it is of a centralized file for an entire business. The correspondence of one department is usually concerned with a relatively small number of subjects with few divisions and subdivisions. These subjects fit into a simple classification that everyone in the department who has occasion to use the file understands thoroughly.

Subject files are frequently found in:

1. Research departments where materials are filed under titles describing particular studies. A research director for new product development, for example, may file research reports first by product name and then by the specific report name.
2. Executive offices where the interest is not so much in a particular correspondent as in the overall picture. A purchasing agent for office equipment, for example, may be more concerned with the types of office equipment available than with the names of the manufacturers of such equipment.
3. Offices that keep instructional information. In teachers' files, for example, information relating to various subjects is filed under topic headings.
4. Companies and institutions where work is handled first by group titles and then by name. Art galleries, museums, libraries, and commercial supply houses are examples.

Subject Filing in a Centralized File

A centralized records department must handle materials relating to customers as well as to business operations.

Some businesses operate a central records department. In such a department, records are kept in one location but the papers may relate to the activities of many different departments. Sometimes a centralized records department must handle materials relating to customers as well as to business operations. In this case, all customer materials are filed according to the names of the customers—sometimes in a separate alphabetic filing system. Then all matters dealing with the operation of the business are filed by subject in a subject system.

The subject filing system brings together all materials from areas such as advertising, sales, personnel, taxes, insurance, and office procedures. These materials are often needed for reference over a longer period of time than customers' correspondence. Holding them in a separate subject file means that important records can be kept without transfer for as long a time as desired.

Arrangement of a Subject File

A subject filing system consists of the same elements as an alphabetic correspondence file.

A subject filing system consists of the same elements as an alphabetic correspondence file—equipment, guides, folders, and procedures—which you studied in Chapter 5. The guides of a subject file may appear in one, two, or three positions, depending on the number of headings and subheadings in the outline of subjects for the activities or departments of the business. For example, primary guides might be used in first position to indicate the subjects representing the main headings of the outline. Auxiliary guides might appear in second position to represent subdivisions of each main heading in the outline. If the subdivisions' headings in the outline are in turn subdivided, guides in third position could carry suitable captions.

All folders in a subject file may be of one type with captions consisting of subject headings only; or folders of a second type may be included for names of individuals and businesses.

General folders similar to those used in an alphabetic file usually are not used in subject systems. Each paper or other document is coded according to its subject title and is filed directly in its properly labeled folder. Tabs on folders used in a subject file are usually third-cut or half-cut.

Outline of a Subject File

The best technique to use in starting a subject file is to develop a detailed outline. Six divisions of a subject filing system are shown in Illustration 9-1. When the file in the illustration was established, a very thorough study was made of the titles under which papers could be requested from the file. The study determined that papers should be filed under six major titles or headings. These six headings were then arranged in alphabetic order on the outline. Further study suggested twenty subheadings under the main headings. On the outline these subheadings were arranged in alphabetic order within the six primary sections.

It was recognized that a third subdivision could be set up if necessary. These third-level divisions could be used if the amount of material filed in the subdivisions already identified would be large. For example, under "Finance" there are many budget reports. A logical subdivision of budget reports can be made by dividing the year into quarters. If the reports are prepared daily, weekly, or monthly, and are frequently requested in these forms, the titles "Daily," "Weekly," or "Monthly" can be used as subheadings. However, the

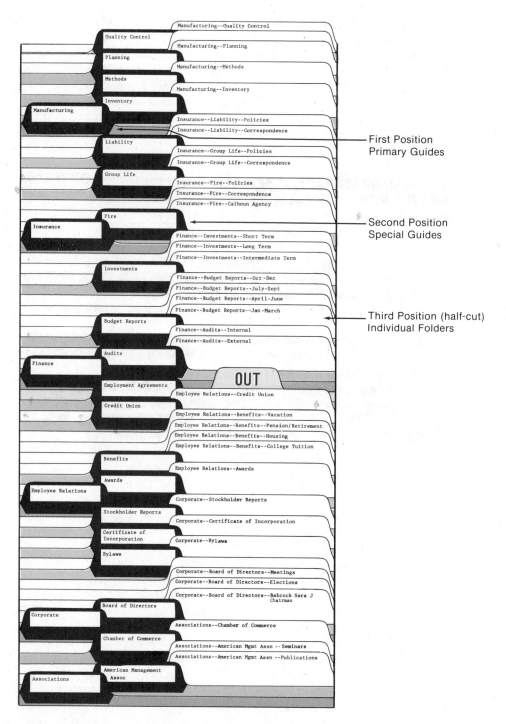

First Position
Primary Guides

Second Position
Special Guides

Third Position (half-cut)
Individual Folders

Illus. 9-1 Portion of a Subject Filing System

reports for this company were prepared quarterly, so quarterly was the logical breakdown.

The third subdivision would also be helpful if certain subtopics were requested frequently but separately from the other papers in the subdivision's folder. For example, also under "Finance," the subheadings "Audits" and "Investments" both had logical subdivisions that might be requested separately. Other possible subdivisions were studied and these were made where helpful.

The third subdivision could also be used for individual name folders. These would be added to the system whenever correspondence with a person concerning a given subject was very active and/or if there was a large amount of correspondence. For example, under the subheading "Board of Directors," an individual folder for the chairman, Sara J. Babcock, was included.

The headings and subheadings on the outline were then studied to see if the titles used were satisfactory. Titles, in order to be useful for headings and subheadings, should be simple. They also need to be readily expandable into further subheadings if necessary at a later time. After this study was completed, the headings and subheadings in the system shown in Illustration 9-1 were outlined as follows:

I. Associations
   A. American Management Association
      1. Publications
      2. Seminars
   B. Chamber of Commerce

II. Corporate
   A. Board of Directors
      1. Babcock, Sara J., chairman
      2. Elections
      3. Meetings
   B. Bylaws
   C. Certificate of Incorporation
   D. Stockholder Reports

III. Employee Relations
   A. Awards
   B. Benefits
      1. College Tuition
      2. Housing
      3. Pension and Retirement
      4. Vacation
   C. Credit Union
   D. Employment Agreements

IV. Finance
   A. Audits
      1. External
      2. Internal
   B. Budget Reports
      1. January-March
      2. April-June
      3. July-September
      4. October-December
   C. Investments
      1. Intermediate Term
      2. Long Term
      3. Short Term

V. Insurance
   A. Fire
      1. Calhoun Agency
      2. Correspondence
      3. Policies
   B. Group Life
      1. Correspondence
      2. Policies
   C. Liability
      1. Correspondence
      2. Policies

VI. Manufacturing
   A. Inventory
   B. Methods
   C. Planning
   D. Quality Control

Primary guides are placed in first position.

The primary guides in the illustration—Associations, Corporate, Employee Relations, Finance, Insurance, and Manufacturing—were placed in first position. After the first primary guide, Associations, the two subdivisions of Associations—American Management Association and Chamber of Commerce—were used as captions on the two auxiliary guides for this section of the file and were placed in second position.

The individual folders were then prepared with half-cut tabs. Long captions are frequently required for a subject system. The captions for the individual folders are complete in order to indicate their exact locations.

Auxiliary guides and individual folders were then prepared for the rest of the subheadings of the outline, and were placed in their proper locations in the file.

Several additional points should be noticed while studying Illustration 9-1:

1. When a folder is removed from the file, an OUT card (or OUT guide) is substituted in the individual folder's position. In Illustration 9-1, note the OUT guide in place of the folder for "Employee Relations—Employment Agreements." If desired, an OUT folder can be used instead of an OUT guide. When an OUT folder is used, materials accumulated while the original folder is out of the file can be held in the proper location. These materials can then be placed in the original folder when it is returned to the files.

2. The months of the year can be used to extend sections in a subject filing system. In Illustration 9-1, the section "Finance—Budget Reports" has a different folder for each quarter of the year and the captions on the folders indicate this breakdown. Dated folders can be used in this same way when needed. An alphabetic breakdown can also be indicated in the same manner. If additional folders with the same subject headings are required in other sections, a second folder can be labeled with a number 2; a third folder with 3; and so on.

3. In the "Insurance" section, there are three folders for holding correspondence. These were added to this subject filing system because there was a volume of correspondence concerning each of these three types of insurance.

   Letters filed in these correspondence folders are first coded by writing subject titles on them. Then they are coded by names of correspondents in the usual manner, that is, by underlining the key unit and numbering the other units to establish the indexing order of the names.

No general folders are needed in this subject system. If, however, general folders are desired, they can be added immediately after the last folder in the appropriate sections and labeled with the captions identifying the sections. General titles in subject systems are usually avoided because of the possibility of error when filing and finding. If a new subject is important enough to be added to a subject system, a new folder should be made for it whenever possible.

SUBJECT FILING PROCEDURES

There are several methods for filing correspondence in a subject system. Some subject files are established primarily to provide up-to-date information on a

There are several methods for filing correspondence in a subject system.

topic. In this case, the information about a topic is more important than a specific document. Correspondence in such a file is stored in the same folder as all other documents pertaining to the same topic.

For other subject files, the main purpose is to arrange a variety of materials according to only a few specific topics. In such a file, main captions are prepared for each major topic, and subheadings are prepared and captioned according to the type of material filed. Examples of such materials are catalogs, contracts, correspondence, employees, invoices, and raw materials.

When document-type records (such as sales slips) are of most importance in one phase of filing and correspondence-type records in another phase of filing, using two systems might be the best approach. The first system might be a subject-document system; the second, a subject-correspondence system.

Filing Procedures in a Subject File

Similar procedures are used in filing materials in a subject file whether the materials are documents or correspondence. To illustrate filing procedures, a subject correspondence file is used in the following discussion.

Inspection. Each incoming letter should be checked to see that it has been released for filing. Inspection procedures were discussed in detail in Chapter 5.

Coding. In many cases, the correspondence is coded by an executive or a secretary before it is sent to the records department. If a letter has not been coded, the filer must read it carefully to determine the subject title to be used as a basis for coding. If the subject appears in the letter in the same form as is used on the caption of the folder in which the letter should be filed, the coding may be done by underlining the subject wherever it appears in the letter. In Illustration 9-2, the subject of the letter is indicated on line 2 of the last paragraph: "Sales." Because of its location within the letter, the subject for coding could be underlined. In most cases, however, it is necessary to code the letter by writing the subject title at the top of the letter, usually in the upper right corner. When there is more than one unit in the subject filing segment, the units are coded by numbering them to indicate their position or rank in the indexing order.

Keep a master record of the subject captions and the kinds of correspondence filed in the folders.

In order to prevent errors in coding, a master record is made of the subject titles of the kinds of correspondence filed in each of the folders bearing these captions. This master record should be available at all times in the records department. The master record may be in the form of a typewritten outline, in the form of a card file with all subject titles arranged alphabetically, or in both forms. Unless some type of supplementary record is kept, two filers may use two different subjects for coding letters of the same type. More differences of opinion arise regarding the coding of letters for a subject file than for any other type of file. Thus, in addition to using a master record, it is advisable to have one person take responsibility for making final decisions on subject coding problems.

Cross-References. A cross-reference should be prepared if more than one subject is involved in the same piece of correspondence or if the correspondence relates to another correspondent whose materials are filed under a different subject heading. In Illustration 9-3, the information on the cross-reference sheet indicates:

1. That the letter was received from the Ching-Yu Chan Personnel Services and discussed the possible sale of SuperChips to be used in training with SuperChips.
2. That the letter was filed in the folder bearing the caption *Sales.*
3. That the cross-reference should be filed in the folder captioned *Branch Offices Branch Office West* so that anyone looking in that folder for the correspondence concerning the use of SuperChips in training will know that the letter is in the *Sales* folder.

In some businesses a photocopy is made of the original letter, and the copy is filed in the cross-reference location. When this is done, a cross-reference sheet is not prepared. The coding of the letter remains the same so that it is evident where the copies are filed.

Sorting. After all material has been coded, it should be sorted first according to the main subjects of the file and then by the first subdivisions. This means that if the file is based on an outline consisting of five main headings, the first sorting is on the basis of such headings. For each of these sorted groups, the second sorting is based on the subdivisions of the main heading in the outline.

Materials in a subject correspondence folder are arranged alphabetically by the correspondents' names.

Placing Materials in Folders. The first basis for arrangement of materials in a subject correspondence folder is the alphabetic order of the names of the correspondents. All correspondence with one person or company is grouped together in the folder. Different pieces of correspondence for the same correspondent are arranged within that group by date, with the most recent date in front. Material that is placed in an individual folder is arranged in the same manner as that in an individual folder for an alphabetic name file; that is, the paper showing the most recent date is filed in front of others within the group.

Index for a Subject File

A subject system is difficult to keep under control, but such a system can hold papers and other records efficiently. In some subject systems, alphabetic primary guides (A, Ba, Bu) are used in a manner similar to that in an alphabetic correspondence file. This makes filing and finding easier under certain conditions. A popular way to control a subject file is to prepare an index card control file and use it along with the subject system. This procedure requires preparing cards that show descriptions of each major subject in the system and also list the subtopics under each subject. For example, it is useful to

A popular way to gain control over a subject file is to prepare an index card control file.

CROSS-REFERENCE SHEET

Name or Subject Branch Offices
Branch Office West

Date of Item 4/17/--

Regarding Training with
SuperChips

SEE

Name or Subject Ching-Yu Chan Personnel
Services

Authorized by J. B. M. Date 4/19/--

HOME OFFICE
12 Tech Circle
Bensenville, IL 60106-2811
(312) 728-1690

Ahead in the Information Age

SUPERCHIP, INC.

April 17, 19--

Mrs. Ching-Yu Chan, President
Ching-Yu Chan/Personnel/Services
935 West Portland
Eugene, OR 97401-3726

Dear Mrs. Chan

We have indeed served many businesses and industrial training programs with SuperChips. Thank
you for writing to us.

Fortunately, one of our branch offices is located
in Oregon. I am sending a copy of your letter
to Mr. Benito J. Cardona, Manager of Branch
Office West. I am sure he will be contacting
you.

Should you wish to see him before he makes a
sales contact, or to visit his office for a
demonstration, you may write to him at 374
Fourth Street, Portland, OR 97208-3817. His
telephone number is 503-466-2800.

Sincerely

Anthony Q. Barker

Anthony Q. Barker
Vice President, Marketing

tbm

cc Benito J. Cardona

Branch
Office
X

Illus. 9-2 **Incoming Letter with Subject and Cross-Reference Coding**

Illus. 9-3 **Subject Cross-Reference Sheet**

prepare a control card for each correspondent showing the correspondent's name and the subject title or titles under which the correspondent's papers are filed.

There are many different types of subject systems, each designed to serve a particular purpose. Some follow a dictionary arrangement so that all main topics beginning with the letter "A," for example, are located behind a primary guide showing "A," just like in a dictionary. Others are more like an encyclopedia, where main subject headings are determined along with their many subheadings, as shown in Illustration 9-1.

Subject Sections in Alphabetic Filing Systems

Subject sections can be added to alphabetic filings systems whenever and wherever they are needed without disrupting the efficiency of the alphabetic system. However, this is true only when correspondence that is to be filed by subject title is properly coded before being filed. Material to be filed by subject must be recognized by code clerks, and the subject title must be underlined if it appears in the paper. If it does not appear in the paper, the subject must be written and underlined on the upper right-hand side of the paper. Preparation of a separate listing of the subject titles being used will ensure that all papers are properly coded.

Questions for Discussion

1. What is a subject filing system? (1)

2. Where is subject filing frequently used? (2)

3. When is it an advantage to use a subject filing system? A disadvantage? (2,3)

4. Why does a subject file look like an outline? (4)

5. In what ways is a subject filing system similar to an alphabetic correspondence filing system? (4)

6. Why does a subject file generally not have general folders similar to those in an alphabetic file? (4)

7. What is the first step in setting up a subject file? (5)

8. How is an OUT guide used in a subject file? (5)

9. How is a letter coded for subject filing? (5)

10. When should a cross-reference be prepared in subject filing? (5)

11. What three items of information are available from a cross-reference sheet? (5)

12. If a photocopy is made of an original document, is a cross-reference sheet necessary? Where is the photocopy filed? (5)

13. After materials have been coded, how should they be sorted? (5)

14. How are materials arranged in a subject correspondence folder? (5)

15. What is the purpose of the master record of the subject guide and folder captions? (6)

16. What is the purpose of maintaining an index to a subject file? (7)

Applications

1. An executive file in the human resource office of the Nitobe Electronics Company contains information grouped under the following general subject captions:

Employee Testing	Employee Selection Devices
Sources of Potential Employees	Employee Training

The following subdivisions are used often enough to require separate folders in the file:

Applications	Present Employee Recommendations
Combination Tests	School/College Courses
Visual Aids	High Schools
Employment Agencies—Private	Instructional Materials
Former Employees	Physical Examinations
Follow-Up on Training	References Submitted by Applicants
Achievement Tests	Aptitude Tests
On-the-Job Training	Walk-In Applicants
Employment Interviews	Supervisory Training
Administration of Training	Employment Agencies—Government
Colleges	Social Interest Tests
Company Courses	Advertisements
Personnel Investigations	

On an $8\frac{1}{2}'' \times 11''$ sheet of paper, prepare a master record of the subject titles and the subdivisions that logically fall under these titles. Arrange both the subject titles and the subdivisions in alphabetic order. (6)

2. The files in the office of the purchasing agent of the Mueller Manufacturing Company need to be rearranged. The purchasing agent wants to use a subject filing system similar to the one shown in Illustration 9-1. Prepare a master record of the primary guides, secondary guides, and folders in alphabetic order on $8\frac{1}{2}'' \times 11''$ sheets of paper. (6)

The primary guides have the following captions:

Office Equipment
Office Supplies
Office Furniture

The secondary guides show the following captions for the subtopics:

Dictating Machines	Calculators
Chairs	Bookcases
Ribbons	Ink
Typewriters	Paper
Bookends	Calendars—Calendar Pads
Copying Machines	Carbon Paper
Binders	Miscellaneous Supplies
Desks	(Place this guide at the end of
Pens	the Office Supplies Section.)

The folders have the following captions:

Secretarial Desks	Metal Bookends
One-Time Carbon Paper	Battery-Operated Dictating Machines
Bond Paper	Xerography Copying Machines
Folding Chairs	Typewriter Ribbons
Tape Dictating Machines	Executive Chairs
Executive Desks	Catalog Binders
Magnetic Ink	Photocopy Paper
Ball Point Pens	Indelible Ink
Address Labels	Letterhead Paper
Cement and Glue	Disk Dictating Machines
Staplers	Paper Clips
Plastic Bookends	Clip and Spring Binders
Felt Tip Pens	Carbon Paper Packs
Printing Calculators	Photocopy Machines
Second Sheet Paper	Receptionist Desks
Drawing Ink	Printing Calculator Paper
Desk Calendar Pads	Secretarial Chairs
Marking Ink	Printer Ribbons
Wooden Bookends	Stamp Pad Ink
Tissue Paper	Cartridges, Ball Point
Display Calculators	Wrapping Paper
Appointment Calendars	Prong Binders
Printing Calculator Ribbons	Wall Calendars
Ring Binders	Facsimile Copying Machines

Job 7   Subject Correspondence Filing   (4,5)

At this time complete Job 7 in OFFICE FILING PROCEDURES, Sixth Edition. Instructions and supplies for this job are included in the practice set.

CHAPTER 10

Numeric Filing

Learning Objectives

After completing Chapter 10, you will be able to:

1. Describe numeric filing.
2. Recommend when to use a numeric file to advantage.
3. List the four parts of a numeric correspondence file and describe what is included in each part.
4. Describe an accession book and its contents.
5. Describe a numeric correspondence file.
6. Explain how a computer can help with an index card control file.
7. List the advantages and disadvantages of numeric filing.
8. Explain how numbers are used in subject filing systems.
9. Describe a decimal-subject file.
10. Explain the differences between decimal-subject filing and duplex-numeric, duplex-alphabetic, and alphanumeric coding.
11. Read and arrange numbers for filing in consecutive digit, terminal digit, and middle digit filing systems.
12. List the advantages of terminal digit filing over consecutive digit filing.
13. Explain the advantages of using color coding in numeric filing systems.

Numbers are important in our lives.

Numbers have become very important in our personal and business lives. If you want to call a friend on the telephone, you need to know a telephone number. You may have a driver's license number, an automobile license number, a credit card number, and a savings account number. As a student you may have a student identification number (See Illustration 10-1). As a worker you will have a social security number and may have an employee number. When you want to buy replacement parts for something you own or order merchandise from mail order catalogs, you ask for these items by number. All parts and merchandise have been assigned numbers and are listed and stored (filed) numerically.

A number is usually the only identification needed to locate a desired item. The name of the item and its size, color, and other distinctive features are all summarized in a single number assigned only to that one item. If the

Illus. 10-1   Student Identification Numbers May Be Stored in a Computer

number is known, the exact item can be located quickly. For example, with the number of your automobile license, a police officer can obtain information about your car by calling the control station. If a computer is available, this number can be entered into the computer which will almost instantly locate the needed information. Using numbers is the quickest way to find information stored in computer files.

A single number can also provide detailed information about a person. For example, from your driver's license number, one can quickly and easily discover your date of birth, address, and driving record from the motor vehicle registration files. Whether you are a student or an employee of a large corporation, your student number or employee number is all that is needed to locate information about you in the school or corporate files.

NUMERIC FILING SYSTEMS

A filing system that records information by number rather than by name is a numeric filing system.

A filing system that stores records and other information by number rather than by name is a **numeric filing system.** Such filing systems are used in many everyday business and personal situations. For example, filing by number may be considered (1) when the filing system is large and the names of many people and/or objects are similar, (2) when it is necessary to maintain secrecy, or (3) when the information needed is stored on a computer.

Nature and Uses of Numeric Filing

Under certain conditions, numeric filing is efficient, quick, and accurate because a number is much easier to read than a long series of words. A number is, therefore, easier to locate in a file drawer, on a shelf, or in a computer. We know that banks identify the checking accounts of their depositors by numbers. An individual account number is assigned to each depositor. This number, along with the number of the bank, is printed with a special ink on a set of blank checks before the checks are given to the depositor. After a check is written and cashed, the bank number ensures its return to the right bank. The depositor's number ensures that the amount is subtracted from the right depositor's account. Many banks keep depositor's account records on a computer. By using just the depositor's account number, all the necessary information about that account can be retrieved almost instantly by the files user.

Some examples of situations in which numeric filing is advantageous are these:

1. Charge accounts for gasoline purchases and for department store buying, credit card purchases, and many other types of transactions involving credit, all of which are identified by number.
2. Orders for merchandise from a mail-order house, which places its items by number on the stockroom shelves and lists its items by number in its catalog.
3. Orders for automobile replacement parts to be sent by manufacturers.
4. Premiums on life insurance policies that are filed by policy numbers.
5. Factory jobs that are identified by numbers.
6. Installment loans and mortgages.
7. Legal cases, which are assigned consecutive numbers in the order in which they are initiated.
8. Jobs undertaken by building contractors.
9. Districts or territories, such as sales districts or distribution areas.
10. Medical case histories, which are usually filed by patient number.
11. Student records filed by student identification number—frequently social security numbers.
12. Mailing lists arranged and filed by ZIP Code numbers.
13. Income tax collections where taxpayers are identified through social security numbers.

Numeric Correspondence File

For convenience and secrecy, correspondence may be coded and filed by number instead of by name. This is referred to as **numeric correspondence filing**. The chief disadvantage is that a numeric correspondence system requires keeping four types of records. This is far too time-consuming for most modern offices where complex manual (hand-operated) systems are avoided whenever possible.

A numeric correspondence file usually consists of four parts.

A numeric correspondence file usually consists of four parts:

1. A main file in which guides and folders bear numeric captions (See Illustration 10-2).

2. A supplementary index card control file in which names or subject titles are arranged alphabetically.
3. A general alphabetic file which contains (1) new materials about new people or subjects for which the volume of future materials is not anticipated to be extensive enough for the immediate assignment of a number or (2) materials from past correspondents or on subjects that have not yet reached the activity requiring a separate folder and an assigned number.
4. An accession book containing a consecutive record of assigned numbers (See Illustration 10-3).

Main File. In the main numeric file, each important topic or name of a correspondent is assigned an individual folder that has only a numbered caption. The folders are numbered in sequence, beginning with a predetermined number such as 100 or 1000, with little or no regard for the alphabetic order of names (See Illustration 10-2).

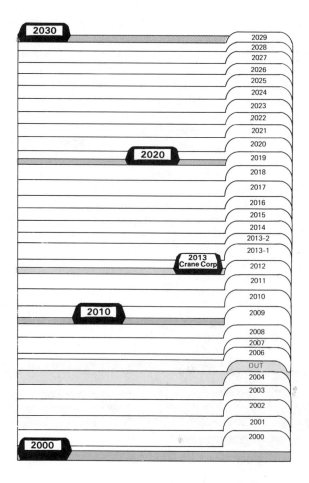

Illus. 10-2 Numeric Correspondence File

An alphabetic card control is essential.

Index Card Control File. Since guide and folder tab notations show numbers only, an alphabetic card control file is essential to the operation of a numeric file. The card control consists of an alphabetic arrangement of the names of the correspondents and subjects. The names are typed on cards which are filed behind alphabetic guides in a special card drawer or in a file box. Each card gives the name of a correspondent or a subject title and shows the number of the folder that has been assigned to the name or subject. If the number of the folder for a company has been forgotten, the filer can consult the index card control file to get the number of the folder. The index card control information can be entered into a computer instead of being written or typed on a card. The computer will contain the same information, but the number of the folder and other information can be found much faster and with little effort.

The index card control information can be entered into a computer.

General Alphabetic File. If the volume of material on a certain topic, or from a particular person or company is small, infrequent, or inactive, the material is kept in a general alphabetic file. But when the quantity of information from a person, company, or topic increases enough to require an individual folder, the folder is given the next unassigned number. All materials to, from, or about this topic or correspondent are always placed in the same folder grouped with other similar material. The most recent material is filed in front.

A number may be assigned to a subject or a group classification. For example, a topic such as "Applications for Employment" could be given the number 2000. This number would appear on the file folder in which applications for work are filed. The kind of numeric filing system in which folder 2000 would be held could be similar to the system shown in Illustration 10-2. Within such "Applications for Employment" folders, the materials are filed in alphabetic order according to the names of the applicants, and all letters and other materials pertaining to each application are arranged by date, with the most recent date in front.

Accession Book. Many users of a numeric system keep an accession book. An **accession book** contains a consecutive record of numbers assigned to folders. One form of accession book is shown in Illustration 10-3. A computer can be used here too. In many cases, a computer can assign consecutive numbers automatically and make a list of all numbers assigned, including the name of the folder given that number. The computer list, then, is the accession "book."

A computer can assign consecutive numbers automatically.

Advantages and Disadvantages of Numeric Filing

There are many advantages to a numeric filing system. The most important are these:

1. All papers pertaining to a certain job or to related activities are brought together.

NUMBER	NAME	DATE
1208	Payroll Register	Feb. 1, 19--
1209	Corwin L. Adams Co.	Feb. 3, 19--
1210	Monthly Production Reports	Feb. 3, 19--
1211	Rogers Collection Agency	Feb. 4, 19--
1212		
1213		

Illus. 10-3   Accession Book

2. A certain degree of privacy is possible because only numbers are visible to someone looking at the files. Ordinarily neither names nor titles are written on the guide or folder tabs.
3. Numbered folders or cards that are out of place can be located more rapidly than is possible in most alphabetic systems.
4. Almost unlimited expansion is possible in a numeric filing system.
5. Cross-references are not needed in the numeric section of the files because they are conveniently located in the alphabetic card index.
6. Identifying information by number makes it easier to use mechanized or automated equipment to store and retrieve information from the files.

In spite of the advantages of numeric filing, there are disadvantages to consider, the most important of which are these:

1. Numeric filing systems are indirect systems in that the filers, before filing or retrieving correspondence, must consult an alphabetic index card control file or a computer list or display to determine the proper code number for each correspondent or subject.
2. Numeric files provide only for active correspondents in a correspondence file. Alphabetic files are still necessary for general folders to accommodate materials received in such limited quantity that individual folders are not necessary.
3. When the numbers in a numeric file become too large, transpositions (reversing the order of the digits) can happen easily. For example, it is more difficult to remember the exact order of a number such as "47213" than a word such as "Moped."
4. Although misfiled papers do not occur frequently, when they do occur, they may be more difficult to detect. For example, a document coded with the wrong number may be hard to find.

Numeric File with Subject Guides

Correspondence files represent only one of the many uses of a numeric filing system. Many types of other materials are held in numeric filing systems. Numeric systems with subject titles are used for many kinds of records, such

A numeric file with subject guides can be used with many types of records.

as invoices, sales brochures, and price lists. Executive filing systems and accounting systems frequently use a combined form of numeric codes and subject titles on guide and folder tabs. Illustration 10-4 shows a numeric file with subject guides. Although the arrangement of the guides and folders is similar to the numeric correspondence file shown in Illustration 10-2, there are a few important differences:

1. The primary guides in first and second positions in Illustration 10-4 are numbered by fives because this is a very active file and several folders bearing the same basic numbers are needed to store the large volume of material. These additional folders are identified by adding a hyphen and numbering them in order (See folders 3009-1, 3009-2, 3018-1, 3018-2, and 3018-3).
2. The special guides are third-cut and are placed in third position. The double-width guide is used because subject titles tend to be longer and need more space. There are five special guides in this system to provide for very active topics that require frequent filing and retrieval.
3. Individual folders and OUT guides are placed in fourth position.

NUMERIC CODES FOR SUBJECT FILING SYSTEMS

Subject filing is a major part of many numeric systems.

Subject filing is a major part of many numeric systems; therefore, it is important to discuss further some of the ways in which businesses use numbers with their subject systems.

Numeric Subject Filing

The use of numeric codes for subject files has increased in recent years. This increase has undoubtedly been caused in part by the rapid adoption of computers and word processors. Computer-produced records are more easily processed by number; computers operate rapidly through numbers; and reference to information is increasingly being done through the use of various numeric systems. Even when there is a clearly labeled alphabetic name on a card or record, the number of that card or record must also be known.

Files are organized primarily by subject, but numbered notations are used.

In many situations the files are organized primarily by subject, but numbered notations on guide and folder tabs are used just as they sometimes are used in alphabetic name files. The simplest type of numbering is that shown in the example on pages 129 and 130 in which the subject titles are the same as those used on pages 109 and 110 of Chapter 9. The numbered notations may be used:

1. As a part of the subject captions to facilitate filing. Subject titles are frequently quite long and seldom appear in their exact form in correspondence. Considerable time can be saved, therefore, if numbers instead of words are used in coding and in locating folders in the files.
2. As a substitute for subject captions. When only numbers are used for captions, then subject headings, divisions, or subdivisions that are closely related can be

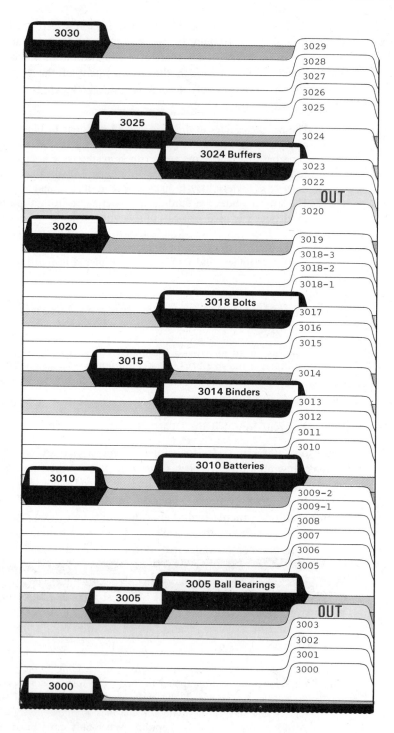

Illus. 10-4   Numeric File with Subject Guides in Third Position

grouped together in the files even though the subject titles do not fall in the same alphabetic section. When this plan is followed, a supplementary index card file, arranged alphabetically by subjects, is necessary and is used in a manner similar to that for numeric correspondence files.

In coordinate indexing, many possible titles are used to refer to the same document.

One example of using only numbers for captions is called **coordinate indexing**, designed by the Office of Aerospace Research, United States Air Force. One meaning of **coordinate** is to set in equal rank. In coordinate indexing, many possible subject or name titles are used to refer to the same document. These subjects or name titles are considered of equal "rank" and any of them could be used when someone is requesting a document. It is helpful, then, to list in the alphabetic index card control file all of the possible titles or subjects which may be used to request a particular file. Each index card would then give the same number for the document needed. You can easily see how placing the alphabetic index card control file on a computer would speed up your search for a document regardless of the title used.

Three things are necessary for a coordinate indexing file:

1. A simple numeric coding according to the subject.
2. A word list containing the filing words (subject titles) and alternate words. This will help the filer locate the key title under which the subject is coded.
3. A word card file consisting of one card for each key title and the indexing numbers of all filed items containing information covered by that title, or a computer list of these titles and numbers. This serves as a cross-reference notation necessary to locate one or more items pertaining to a particular subject.

No.	Heading	No.	Division	No.	Subdivision
100	Accounting	110	Audits		
				111	Cash Payments
				112	Cash Receipts
				113	Management Statements
				114	Payroll
		120	Budgets		
				121	Branch
				122	Corporate
		130	Costs		
				131	Administrative
				132	Manufacturing
				133	Office
		140	Credit		
				141	Secured
				142	Unsecured
		150	Expense		
				151	Administrative
				151	Executive
				151	Office
				152	Marketing
				152	Advertising
				152	Research
				152	Sales

160	Financial		
		161	Bonds
		162	Investments
		163	Stocks
170	Taxes		
		171	Federal
		172	Local
		173	State

200   Administration
300   Construction
400   Engineering
500   Insurance
600   Legal
700   Manufacturing
800   Marketing
900   Office
1000 Personnel
1100 Public Relations
1200 Purchasing

Decimal-Subject Filing

When the outline of a subject filing system is detailed, a decimal system is advantageous.

A simple numbering system is adequate for most subject files. When the outline on which a subject filing system is based is more complicated or detailed, however, a decimal system is advantageous.

Perhaps the most widely known and used decimal system is that devised by Melvil Dewey and called the *Dewey Decimal System*. It is used by libraries to classify books, catalogs, pamphlets, and all related materials. Dewey's system divides all human knowledge into nine main groups and one general group. These major groups, in turn, are divided into nine subdivisions and one general division. The subdivisions are further subdivided into groups of ten. Then by the use of decimals, the subdivisions can continue indefinitely.

The Dewey Decimal System, or some adaptation of this system, can be used to advantage in business filing when provisions for expansion in the files must be made, and when detailed subdivisions in a filing system are needed. For example, referring to the simple numbering system for the outline on pages 129 and 130, *Accounting* was assigned number *100*. The subdivision *Administrative* (following *150 Expense*) was numbered *151*, and under this the subheadings *Executive* and *Office* were also numbered *151*. Using the decimal-subject system, the arrangement would be numbered as follows:

100 Accounting
     150 Expense
          151 Administrative
               151.1 Executive
               151.2 Office
          152 Marketing

In many files, a hyphen is used instead of a decimal. The number 151.1 would then be 151-1. Many computers can *read* 151-1 more easily than 151.1.

For efficiency, such filing systems must be carefully organized and the filers must be thoroughly familiar with the subject outline on which the system is based.

Direct Decimal-Subject Filing

The principal advantages of the direct decimal-subject system over the alphabetic system for certain kinds of materials are illustrated by the direct subject filing system shown in Illustration 10-5. It is possible to group related materials in this file, as shown by the series of folders in Sections 102 and 202. The folders in Section 102, if arranged in a straight alphabetic system, would be spread from the *B* to the *O* sections of the system. Section 202 folders would be spread from *F* to *S*. Also, coding papers for the decimal-subject

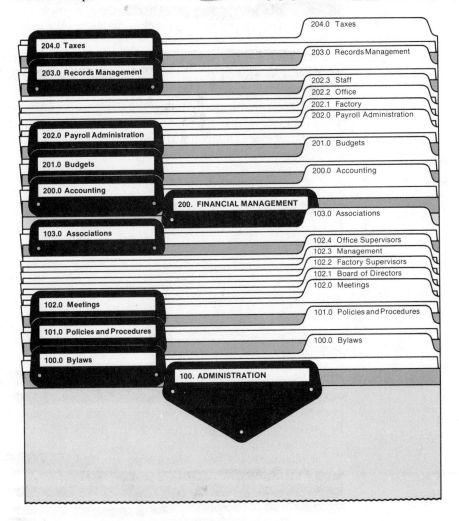

Illus. 10-5   Direct Decimal-Subject Filing

*Coding in a decimal-
subject system is
easier and faster
than in an alphabetic
system.*

system is easier and faster than coding in an alphabetic system because only the code numbers need to be written on file materials. It is helpful to have decimals showing on guide and folder tabs so that numbers and titles can be identified as a unit. The direct decimal-subject filing system is based on no more than ten primary groups (100. Administration in Illustration 10-5), but the primary groups can be subdivided as needed—102.2, 102.21, 102.211.

Other Coding Systems for Subject Filing

Other coding systems may also be used in subject filing. Three of these coding systems are duplex-numeric, duplex-alphabetic, and alphanumeric.

Duplex-Numeric Code. Several other number-based and related systems for subject titles are in common use. One of these is known as Duplex-Numeric. The example shown below indicates the nature and use of the system.

This system is capable of indefinite expansion and can be used to advantage when subject classifications are numerous and detailed, or when an alphabetic arrangement would be impractical. For example, in an architect's office, a file would logically follow the sequence of the erection of a building. The system is extensively used in law offices, where the client is assigned a number and every case handled for the client is assigned an auxiliary number based on the client's number.

Subject Outline	Primary Guide Notations	Secondary Guide Notations	Tertiary Guide Notations	Folder Notations
Accounting	10			
Expense		10-5		
Administrative			10-5-1	
Executive				10-5-1-1
Office				10-5-1-2
Marketing			10-5-2	
Advertising				10-5-2-1
Research				10-5-2-2
Sales				10-5-2-3
Financial		10-6		

Duplex-Alphabetic Code. If letters are substituted for numbers in the Duplex-Numeric system, the method is known as Duplex-Alphabetic. In the example used for the Duplex-Numeric system, the Duplex-Alphabetic caption for *Accounting* would be *A*; for *Expense, A-e*; for *Administratve, A-e-a.*

Alphanumeric Code. Another system, the Alphanumeric, is a combination of the two preceding systems in that capital letters are used for the main headings of the outline; numbers are used for the first division of the main headings; and lowercase letters are used for the subject subdivisions. For example, *Executive* would be *A-5-a-1.* In other words, letters and numbers are alternated to determine the captions.

Illustration 10-6 shows the application of five different systems of coding the same items in a portion of our subject outline. Notice that some of the coding systems are not adapted to the subject outline given in the first column. The simple numeric outline is not adequate, and some of the duplex outlines appear cumbersome. However, these systems are very useful in certain situations.

Subjects and Subdivisions	Simple Numeric Code	Decimal Code	Duplex-Numeric Code	Duplex-Alphabetic Code	Alpha-Numeric Code
ACCOUNTING	100	100.	10	A	A
Audits	110	110.	10-1	A-a	A-1
Cash Payments	111	111.	10-1-1	A-a-a	A-1-a
Cash Receipts	112	112.	10-1-2	A-a-b	A-1-b
Management Statements	113	113.	10-1-3	A-a-c	A-1-c
Payroll	114	114.	10-1-4	A-a-d	A-1-d
Budgets	120	120.	10-2	A-b	A-2
Branch	121	121.	10-2-1	A-b-a	A-2-a
Corporate	122	122.	10-2-2	A-b-b	A-2-b
Costs	130	130.	10-3	A-c	A-3
Administrative	131	131.	10-3-1	A-c-a	A-3-a
Manufacturing	132	132.	10-3-2	A-c-b	A-3-b
Office	133	133.	10-3-3	A-c-c	A-3-c
Credit	140	140.	10-4	A-d	A-4
Secured	141	141.	10-4-1	A-d-a	A-4-a
Unsecured	142	142.	10-4-2	A-d-b	A-4-b
Expense	150	150.	10-5	A-e	A-5
Administrative	151	151.	10-5-1	A-e-a	A-5-a
Executive	} No Number	151.1	10-5-1-1	A-e-a-a	A-5-a-1
Office	Available	151.2	10-5-1-2	A-e-a-b	A-5-a-2
Marketing	152	152.	10-5-2	A-e-b	A-5-b
Advertising		152.1	10-5-2-1	A-e-b-a	A-5-b-1
Research	} No Number	152.2	10-5-2-2	A-e-b-b	A-5-b-2
Sales	Available	152.3	10-5-2-3	A-e-b-c	A-5-b-3
ADMINISTRATION	200	200.	20.	B	B

Illus. 10-6   Comparison of the Various Codes Used in Subject Filing Systems

SPECIAL METHODS OF NUMERIC FILING

Numbers added to an alphabetic system help to reduce misfiling.

We have discussed assigning numbers to various materials to help avoid misfiling. Numbers, when added to an alphabetic system, provide a quick check that a particular document is at least in the correct general location. Illustration 10-7 uses a straight numbering system for each primary guide. The first guide, *A*, is numbered *1*; the second primary guide, *An*, is numbered *2*; the third primary guide is *3*; and so on throughout the major divisions of the file.

All folders behind a particular guide have the same number as the primary guide; hence, *Adams* is number *1* as is *American Can*. This use of numbers aids the filer in returning materials to the same section of the file, but it does not aid in placing the material in proper order within the major sections.

Illus. 10-7   Numbers with Alphabetic Name Filing

Up to a certain number of digits, the use of additional numbers increases the accuracy of locating the precise spot in the file for each item. Subject filing can therefore be made more accurate through coding systems similar to one of those presented in Illustration 10-6. Beyond a certain number of digits, however, numbers become more difficult to read and remember accurately. This difficulty increases the possibility of misfiling. To reduce the memory load and improve accuracy in numeric filing, various methods are available. These methods include terminal digit filing, middle digit filing, and color coding.

As numbers get larger, they become more difficult to read and remember.

Terminal Digit Filing

Terminal digit filing is a method of numeric filing designed to reduce the possibility of misfiling because of the difficulty in reading and remembering large numbers. In terminal digit filing, the numbers are assigned in the same manner as described for consecutive digit filing. However, the numbers are read from *right to left* in small groups beginning with the terminal (final) group, hence the name *terminal* digit filing.

In terminal digit filing, the last series of digits is considered first.

Terminal digit filing is used when numbers contain five or more digits. In the number 483674, for example, the digits could be separated into two groups of three digits each (483 674) or three groups of two digits each (48 36

74). Frequently the groups within the numbers are separated by hyphens, 48-36-74. The two-digit groups are filed in this manner:

3	*2*	*1*
Final	*Secondary*	*Primary*
48	36	74

To secure a folder numbered 48-36-74, the filer first locates the drawer containing those materials or records with numbers ending in 74—the primary digits. A search is then made of the guides in that drawer for guide No. 36—the secondary digits. Lastly, the material is located in the folder immediately following folder number 47 because 48 are the final digits of the folder needed. Numbers of less than six digits are brought up to that figure by adding zeros to the *left* of the number. For example, the number 12623 would be written 012623.

Terminal digit filing is used in filing items such as checks, mortgages, letters of credit, insurance policies, medical case records, purchase orders, and government documents.

Terminal digit filing has several advantages over consecutive digit filing. These are listed below:

1. Filing errors are more easily avoided because only the primary digits need to be considered in locating the drawer and only the secondary digits need to be considered in locating the guide.
2. Records are more easily obtained because the most current materials are more evenly distributed throughout the files. New numbers are assigned in consecutive order, therefore, each new number will be in a separate drawer. (For example, if 983672 is the next number to be assigned, 98-36-72 will be filed in a different drawer from 98-36-71.) If several filers are working at the same time, they are less likely to need the same file drawer at the same time.
3. Sorting and handling of records is more efficient because the first sorting is only two digits. Time savings of 25 to 50 percent have been realized by some companies that have changed to terminal digit filing.

Middle Digit Filing

In middle digit filing, the middle series of digits is considered first.

Middle digit filing is a modification of terminal digit filing. In middle digit filing, the *middle* series of digits is considered first, then the series at the *left*, and lastly, the series at the *right*. The primary guides are prepared for the middle series of digits.

In using the middle digit system, the number 483674 would be filed in this order:

2	*1*	*3*
Secondary	*Primary*	*Final*
48	36	74

The filer would first locate the drawer or primary guide for those materials or records whose primary digits are 36 and search the guides for guide No.

48–the secondary digits. The materials would then be filed in the proper order according to the number 74–the final digits.

Middle digit filing has the same advantages and uses as terminal digit filing. In addition, the following advantages are claimed for it:

1. A consecutive digit system is easier to change to middle digit filing than terminal digit filing because entire blocks of 100 numbers are moved as a single group. For example, all records numbered 86-19-00 through 86-19-99 remain in the same sequence after the move and can therefore be moved at one time.
2. In terminal digit filing it is necessary to consider ten different places to find ten documents already numbered in consecutive order. In middle digit filing, only one place needs to be considered. Each place represents 100 consecutive numbers as the folders are already arranged in consecutive order by the middle digits.
3. If the numbers are assigned in blocks rather than individually, in middle digit filing it is possible to have the entire block of middle digit numbers filed in one place. For example, a sales organization may wish to assign all records with the middle digits of 50 to a main branch in Ohio; all records with the middle digits of 51 to Oregon; and so on. In middle digit filing, 100 different folders could have the middle digit of 50, and all would be located in the same section of the files.

Comparison of Consecutive, Terminal Digit, and Middle Digit Sequences

The following table compares the sequence of the number on seven documents filed in consecutive, terminal digit, and middle digit files. The same numbers are used in the three columns.

Order of Filing	Consecutive Number Filing	Terminal Digit Filing	Middle Digit Filing
1	8-23-38	46-23-21	13-19-28
2	13-19-28	23-48-21	57-19-28
3	13-23-28	13-19-28	08-23-38
4	23-48-21	57-19-28	13-23-28
5	23-48-35	13-23-28	46-23-21
6	46-23-21	23-48-35	23-48-21
7	57-19-28	08-23-38	23-48-35

Folder or Card Guide / Drawer or Shelf

Guide / Drawer or Shelf / Folder or Card

Illustration 10-8 shows a folder designed for an open-shelf file. Full-cut tabs are generally used on the folders which are stored with the tabs facing the outside of the shelf. The guides are usually cut for first or second position and, therefore, extend out from the top of the open shelf (See Illustration 10-9).

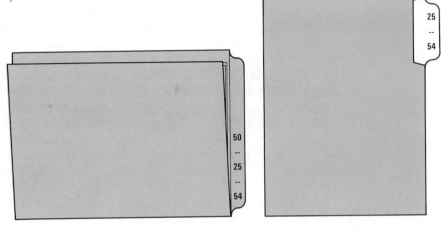

Illus. 10-8   **Folder for Open-Shelf File**   Illus. 10-9   **Guide with First Position Tab for Open-Shelf File**

Illustrations 10-10 and 10-11 show portions of terminal digit systems. A drawer file is shown in Illustration 10-10; an open-shelf file is shown in Illustration 10-11. Notice in this drawer file system, the drawer label 54 is the

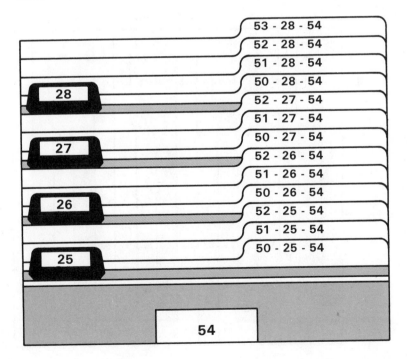

Illus. 10-10   **Terminal Digit Drawer File**

terminal group number. The first position guide shows the secondary numbers of 25, 26, 27, and 28. The captions on the folder tabs show the complete number. The first folder is 50-25-54; the second is 51-25-54, and so on.

In the open-shelf file the bottom number on the guide tab is the terminal digit number, 54. The top number is the secondary number, 25. The folder labels show the entire number, 50-25-54.

To use a terminal digit file, the filer notes the terminal digit and locates the drawer (or shelf) guide. The secondary number is then noted and located on the guide (top number on open-shelf guides). Lastly, the final number is checked, and the folder label bearing these first two digits is located.

With terminal digit filing, it is easy to see a folder that is out of order as all folders in a drawer or shelf section have the same terminal numbers. In addition, all folders within a secondary segment have the same secondary numbers.

A similar system can be used with middle digit files. For example, using a middle digit system, the number 73-14-98 would be arranged so that the shelf or drawer is labeled with the middle digits, 14; the guides are labeled with the first two digits, 73; and the folders are arranged by the final two digits, 98. With the format used for the open-shelf file in Illustration·10-11, the top numbers on the guide would be 73 and the bottom numbers would be 14. Folder number 73-14-98 would follow 73-14-96 and 73-14-97. If the drawer file were used, the drawer number would be 14 and the guide would be 73.

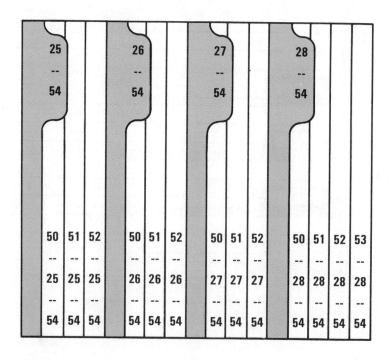

Illus. 10-11 Terminal Digit Open-Shelf File

Numeric Name System

In the system shown in Illustration 10-12, numbers are printed on the folder tabs. The tabs are wide enough to accommodate gummed labels indicating the name or subject of the folder.

By showing both a number and a name, additional identity is given to each folder and makes filing and finding faster and surer. Another feature of this system is that even numbers are given to folders with tabs on the left side and odd numbers are given to folders with tabs on the right.

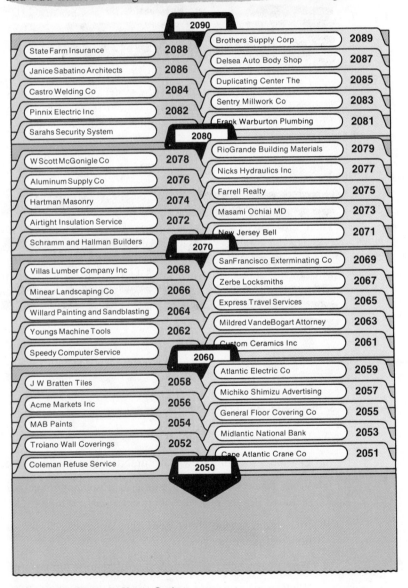

Left tab	Number		Right tab	Number
	2090			
			Brothers Supply Corp	2089
State Farm Insurance	2088		Delsea Auto Body Shop	2087
Janice Sabatino Architects	2086		Duplicating Center The	2085
Castro Welding Co	2084		Sentry Millwork Co	2083
Pinnix Electric Inc	2082		Frank Warburton Plumbing	2081
Sarahs Security System			2080	
W Scott McGonigle Co	2078		RioGrande Building Materials	2079
Aluminum Supply Co	2076		Nicks Hydraulics Inc	2077
Hartman Masonry	2074		Farrell Realty	2075
Airtight Insulation Service	2072		Masami Ochiai MD	2073
Schramm and Hallman Builders			New Jersey Bell	2071
			2070	
Villas Lumber Company Inc	2068		SanFrancisco Exterminating Co	2069
Minear Landscaping Co	2066		Zerbe Locksmiths	2067
Willard Painting and Sandblasting	2064		Express Travel Services	2065
Youngs Machine Tools	2062		Mildred VandeBogart Attorney	2063
Speedy Computer Service			Custom Ceramics Inc	2061
			2060	
J W Bratten Tiles	2058		Atlantic Electric Co	2059
Acme Markets Inc	2056		Michiko Shimizu Advertising	2057
MAB Paints	2054		General Floor Covering Co	2055
Troiano Wall Coverings	2052		Midlantic National Bank	2053
Coleman Refuse Service			Cape Atlantic Crane Co	2051
			2050	

Illus. 10-12   Numeric Name System

In Illustration 10-12, notice that you can determine the arrangement by the numeric sequence, not by the alphabetic sequence of names. Thus, the system is primarily numeric and indirect. It requires a supplementary alphabetic card file for identification purposes.

Soundex Alphanumeric Filing System

There are many possible variations of alphanumeric filing systems. One such variation is the Soundex System, manufactured by Kardex Systems, Inc. The Soundex System is designed to bring all names that sound the same but are spelled differently (such as Patin, Paton, Patten, and Patton) into one section of a file. By assigning alphanumeric codes to the names on the basis of pronunciation rather than spelling, this is possible.

Soundex is a highly specialized system and is typically used with large files with special problems that the system is designed to solve. A filer who is assigned the operation of such a system is given careful on-the-job training. For that reason Soundex and similar systems are not covered in detail in this book.

Use of Color in Numeric Filing

There are many color systems in use for numeric filing systems.

Color coding is frequently used in numeric filing systems as an aid in quick identification of groups of numbers and in identification of misfiled folders. There are many color systems in use for numeric filing systems. One popular color-coded system used in terminal digit filing prints each terminal digit group in a different color. A folder in the wrong drawer or on the wrong shelf will quickly stand out from the folders that use a different color. This color coding is frequently extended to use colors for the secondary digits, thus making misplaced folders stand out when misplaced in the wrong group between guides.

Questions for Discussion

1. What is numeric filing? (1)

2. List ten situations in which numeric filing may be used to advantage. (2)

3. What four parts does a numeric correspondence filing system usually include? Briefly describe what each part contains. (3)

4. In a numeric file, how does the alphabetic order of names affect the number assignment? (3)

5. Why is a general alphabetic file used in a numeric filing system? (3)

6. What is an accession book? What does it contain? (4)

7. Describe the arrangement of the numeric correspondence file in Illustration 10-2. (5)

8. What is an index card control file and how can the use of a computer help with this file? (6)

9. What are the advantages of numeric filing? (7)

10. What are the disadvantages of numeric filing? (7)

11. Explain how numbers are used in the numeric file in Illustration 10-4. (8)

12. How are numbers used in subject filing? (8)

13. What is a decimal-subject file? (9)

14. In what ways do decimal, duplex-numeric, duplex-alphabetic, and alpha-numeric coding systems for subject filing differ? (10)

15. How is the number 526710 read for filing in consecutive digit filing? In terminal digit filing? In middle digit filing? (11)

16. What are the advantages of terminal digit filing over consecutive digit filing? (12)

17. What are the advantages of using color coding in numeric filing systems? (13)

Applications

1. Assume that individual folders are to be opened in a numeric file for the names in the following list in the order in which the names are shown. Type or write each name on a separate 5″ × 3″ card or on a slip of paper cut to that size. Keep the names in the order listed. Assume that the accession book indicates that the next number to use is 724. Assign a number to each name and write that number in the upper right corner of the card. (4)

After you have typed or written the names on the 25 cards and assigned the numbers, arrange the cards in alphabetic order in preparation for filing in the supplementary card control file. (5)

Prepare an answer sheet by typing or writing the numbers 1 to 25 in a column at the left of the sheet. After the numbers, list the folder numbers assigned to the names you have arranged in alphabetic order.

Dancer Ski Resort
Alberta J. Reuters
DuVal's Collection Agency
D'Arcy Department Store
  Canton, Missouri
Gerry South & Sons Plumbing
A & D Towing Company

Bark River Fishing Bait
Reuter's Bowling Lanes
Nesbit Coats Emporium
East Side Beauty Salon
Gee Wizz Pizzas
Rae-Lynn Bridal Shoppe
Southeast Orange Groves

Gerry's Barbershop
Duo-Fast Corporation
East Street Laundry
Archie T. Nesbitt, M.D.
Georgette St. John, Catering
Tiny Tot Clothes
Tar Paper Manufacturing Co.

Duvall Gas Stop
Zero Base Freezer Lockers
Nonstop Auto Repair
A-A Electric Utility
D'Arcy Department Store
Canton, Minnesota

2. Assume that each of the following 30 numbers is the numeric code for a document that has been removed from the files. The files are arranged according to a consecutive digit system. Type or write each number on a separate 5″ × 3″ index card or on a slip of paper cut to that size. Type the digits in each number in pairs by typing a hyphen after the second and fourth digits.

After you have typed or written all the names on the cards, arrange the cards in order for consecutive digit filing. Your first number will be 08-24-11, the lowest number.

Prepare an answer sheet similar to the one you prepared for Application 1, except that you will number from 1 to 30. Beside the 30 numbers on the answer sheet, list the card numbers in the order of their arrangement. Number 08-24-11 will appear after number one on the answer sheet. (11)

12-41-25	50-54-14	30-49-15	43-15-12	44-54-22
12-48-37	68-30-45	12-44-01	44-50-14	68-36-13
21-35-13	12-48-46	30-24-08	28-40-12	63-50-18
28-02-26	30-18-01	43-44-25	12-41-20	08-24-11
30-24-02	43-22-35	44-55-22	21-52-02	50-55-38
37-31-46	63-22-25	63-31-46	68-30-21	37-31-39

3. Using the same index cards that you prepared for Application 2, rearrange the numbers for a middle digit file. Your first number will be 28-02-26.

Prepare an answer sheet similar to the one you prepared for Application 2. List the card numbers in middle digit order. Your first number on the answer sheet will be 28-02-26. (11)

4. Using the same index cards that you prepared for Application 2, rearrange the numbers for a terminal digit file. Your first number will be 30-18-01.

Prepare an answer sheet similar to the one you prepared for Applications 2 and 3. List the card numbers in terminal digit order. Your first number on the answer sheet will be 30-18-01. (11)

Job 8 Numeric Correspondence Filing (5)

At this time, complete Job 8 in OFFICE FILING PROCEDURES, Sixth Edition. Instructions and supplies for this job are included in the practice set.

CHAPTER 11

Geographic Filing

Learning Objectives

After completing Chapter 11, you will be able to:

1. Define a geographic filing system.
2. List types of organizations that make use of geographic filing systems.
3. Distinguish between the dictionary and the encyclopedia arrangements of geographic files.
4. Distinguish between a lettered guide plan and a location name guide plan in the geographic file.
5. Inspect, code, cross-reference, sort, file, and retrieve records in a geographic file.
6. Explain the use of a supplementary card index file in a geographic filing system.
7. Explain when and how to expand the geographic file.
8. List advantages and disadvantages of geographic filing.
9. Arrange cards alphabetically by states, cities, and correspondents' names.

Geographic filing is an alphabetic method of filing based primarily on the geographic location of individuals, organizations, reports, or projects. A geographic filing system is useful when the operations of a business are related primarily to locations rather than to names of persons and companies. Examples of such operations are found in many areas of social and political life, as well as in business and industry. Political groups, social clubs, and societies having national or regional memberships make use of geographic filing systems as well.

GEOGRAPHIC FILING SYSTEMS

Geographic filing systems are extensively used by business and industrial organizations with branch offices, and businesses spread over wide geographic regions. For example, a company that sells or buys in various regions may use

It is useful to group records by location.

geographic files in its sales and purchasing departments; a large department store with branch stores throughout the country, or even the world, may find it useful to group its records by location; many mail-order companies, publishers, airlines, railways, wholesale houses, and travel-related companies use geographic filing systems in one form or another.

Arrangements of Geographic Filing Systems

Since so many kinds of organizations make use of geographic systems, there is no one type of system that is best for every organization. Geographic systems are among the most adaptable systems in general use. The systems can be tailored to fit almost any kind of geographic area, from regions in the world to streets in a city: The scope of the file depends on the territorial range of business operations, with geographic units flowing from major to minor geographic units.

There are two basic arrangements of geographic filing systems: (1) the dictionary arrangement and (2) the encyclopedia arrangement. You are already familiar with a dictionary and an encyclopedia; this knowledge will aid you in understanding these two basic arrangements.

The dictionary arrangement is a single alphabetic arrangement.

Dictionary Arrangement. The **dictionary arrangement** consists of a *single* alphabetic arrangement (A-Z) into which all records are filed. If folders and special guides are part of the system, then location titles are used on them. Study the sample files in Illustrations 11-1 and 11-2. Both are dictionary arrangements of geographic files. Illustration 11-1 is a reference card file used in a newspaper circulation office. The file lists streets in the city and identification numbers of carriers who deliver papers to those streets throughout the city. Changes in delivery routes are made easily with this type of geographic card file. Territories can be rearranged and additional streets added when

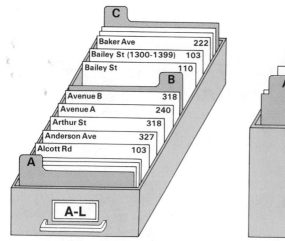

Illus. 11-1 Dictionary Arrangement of Cards   **Illus. 11-2 Dictionary Arrangement of Folders**

expanded newspaper circulation warrants it. This is a simple type of geographic file in a dictionary arrangement: a single alphabetic file arranged by streets from A to Z!

Illustration 11-2 is a dictionary arrangement of folders by state. A variety of correspondence and/or reports can be filed by state in these general state folders. This geographic file also contains only one arrangement of alphabetic guides, labeled from A to Z. Additional folders for states are prepared and added to the file as they are needed.

The encyclopedia arrangement is one alphabetic arrangement plus subdivisions.

Encyclopedia Arrangement. The **encyclopedia arrangement** of a geographic file, on the other hand, contains more than one alphabetic arrangement of information. The encyclopedia arrangement has one major geographic division arranged in alphabetic order *plus* one or more geographic *subdivisions* also arranged in alphabetic order.

Guide Plans in Geographic Filing Systems

In general, there are two basic guide plans used in the encyclopedia arrangement of geographic files: (1) the **lettered guide plan** and (2) the **location name guide plan.** The files in illustrations 11-3 and 11-4 hold identical records. However, Illustration 11-3 uses the *lettered guide plan* and 11-4 uses the *location name guide plan.*

The primary guides are LETTERED.

Lettered Guide Plan. The lettered guide plan (Illustration 11-3) is very similar to an alphabetic filing system in that free use is made of alphabetic guides. The guide plan must allow for the entire filing segment, which considers first the geographic divisions (largest to smallest) covered by the system. In Illustration 11-3, the filing segment includes (1) the state name, (2) the city name, and (3) the name of the correspondent indexed in the usual manner. Although variations in guide placement are possible, this system is designed as follows:

1. The key unit—a state name in this instance (California)—is indicated by a state name guide with a double-width tab in central position.
2. The primary guides are alphabetic guides staggered in first, second, and third positions. Each primary guide indicates the alphabetic range of the city names filed behind it. Notice that the primary guides are numbered consecutively to aid the filer in keeping them in proper alphabetic sequence.
3. A general folder is provided for each alphabetic primary guide. It bears the same captions and appears in the same position as the lettered guide and is placed at the end of the alphabetic section. Notice in Illustration 11-3 that primary guide A 1 and general folder A 1 are both in first position; guide B 2 and general folder B 2 are in second position, and so forth.
4. Special guides are in fourth position. Two kinds of special guides are illustrated: (a) special name guides that identify the cities for which there is considerable material and (b) special lettered guides (A-M and N-Z) that follow the special name guides to provide an alphabetic breakdown of the names of correspondents within the cities.

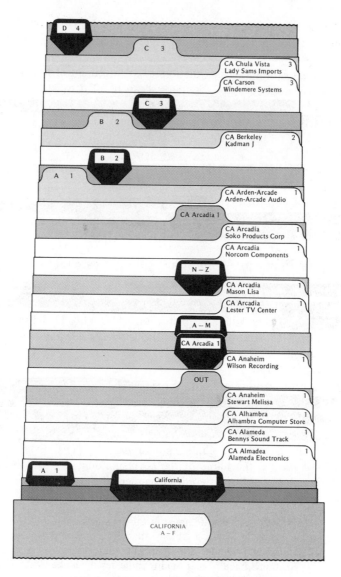

Illus. 11-3 Lettered Guide Plan for Geographic Arrangement

5. General city folders corresponding to the special city guides are in fourth position also.
6. OUT guides to indicate that materials have been borrowed from the files also occupy fourth position.
7. Individual folders with third-cut tabs are in the fifth position in the file drawer. Note that the tab for an individual folder has a two-line caption: The names of the state and city are typed on the first line, and the name of the correspondent is typed on the second line.

Location Name Guide Plan. Illustration 11-4 shows the same file as that in the lettered guide plan just described, except that the location name guide plan is used. Notice that the primary guides are location names (Alameda, Berkeley, Carson) rather than letters (A, B, C). Although other guide positions are possible, this system is designed as follows:

The primary guides are location names.

1. The key unit (California) is indicated by a state name guide with a double-width tab in second and third positions.
2. The primary guides are city name guides placed in first position— Alameda, Alhambra, Anaheim, Arcadia, Arden-Arcade, Berkeley, Carson, Chula Vista, and Daly City. These guides represent cities from which correspondence is sufficient to warrant the use of primary city name guides.
3. Special letter guides, if needed, are placed in second position to denote alphabetic breakdowns of correspondents' names filed behind city name guides. Note the guides A-M and N-Z behind the primary city name guide Arcadia.
4. General folders are located in third position. The general folders in Illustration 11-4 are of three types:

   a. A general city folder for each city guide is placed immediately behind the last individual folder in the city section: Alameda, Alhambra, Anaheim, and so forth.
   b. A separate general folder is provided for each special letter guide. Notice that the special letter guides A-M and N-Z have accompanying general folders in the Arcadia section of the file.
   c. General state folders for each alphabetic subdivision end each alphabetic section. Note, in Illustration 11-4 the general state folders—labeled CA A-Az, CA B-Bz, and CA C-Cz.

5. Individual folders with double-width tabs span the fourth and fifth positions of the file drawer. These folders are prepared for clients with whom correspondence is active enough to warrant the use of individual folders. The tabs for these folders show state and city names on the first line and the client name on the second line.
6. OUT guides with single-width tabs appear in the individual folder position: The tabs are centered over the fourth and fifth positions.

Although other arrangements of guides and folders exist in geographic filing systems, a thorough understanding of the two just illustrated will allow you to adapt easily to alternate arrangements.

Supplementary Card Index to Control Geographic Filing

When geographic filing systems are used, problems sometimes arise because records are not filed according to the names of correspondents. They are arranged first by location of those companies or persons. If the address is not known, the record cannot be found. Sometimes correspondents write from a location different from their usual business address. To solve problems such as these, an organization may maintain a supplementary card index file with names of correspondents arranged in alphabetic order. This card file is not needed as an aid in filing materials when the locations are known. The file is

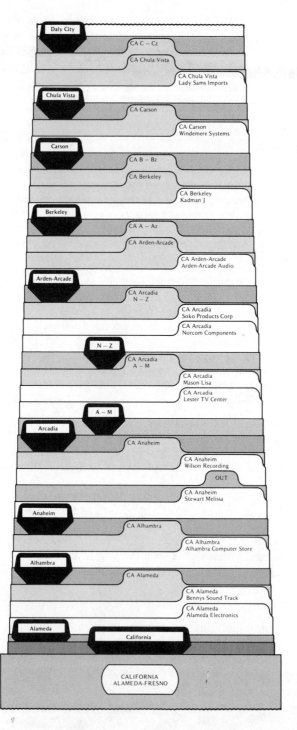

Illus. 11-4 Location Name Guide Plan for Geographic Arrangement

When a correspondent's name is unknown, use a card file.

helpful, however, in finding filed materials when the correspondent's address is unknown or in doubt.

Cards for the supplementary card index system (See Illustration 11-5) are prepared and used in the following manner:

1. Before filing a record, refer to the supplementary card index to see if a card has been prepared for that person or company. If there is none, prepare one by typing the name and address of the correspondent on a file card. Because the correspondent is new, type the letter G (for general) in the upper right corner of the index card. This G indicates that records relating to the person or company concerned are in a general folder. Place the index card in the supplementary card index. Place the record in the appropriate general folder.

2. Later, when the volume of correspondence is sufficient, prepare an individual folder for this same correspondent. Move all records for this correspondent from the general folder to an individual folder. Remember to remove the G from the index card and type an I in its place. This signifies that the correspondent's records are now held in an individual folder.

   Follow a similar procedure if a general state folder holds sufficient material from a particular city: prepare a general city folder and transfer to it all materials to and from that city. In this example, do not change the G on the index card. The records are still in a general folder.

```
 ┌─────────────────────────────────────────────────┐
 │  BoMars Video Corp                          G     │
 │                                                   │
 │  Bo-Mars Video Corp.                              │
 │  1414 Wheeling Drive                              │
 │  Santa Clara, CA  95051-7816                      │
 │                                                   │
 │                                                   │
 │                                                   │
 │                                                   │
 └─────────────────────────────────────────────────┘
```

Illus. 11-5 Supplementary Index Card

GEOGRAPHIC FILING PROCEDURES

Although procedures in geographic filing are similar to those used in alphabetic filing, there are sufficient differences to justify the discussion that follows. When it is necessary, distinctions are made between the lettered guide plan and the location name guide plan.

Inspecting

Inspect each incoming letter to see that it has been released for filing. Check each paper to see that it has been dated. If no date appears on the record, write or stamp the current date on the paper and use it for filing purposes.

Coding

Because the names of geographic locations are considered the first part of the filing segment, mark the locations clearly. An effective way to code is to *circle* units in the geographic name and to number them to show their importance in the indexing order (See Illustration 11-6).

After coding the location name, code the correspondent's name in the usual manner: Use diagonal lines to separate the filing units and number the units to show their indexing order.

Cross-Referencing

Cross-references are made from one location to another.

In geographic filing, as in alphabetic filing, there are times when a cross-reference is helpful. For example, if a letter gives useful information about another company, a cross-reference should be prepared for that letter. In a geographic system, cross-references are made from one geographic location in the file to another. The name of the correspondent is given second consideration.

When necessary, a cross-reference can be made in any of three different ways: (1) by using cross-reference sheets or photocopies, (2) by using cross-reference guides, or (3) by making cross-reference notations on folder tabs.

Study Illustration 11-7 for an example of a cross-reference sheet used in a geographic file. If a letter that requires a cross-reference is photocopied, then the copy of the letter is used in place of the cross-reference sheet.

Cross-reference guides are used when there is a more-or-less permanent reason for calling attention to a cross-reference. An example is when a correspondent has offices in several locations. This problem can also be handled by using a permanent cross-reference notation on the tab of each folder that contains information relating to materials in other folders. Assume, for example, that a correspondent, Economy Stores, Inc., has its main office in Carson, California, but has branch offices in Daly City and Alameda as well. In the main files, the tabs on each folder for each office of this company would show references to the other offices in this manner:

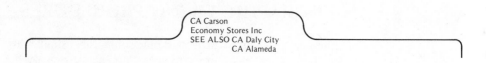

CA Carson
Economy Stores Inc
SEE ALSO CA Daly City
CA Alameda

Sorting

Sort letters and other records by geographic units, starting with the major geographic unit and continuing until all units in the filing segment have been used. For example, the first sorting might be on the basis of states; the second, cities; and the third, names of correspondents.

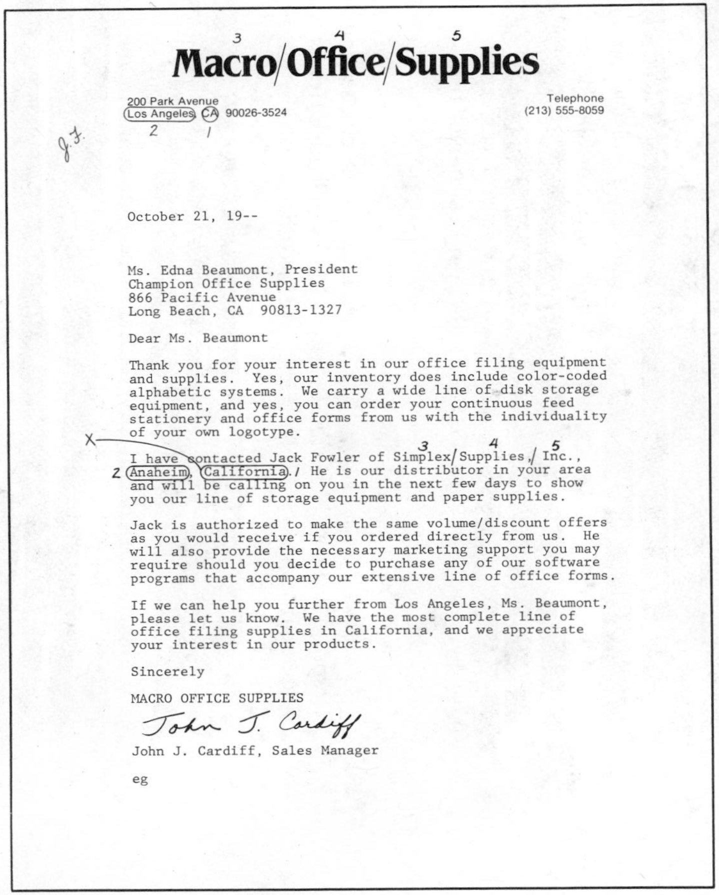

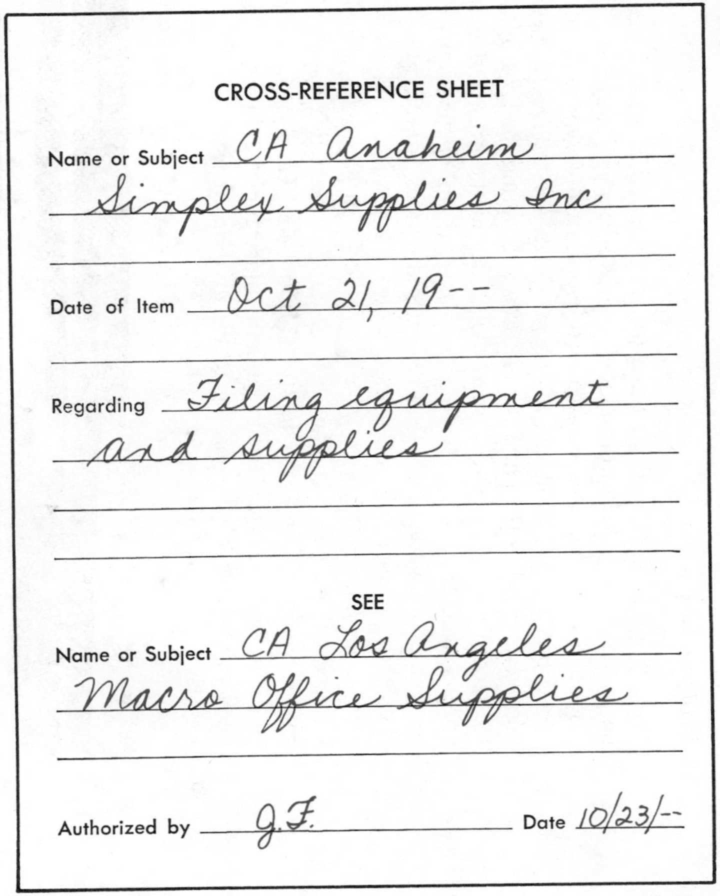

CROSS-REFERENCE SHEET

Name or Subject CA Anaheim Simplex Supplies Inc

Date of Item Oct 21, 19--

Regarding Filing equipment and supplies

SEE

Name or Subject CA Los Angeles Macro Office Supplies

Authorized by J.F.   Date 10/23/--

Illus. 11-7   Cross-Reference Sheet for a Geographic System

Macro/Office/Supplies

200 Park Avenue
Los Angeles, CA 90026-3524
Telephone
(213) 555-8059

October 21, 19--

Ms. Edna Beaumont, President
Champion Office Supplies
866 Pacific Avenue
Long Beach, CA 90813-1327

Dear Ms. Beaumont

Thank you for your interest in our office filing equipment and supplies. Yes, our inventory does include color-coded alphabetic systems. We carry a wide line of disk storage equipment, and yes, you can order your continuous feed stationery and office forms from us with the individuality of your own logotype.

I have contacted Jack Fowler of Simplex/Supplies/Inc., Anaheim, California. He is our distributor in your area and will be calling on you in the next few days to show you our line of storage equipment and paper supplies.

Jack is authorized to make the same volume/discount offers as you would receive if you ordered directly from us. He will also provide the necessary marketing support you may require should you decide to purchase any of our software programs that accompany our extensive line of office forms.

If we can help you further from Los Angeles, Ms. Beaumont, please let us know. We have the most complete line of office filing supplies in California, and we appreciate your interest in our products.

Sincerely

MACRO OFFICE SUPPLIES

John J. Cardiff

John J. Cardiff, Sales Manager

eg

Illus. 11-6   Incoming Letter Coded for a Geographic System

Storing Records

The procedures involved in storing (or retrieving) records in a geographic filing system are similar to those used in any other type of system. This process is most effective when a well-planned, well-cared-for system is maintained.

Guides help to locate folders.

The first step is to locate the proper folder for the record. Begin by reading the drawer labels to find the file drawer covering the geographic range for the record to be filed. Next, scan the guides in the drawer that indicate the subdivisions. The guides usually show either an alphabetic arrangement of letter guides (Illustration 11-3 uses lettered guides for city location) or an alphabetic arrangement of name guides (Illustration 11-4 uses city name guides). Ordinarily this is as far as the guides can be used in locating folders. However, there may be other helpful subdivisions: See the A-M and N-Z guides behind CA Arcadia in Illustration 11-3; see also the A-M and N-Z guides behind the Arcadia city guide in Illustration 11-4. From this point the filing procedures vary according to the guide plan used.

Lettered Guide Plan. In the lettered guide plan, locate the alphabetic section in which the city name falls to see whether there is an individual folder for the correspondent. If there is a folder, place the record there with the most recently dated record in front.

If there is no individual folder, look for a general city name folder. If there is one (Arcadia, for example, in Illustration 11-3), place the record there in alphabetic order by the correspondent's name.

If there is no general city name folder, place the material in the proper general alphabetic section folder (A for Anaheim, C for Carson, and so forth).

At this point, follow the rules for alphabetic correspondence filing: Group letters in general folders alphabetically first by the city names, then by the names of the correspondents, and finally in each group by date with the most recently dated letter in front. If there are several correspondents with the same name in the same city, follow the identical names rule, Rule 8.

Location Name Guide Plan. After locating the city section in which the correspondence should be located, look for an individual folder for the correspondent. If there is a folder, file the record there with the most current record in front.

If there is no individual folder, look for a general city folder. In this folder the letters are grouped first in alphabetic order by correspondents' names and then in each group by date, the most recent record in front.

If there is no general city folder, place the record in the general state alphabetic folder (such as CA A-Az or CA B-Bz). Group records in the general state folders first by city or town; next, in each city group by names of correspondents; and finally, in each correspondent's group by date with the most recent record in front.

PROVISIONS FOR EXPANSION IN GEOGRAPHIC FILING SYSTEMS

The geographic arrangement adapts readily to changes.

Geographic systems are readily adaptable and can be reduced and expanded with relative ease. The alert filer knows when changes in the system are necessary and how to make them. When customers are lost or vendors changed, sections of the file are simply eliminated at, or before, transfer time. Expanding the filing system, however, is more challenging.

When to Expand

As business operations continue throughout a year, changes occur that require adjustments in the records control system. For example, a business will correspond with new customers and will buy from new vendors; therefore, new names or sections will need to be added to the filing system.

The first indication of a need for expansion in a system is an increase in the volume of incoming and outgoing records being processed for filing. However, an overcrowded folder is perhaps the best indication that expansion is necessary.

How to Expand

If a records department is efficiently managed, space for expansion will have been anticipated at transfer time. Free space will have been left in every file drawer and on every shelf section. This space is used to hold additions to the system.

For example, as general folders for a state become overcrowded with materials from correspondents from the same cities in that state, perhaps it is time to add general city folders to the system. That way, blocks of records are removed from the crowded general *state* folders and refiled in the new general *city* folders.

When general *city* folders begin to bulge, look for groups of correspondents that can be transferred to newly prepared *individual* folders.

Special guides and folders make the system more efficient.

In Illustrations 11-3 and 11-4, review the positions within the file drawer that have been used for special guides and folders. These special sections help to alleviate crowding and make the system more efficient. New sections may include a series of dated, lettered, or name guides, intended to reduce crowding in the individual folders. Also, these open positions can be used to identify sections that will hold especially active materials—records that are frequently requested.

ADVANTAGES AND DISADVANTAGES OF GEOGRAPHIC FILING

Advantages of geographic filing have already been mentioned. They include the abilities to group business activities by location; to evaluate business activities by location in order to improve total operations; and to use a filing system that makes it easy to add, delete, divide, or rearrange territories as necessary changes are made to improve overall business operations.

Geographic filing has certain disadvantages too. The need for a supplementary card index means that time must be spent preparing and maintaining it. It also means that filers occasionally must search through the card system, as well as the main geographic system, to locate needed records.

Provide for internal communications with primary guides.

Another disadvantage of the geographic file is that it provides no place to file papers relating to the internal operations of a company. Where would papers relating to the hiring of new employees be filed? A solution might be to add appropriate primary guides to handle internal communications. For example, add a primary guide that has been labeled with the name of the place where a company is located; then, behind this guide, add other guides and folders, such as Accounting, Applications, Personnel, and Purchasing.

Questions for Discussion

1. Define a geographic filing system. (1)

2. Name two types of organizations that might find a geographic filing system useful. (2)

3. What is the primary difference between a dictionary arrangement and an encyclopedia arrangement of a geographic file? (3)

4. What is the difference between a lettered guide plan and a location name guide plan used in geographic filing? (4)

5. How are papers arranged in individual folders in a geographic file? (5)

6. How are papers arranged in general city folders? (5)

7. How are papers arranged in general state folders? (5)

8. How is a supplementary card index file used in connection with a geographic file? (6)

9. If some general city folders in your filing system are becoming overcrowded, what can you do to relieve this condition? (7)

10. If an individual folder becomes overcrowded, what can you do about it? (7)

11. List two advantages and two disadvantages of geographic filing. (8)

Applications

1. A. Type or write each of the following names and addresses on a 5″ × 3″ index card or on paper cut to that size. Follow the same format as that shown in Illustration 11-5 on page 149. These cards are for the supplementary card index that accompanies the geographic file. Place a G in the upper right corner of the card to show that the record will be placed in a general folder. Type the name in indexing order at the top; then type the name and mailing address below as the correspondent writes it. Number each card at the bottom as you type it (1 to 24). You will use these numbers later to report your card order on an answer sheet. (9)

Rec#	Client	Street	City	State	Zip Code
1	Nu-Way Dry Cleaners	3718 Silver Ln	Lancaster	NY	14086-3544
2	Charles S Chambers	132 College St	Oswego	NY	13126-3362
3	North Side Jewelers	918 Ace Ave	Bethlehem	PA	18017-3211
4	Oliver Stoffer Electronics	230 Lark Ln	Norristown	PA	19401-2213
5	Dun's Diner	23 Main St	Johnstown	PA	15901-3328
6	Wil-Kil Pest Control Co	3602 Washington Ave	Newberry	SC	29108-8266
7	Northside Department Store	739 W North St	Bethlehem	PA	18018-8355
8	North Star Car Wash	97 Copeland Ave	Altona	NY	12910-3351
9	B & B Root Beer	18376 Hwy 12	Newburgh	NY	12550-4422
10	Bond-Well Dry Walls	415 Nelson Pl	New Castle	PA	16101-5561
11	Larry S Nutall	1819 E Madison St	Lancaster	PA	17602-3381
12	John Dundee Construction	1613 Hawthorne St	Johnstown	NY	12095-9113
13	Andy's Duraclean Services	1973 A St	Buffalo	NY	14211-1661
14	Boyds Sporting Goods	7231 W Salem Rd	Williamsport	PA	17701-3577
15	Marie's Women's Wear	176 Market St	Schenectady	NY	12302-4222
16	Oswego Chamber of Commerce	712 Main St	Oswego	NY	13126-4227
17	Rev T P Bruce	527 Cass Bldg	Charleston	SC	29401-6299
18	Bruce Termite Protection	417 Exchange Bldg	Charleston	SC	29401-2241
19	John P Dundee	1613 Hawthorne St	Johnstown	NY	12095-3341
20	Nut-All Peanut Shop	2615 Washington Ave	Lancaster	PA	17602-3811
21	Wilki Leather Shop	94 Race St	Newberry	SC	29108-2255
22	Tom Cat Hamburgers	401 Maple St	Greenville	SC	29609-3771
23	Tom's Speedometer Shop	27 Elm Cir	Greenville	PA	16125-3721
24	Tom Speed	4819 Jefferson Cir	Greenville	SC	29602-5271

B. After you have typed or written all the cards, arrange them alphabetically by correspondents' names. Prepare an answer sheet by numbering 1-24 on a clean sheet of paper. Opposite each number record the numbers representing the names in the order in which you have arranged the cards.

C. Now arrange the cards alphabetically first by states, then according to cities, and finally according to correspondents' names. Prepare another column of numbers 1-24 and record the numbers representing the names in the order in which you have arranged them.

D. Fold an 8½″ × 11″ sheet of paper to simulate folder labels. This is easily done by folding the sheet once lengthwise so that the labels measure 4½ wide. Then fold it in half, then again, and again until you have creased eight "labels" down the page. Two sheets of paper folded will supply you with 32 labels, 8 extra in case you make an error. Now type a label for each correspondent in correct alphabetic order to place on individual folders in a geographic file. Type down the first column of labels, then reinsert your paper and type down the second column. This arrangement will make checking your work easier. Use state abbreviations. Hypens may be included on folder labels for readability. The labels should look like those in Illustrations 11-3 and 11-4.

2. Use the file sample in Illustration 11-4 to explain the location of each of the following incoming letters. (4)

In which folder would you place:

A letter from Norcom Components, Arcadia, CA
A letter from Monument Computer Service, Arcadia, CA
A letter from Tudor Systems, Inc., Burbank, CA
A letter from Lisa Mason, Oakdale, CA

Job 9   Geographic Correspondence Filing   (5)

Complete Job 9 in OFFICE FILING PROCEDURES, Sixth Edition. Instructions and supplies for this job are included in the practice set.

PART 5

Special Records Storage and Retrieval

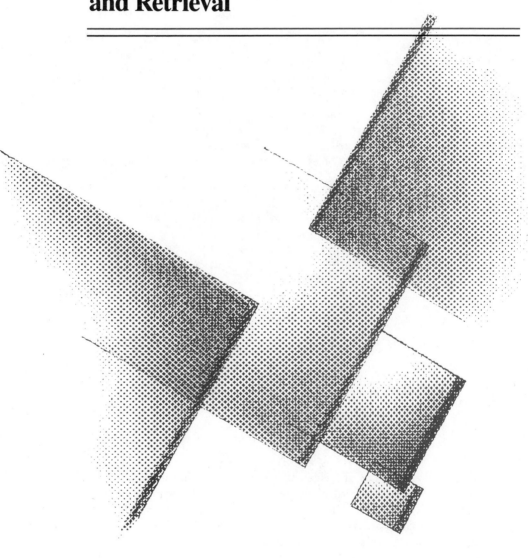

CHAPTER 12

Card Record Systems

Learning Objectives

After completing Chapter 12, you will be able to:

1. List characteristics of cards that make them suitable for information storage and retrieval.
2. List uses of card record systems.
3. Distinguish between a reference card file and a posting card file.
4. Describe the two general classifications of equipment used for card record files.
5. Describe a guide arrangement for an alphabetic vertical card file.
6. Describe a guide arrangement for a subject vertical card file.
7. Describe types of storage equipment used for vertical card files.
8. Describe types of storage equipment for visible card files.
9. List advantages of a horizontal, visible card file.
10. List uses of signaling devices in vertical and visible card files.
11. List advantages of a wheel card file.
12. List important factors to consider when selecting a card record system or equipment.

CARD RECORD SYSTEMS

When fast and efficient reference to current information is needed, some kind of card record filing system is undoubtedly in use. Card record systems are vital to operations in many organizations. In this chapter you will learn why cards are so useful in records systems, how they are used, and some common types of systems and equipment.

Card Characteristics

The physical characteristics of cards make them suitable for a variety of uses in record systems. Cards are available in a variety of sizes, colors, and designs to fit the requirements of the job to be done. Common sizes are 5″ × 3″, 6″

CARDS are Compact, easily Arranged and Rearranged, Durable, and Self-Supporting.

× 4″, 8″ × 5″, and 14″ × 12″. Cards are *compact* so that a great number of them can be stored in a relatively small space. Cards are easily *arranged* and *rearranged* when additions, deletions, and changes in the file become necessary. Cards are *durable*; they can withstand frequent handling. Finally, their added substance makes cards *self-supporting*—they do not require folders to keep them upright in the file. Although guides are needed to divide the file into sections for filing purposes, guides are not required to support the cards in an upright position.

Uses of Card Record Systems

Some commonly used card files have already been described in previous chapters of this text. In Chapter 2, an alphabetic card file for names and addresses is described and illustrated. In the chapters on geographic, subject, and numeric correspondence filing, other card indexes are described as auxiliary parts of the system—these are only a few of the many uses of card systems.

A wide variety of information is stored on cards.

Card files are used extensively by business, industrial, professional, and governmental organizations. They are used as well in libraries, schools, hospitals, and homes. Businesses store on cards a variety of information, such as stock records, payroll records, personnel records, shipping and receiving records, and accounting records. Libraries make use of cards in the card catalog file. This familiar card file is a log of all the books stored and shows where they are located in the library. The cards are arranged in alphabetic order and grouped by title, by author, and by subject. The librarian refers to these cards as title cards, author cards, and subject cards. Illustration 12-1 shows a typical card catalog file, which consists of 5″ × 3″ cards filed in a standard closed vertical card file.

Illus. 12-1   Card Catalog File in a Library

Schools and colleges often keep students' permanent records on cards. Hospitals, doctors, and dentists keep patient information on cards. At home, recipes are often kept on cards and filed in a small card file box. After your study of numeric filing, you may have arranged your record or tape collection by number. In that case, you refer to a supplementary card file arranged alphabetically by title, vocalist, or musical group to find the number assigned to a particular record or tape.

Regardless of how cards are used in a records control system, this is certain: Card records make a significant contribution to the total record control system as useful *reference* and *posting* files.

Reference Card File. A **reference card file** is one from which information such as record or cassette tape location, current addresses, or current merchandise price lists is retrieved. The supplementary card file used in a numeric correspondence file is a good example of a reference card file. Reference to a supplementary, or auxiliary, card file reveals the number assigned to a particular folder in the system. The card catalog file already mentioned and pictured in Illustration 12-1 is a reference file also. The file is used to retrieve information that helps to locate a particular book in the library.

Posting Card File. A **posting card file**, on the other hand, is one in which current information is recorded on the file cards, either by hand or by machine. An accounts receivable records file (money owed a company) is an example of a posting card record file. Clients' names are listed on large ledger cards and amounts due and paid are recorded on the cards either by hand or with a posting or bookkeeping machine. Stock and inventory records are posting files also. Information is posted on these cards as stock is received, used up, or ordered.

Card Storage Arrangements

Cards are stored in both vertical and horizontal arrangements.

The very nature of cards allows them to be stored in several useful arrangements. They can be stored in an upright, vertical position. They can be stored in a flat, horizontal position so that some part of each record is visible to the filer. They can also be attached to wheels that rotate like a Ferris wheel. The storage media and arrangement of cards depends on how the file is being used. For example, the visible horizontal file is an ideal posting file. Because the cards are filed flat, notations can be made on them without removing the cards from a tray file or binder. Vertical, horizontal, and visible files are all explained and illustrated in this chapter.

VERTICAL CARD FILES

The development of a vertical card record system requires (1) a guide arrangement and (2) suitable equipment. In general, guide arrangements used for card record systems are similar to those used for correspondence files. Thus, a guiding arrangement can be alphabetic, geographic, subject, or numeric; or a combination of any of these familiar arrangements.

Guide arrangements vary.

The arrangement of guides in card files varies. In Chapter 2 you saw a staggered, third-cut alphabetic guide arrangement. Illustration 12-2 shows a staggered fifth-cut alphabetic arrangement. This arrangement is ideal for a small record file. Even when the number of cards in the system is too few to separate the guides, the five staggered positions make the guides clearly visible. Illustration 12-3 shows alphabetic guides staggered between the first and fifth positions. A staggered arrangement in only two positions, like that in Illustration 12-3, requires fewer eye movements to scan the file than does the arrangement in Illustration 12-2. The arrangement allows more efficient and rapid reference to records when sufficient numbers of cards in the file separate the guides for easy scanning.

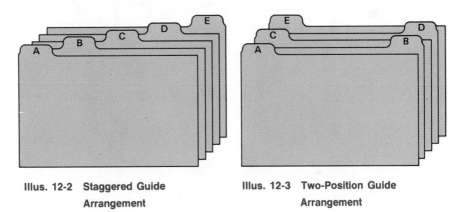

Illus. 12-2   Staggered Guide Arrangement   **Illus. 12-3   Two-Position Guide Arrangement**

Study the two typical vertical card record systems that follow. Both files are vertical card files. However, the alphabetic card record shown in Illustration 12-4 is a *reference* card file, and the subject card file in Illustration 12-5 is a *posting* card file.

Alphabetic Card Files

Alphabetic systems for card files are used extensively to hold records relating to names of customers, personnel, or suppliers of goods and services. The large alphabetic card file in Illustration 12-4 makes use of the efficient straight-line arrangement of primary guides. This alphabetic guide arrangement is suitable for records relating to names of firms or of individuals. Notice that the system includes the following guide arrangement:

1. Primary alphabetic section guides are located in first position and show single-unit notations from A to Al.
2. Special guides for commonly found names occupy the second and third positions.

3. Common name sections are further subdivided by guides in fourth position for frequently occurring second units in names.
4. END guides are shown in fifth position. These guides are used to mark the close of particular name groups and the resumption of the next major alphabetic sequence. For example, the last index card bearing the name "Abrams" is filed before an END guide, and a name such as "Abram<u>son</u> T L" is placed in the next section of cards after the END guide.

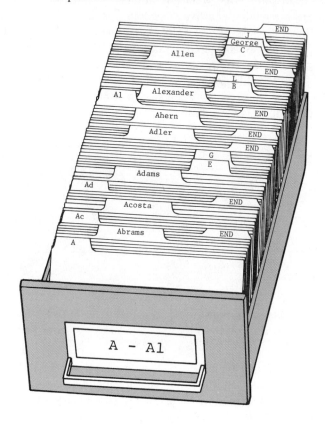

Illus. 12-4 Alphabetic Card File

Subject Card Files

Subject systems may be useful arrangements for card records relating to purchasing and stock records, inspection and maintenance records, or quality control data. The subject file shown in Illustration 12-5 holds stock record cards for items held for sale by a filing equipment and supplies dealer. In this system, there is a card for each type of stock that is carried. These cards are designed to show information such as how many units of a particular item are on hand, how many units to order, when to reorder, and from whom to reorder.

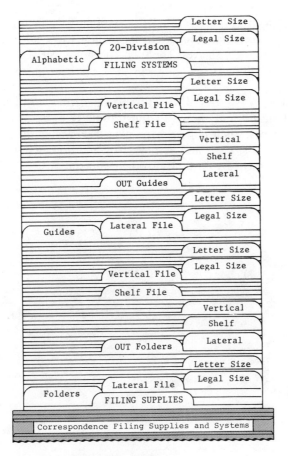

Illus. 12-5   Subject Card File

A person seeking a particular card in a subject system proceeds as follows: (1) Locates the desired drawer in the system by scanning the drawer labels, (2) scans the primary guides and locates the desired major divisions, (3) finds the block of cards that includes the one wanted by scanning from left to right across the drawer, and (4) locates the card bearing the desired title by flipping through the cards that are arranged in alphabetic order by stock title.

In a large stock record system, numeric notations in the form of stock record numbers usually are included as titles on cards, and the cards are arranged in numeric order.

Equipment for Vertical Card Files

A variety of equipment is available for use in vertical card filing. The volume of cards, the reference needs of the users, and cost of equipment are considered when the selection of equipment for card files is made. Generally equipment for vertical card records is stationary, portable, or automated.

Stationary Cabinets or Shelves. Stationary cabinets are commonly used for both large and small filing systems. Shallow trays holding cards are placed in rows on stationary shelves. The trays can hold over 600,000 signature cards at a metropolitan bank.

Portable Trays and Bins. Portable open trays or open bins, similar to the open housing unit shown in Illustration 12-6, are available in different sizes and shapes. Such units can be placed conveniently at any workstation for information storage and retrieval. In addition, individual trays can be removed and carried to a desk or other workstations.

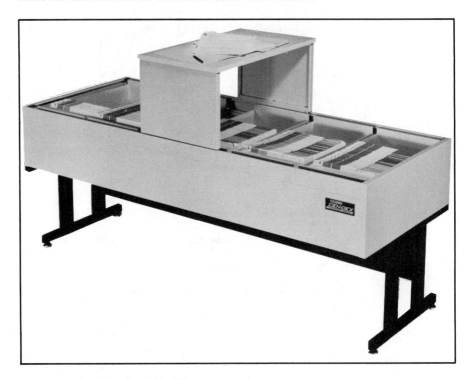

Illus. 12-6 Portable Open-Bin File

Automated equipment saves time and space.

Automated Shelves. Most interesting of all equipment for card records is the automated shelf equipment. An example of an automated card file is the Kardveyer by Kardex Systems, Inc., shown in Illustration 12-7. Cards are held in shallow trays placed on movable shelves inside a cabinet shell. Entire trays can be removed if desired. The unit shown has the storage space equivalent to 12 four-drawer file cabinets, yet requires only the floor space of an average office desk. The shelves revolve in a manner similar to a Ferris wheel. Any shelf can be moved to a position for easy storage and retrieval in only four seconds by pressing a button on an electronic keypad. The keypad is mounted on the work counter in front of the unit and is labeled in Illustration 12-8.

Illus. 12-7   Automated Card File

Computer control of card records is an option.

A computer-assisted storage and retrieval option, shown in Illustration 12-8, may be interfaced with the Kardveyer. The computer at the records control workstation instantly shows availability of records or indicates where they are currently being used. The computer system controls the rotation of the file, reserves records, sorts information, and generates reports from the stored information.

The advantages of automated equipment over manually operated equipment vary according to conditions existing in particular types of business operations. For example, in some companies, reference to card records is infrequent; while in others, card records are vital to operations and are referred to continually. Also, in some organizations, relatively few card records are needed; while in others, card systems are large and complex. Therefore, as business conditions vary, so does the relative value of automated equipment for card systems. When records are required in volume and/or are very active, automated equipment, although more expensive than manual equipment, has these advantages: Floor space is saved because a large volume of cards is held in compact, easily accessible storage. Time is saved because the cards are brought to the filer quickly. Information is transmitted rapidly, and service to customers or to company personnel is therefore more efficient.

Electronic Keypad

Illus. 12-8 Computer-Assisted Storage and Retrieval

There are disadvantages to automated equipment also: Only a portion of the file is accessible at one time, and only one person can operate the equipment at a time. It is possible to remove trays from the file for use at an individual workstation; however, in situations where different parts of the file are needed by many different users, automated shelf filing may not be efficient at all.

Signals for Vertical Card Files

The more important data held in card record systems can be highlighted by using signaling devices. Here are a few examples of the many types of signaling devices available for card systems.

1. Cards of different colors can be used. For example, a manufacturing company that sells to both wholesalers and retailers might use cards of one color for wholesalers and cards of a second color for retailers.

Signals flash the important data.

2. Small, movable color signals may be attached to the tops of cards so that the position, as well as the color, signifies specific information on the card. In a credit file, a red signal can be attached in a particular position to indicate that an account is one month overdue. In this way a credit manager can tell at a glance the number of delinquent accounts and the age of each account. Furthermore, credit references can be checked more easily than if each card had to be pulled from the file and read in detail to secure the payment record of each account.

3. Adhesive color strips, dots, or labels can be attached to cards in an address file to represent a geographic region, branch office, or department of an organization. In a stock or inventory card file, color signals might represent specific product lines or departments where stock is located.

VISIBLE CARD FILES

All cards are visible. Visible card files are formed by a series of cards or sheets held flat and set in an overlapping position. Because an edge of each card or sheet is always visible, scanning and retrieving information in such a file is rapid. The card records are generally held in card cabinets or in card binders.

Visible Card File Cabinets

Illustration 12-9 shows a typical visible card file cabinet, thousands of which are in use today. The primary guide notations appear on labels on the outside of the drawers or trays in the cabinet. Captions on these labels relate to the records held in the cabinet, such as personal names, names of stock items, dates, decimal or serial numbers, geographic names, and subject titles. Each drawer label indicates the range of cards held in it.

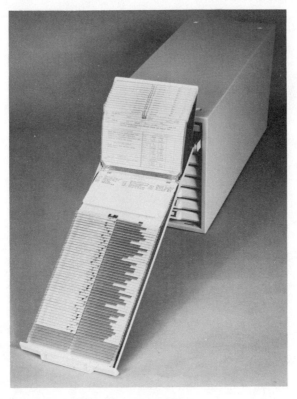

Illus. 12-9   Visible Card File Cabinet

Inside each drawer or tray, the visible edge of each card shows an identifying mark that assists in finding cards and keeping them in order. The mark of identification corresponds to the arrangement of information stored in the file, whether it is alphabetic, numeric, geographic, subject, or a combination of these. Notice that one of the shallow trays held in the cabinet has been pulled out and positioned for reference or for posting purposes. The cards are held in an overlapping position. The lowest line on each card can be read, providing the visible element in this type of card system.

Visible Card File Binders

Visible card records are arranged in books and loose-leaf binders as well. Some binders hold cards so that the bottom edges are visible. Others hold them so that the top edges show. Others may be arranged so that the side edges are visible.

The types of records kept in bound form are as varied as those kept in visible card file cabinets. They include cards for stock records, purchasing data, accounting or record-keeping data, and many other types of records. An advantage of using binders to hold visible card records is the portability of the records—they are easily carried to wherever they are needed. Illustration 12-10 shows such a binder.

Illus. 12-10   Visible Card File Binder

Signals for Visible Card Files

One of the most useful and distinctive features of visible card records is that they, like the vertical card records, can be signaled (marked) to summarize a variety of information; for example, (1) the amount of stock on hand (stock record cards), (2) the volume of sales or percentage of quota on sales (sales records cards), (3) the number of overdue accounts and the length of time each is overdue (credit and collection cards), or (4) the date or time period for following up on any matter of importance concerning accounts, contracts, inspections, and so forth. Two types of signaling devices shown in Illustration 12-9 are (1) the lock-in chain signal and (2) the progressive signal.

Lock-In Chain signals, produced by Acme Visible Records, Inc., consist of four color signals placed near the descriptive title on the card. These four movable plastic tabs can be locked in an up or a down position to summarize important facts without having to review the entire card record; for example, the particular week of the month or quarter of the year (1st, 2d, 3d, 4th) an inspection is due or other action must take place. Or a particular color signal locked in a down position may indicate at a glance an unlimited credit-line customer, a slow paying customer, a poor credit-risk customer, or any other helpful fact or aspect of that particular record.

Progressive signals are those that slide horizontally from one notation to the other at the bottom of the card. Many variations of signaling stock and sales control records are possible with progressive signals. For example, the signal can be moved to show the depletion of stock on a weekly or monthly basis. Or the signal might be used to show the increase in sales for a particular product at specific time intervals. Those who refer to the card files can determine at a glance when to reorder a particular item or how well a product is selling.

WHEEL FILES

Wheel files provide maximum card storage in minimum space.

An adaptation of visible card record equipment is the wheel file. Wheel files come in a variety of forms in which cards are attached directly to wheel-like frames that are manually or motor operated. Wheel files (1) provide maximum card storage in a minimum amount of space, (2) are relatively simple to operate, and (3) are capable of showing all faces of cards for posting or reference. Understandably, they are popular card record equipment in most offices.

Wheel files are generally of two types: Desktop or deskside. The desktop wheel file can be an open or enclosed file. The wheel file shown in Illustration 12-11 is an open, portable unit that holds 2,000 cards (5″ × 3″) and an A to Z index of 60 divisions. Both larger and smaller units are available in this type of equipment for cards of varying sizes and in capacities from 1,000 to 7,000 cards. The cards and guides used on wheel files are cut and perforated to fit around the twin rails formed around the core of the revolving central section of the wheel. The file is rotated by hand action and locks in the desired position, separating the cards into a wide V section. This permits direct access to a given card for reference or posting without having to remove the card from the wheel file.

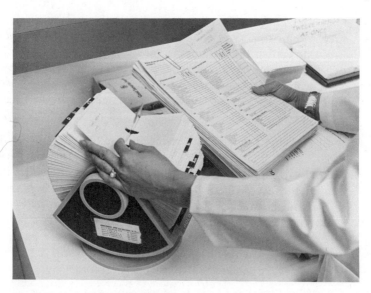

Illus. 12-11   Desktop Wheel File

The deskside wheel file is held in a cabinet equipped with a workstation shelf area. Cards are brought into alignment in the same manner as that described for the portable desktop wheel file. Deskside units usually hold more cards of larger sizes than those held in the desktop types. They are usually of desk height, may include a shelf-like workstation, and can be operated from a desk station (See Illustration 12-12).

If there are advantages to a wheel file that turns like a Ferris wheel, what about one that turns like a carousel, or merry-go-round? That kind of wheel equipment is available too. Illustration 12-13 shows a Delco card file. The carousel-rotating shelves move independently. Tiers of shelves can be added as they are needed. Space is compact. The equipment provides the added advantage of multiple accessibility—more than one person can use the file at one time.

FACTORS AFFECTING CHOICE OF CARD RECORD SYSTEM AND EQUIPMENT

What is the best system and the best equipment for card records? Obviously there is no simple answer to this question. A choice of system and equipment for card records requires consideration of many factors:

1. What kind of card records are needed?
2. How and by whom will the cards be used?
3. What is the volume of cards to be stored?
4. How much money is an organization willing to invest in the system?
5. What systems and equipment are available?

Illus. 12-12   Deskside Wheel File

Illus. 12-13   Delco Card File

Knowledge, liberally supported by experience, is required to build the best card record system for a particular organization. The more knowledge you have about card record systems and equipment, the better you will be able to handle the challenges of card storage and retrieval.

Questions for Discussion

1. Name at least three characteristics of cards that make them suitable for information storage and retrieval. (1)

2. How are card record systems most commonly used and by whom? (2)

3. How does a reference card file differ from a posting card file? (3)

4. What are the two general classes of equipment for card record systems? (4)

5. Describe the typical guide arrangement for the alphabetic name vertical card file shown in Illustration 12-4. (5)

6. Why are END guides used in card files? (5)

7. Describe the typical guide arrangement for the subject vertical card file shown in Illustration 12-5. (6)

8. How do stationary and portable card record equipment differ? (7)

9. What are some advantages in using automated equipment for card files? (7)

10. Would an automated file be a good choice of equipment for a library card catalog file? Why or why not? (7)

11. Describe two types of storage equipment used for visible card files. (8)

12. What two advantages do horizontal visible card files have over vertical card files? (9)

13. Describe how signaling devices are used in vertical and visible card files. (10)

14. What advantages make wheel files so popular? (11)

15. What five important factors should be considered when selecting a card record system or equipment? (12)

CHAPTER 13

Microcomputers, Word Processing, and Micrographics

Learning Objectives

After completing Chapter 13, you will be able to:

1. Explain how mechanical and electronic machines have affected records creation, as well as filing and finding tasks.
2. Describe unit record storage and retrieval.
3. List and describe various electronic data processing (EDP) storage media.
4. Explain indexing and coding procedures for EDP media.
5. Describe the role and responsibilities of the tape librarian.
6. Define word processing.
7. Describe the various word processing storage media.
8. Describe the effects of word processing on records control.
9. Describe microfilming and micrographics, their value and use, as well as their effects on records control.
10. List and describe the various micrographic storage media.

The huge amounts of information needed to run modern businesses require mechanical and electronic filing and retrieval.

Modern businesses need and demand increasing amounts of information rapidly in order to compete successfully in today's world. Management needs more information to make better and quicker decisions. Operation of government agencies requires more information from businesses and individuals. Tax laws are becoming more complicated and require that more records be kept by the public. New laws, such as those related to employee hiring, promotion, assignments, and pay, require large volumes of records.

This accumulation of information demands precise filing techniques and very rapid retrieval. Manual methods to create, process, store, and retrieve this quantity of information are in many cases too slow and costly to satisfy the needs of business operations. Mechanical and electronic machines have, therefore, been developed to help with records creation and the filing and finding tasks. This chapter will describe some of the data processing, word processing, micrographic, and other related systems designed to help control the growing volume of information.

Coding and indexing are still vitally important.

Even with the use of these newer systems, it is important to understand that the tasks of coding and indexing information are of even greater importance than with manual systems. The information created and processed by each system must be prepared accurately for machine processing. The equipment is merely a tool to speed up the processes of filing and finding. In fact, the cards, magnetic tapes, magnetic disks, and films produced by electronic means and by micrographics must still be stored and retrieved. The methods used for this storage and retrieval are similar to those used to control materials produced by and held in systems like those already studied. The real changes are in the form of the media (for example, magnetic disks and microfilm instead of paper), not in the indexing systems.

DATA AND WORD PROCESSING

Data processing refers to the manipulation of information.

The term **data processing** refers to the manipulation of information. People have been doing that since they used chisels and stone tablets to keep records. As the volume of and need for these records increased, faster and more accurate tools were invented to record and process the information. Pen and paper, typewriter, adding machines, computers, and the small pocket calculators many of us use are all examples of these tools.

The major impact of these data processing tools and systems on filers is in the form of the records produced and in the increased use of automated equipment for sorting and retrieving the records. The development of smaller, more powerful, yet less expensive equipment (the microcomputer, for example) has made it possible for even the smallest business to have its own equipment.

Punched Card Systems

Punched card systems are systems that record information in the form of holes in cards and that use machines to "read" the holes and process the information thus read (See Illustration 13-1). Information is punched into cards in

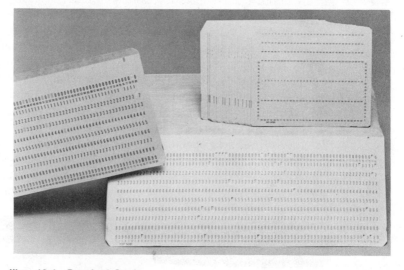

Illus. 13-1 Punched Cards

many ways. Various types of office machines record the information and verify the accuracy of what was recorded in the form of punched holes. An introductory book on data processing will give details for those interested.*

Punched cards are unit records.

Punched cards are known as **unit records** because each card contains one unit of information (for example, a name and address), and each card is handled as a single item or record unit. As such, the cards can be sorted into alphabetic or numeric order either by hand through reading the information printed on the top of the card, or by a machine called a **sorter**. The sorter operates somewhat along the same principles as terminal digit filing, sorting from the right to left, one letter or number at a time.

Information about prospective customers, for example, might be punched into a series of cards, one customer on each card. The cards can then be sorted according to postal ZIP Codes, sales representatives' territories, or the cities and states in which the prospective customers live. Since hundreds, and even thousands, of cards can be sorted by machine in one minute, this operation is much faster than hand filing and retrieving.

Punched cards are placed in long trays or drawers.

Punched Card Filing. Punched cards are placed in long trays or drawers held in specially constructed cabinets. Illustration 13-2 shows open-shelf filing using three indexing systems: (1) in the lower two rows, *numeric filing*, a system that is frequently used for parts inventory records; (2) in the second row

Illus. 13-2 Punched Card File

---

*A good book in this area is James F. Clark and Judith J. Lambrecht, *Information Processing: Concepts, Principles, and Procedures* (Cincinnati: South-Western Publishing Co., 1985).

from the top, *alphabetic filing*, a system that is used for material such as customer name and address cards; and (3) in the top row, *grouped card sets*, a system that is used for applications such as sales records where individual cards arranged alphabetically or numerically are less important than a collection of all sales for a particular department or a particular item.

Each tray or drawer bears a label on which is written a description or code showing the contents. The labels are similar in use to labels on the front of file drawers in cabinets. A variety of specially constructed equipment is available for punched card filing systems, all designed to assemble systems comparable to those used for index card systems.

The desired card or cards may be retrieved in the same manner as other materials by locating the proper drawer or tray by looking at the labels. The guides in the drawers are then scanned. Finally, the proper card is found by reading the printed coding on the top of each card. When many cards are needed, or when printed coding is not placed on the top of the cards, all cards from the appropriate section of the tray or drawer may be placed in the sorter and mechanically located.

If a listing of the information punched into the cards is desired, the sorted cards may be fed through a **tabulator**. The tabulator reads the holes punched into the cards and prints out the information on paper or cards. It is capable of reading all or just selected information punched into the cards, depending on what information is needed.

Tabulator printouts can be filed in a variety of ways.

Tabulator Printout Filing. Tabulator printouts can be filed in a variety of ways. If the printout is in the form of individual records such as invoices, the records are indexed and filed in folders in the same manner as other similar-sized documents. Alphabetic, numeric, or combination indexing systems are used. On the other hand, if the printout is on a large continuous form, the material is usually bound into a specially designed report-type folder and is labeled on the back like a book, or on a tab of a special file folder or guide. The folders can be placed in a vertical file shelf or drawer or placed on tracks in hanging folders. One such system is shown in Illustration 13-3. Special report folders with attachments for hanging are used in this open-shelf system. Alphabetic (subject) indexing, numeric indexing, or a combination of alphabetic and numeric indexing can be used.

Electronic Data Processing

Electronic data processing (EDP) refers to the processing of information at a high speed by using electronic means. The growing popularity of microcomputers by all sizes of businesses (and by families) is one of the great advances of our times. Microcomputers have made the electronic recording of information easy and fast. The information explosion through the use of microcomputers as well as larger computers has had a great effect on filing work. This effect has been brought about by the vast amounts of data that have been developed and must be sorted for future use, and by the various storage

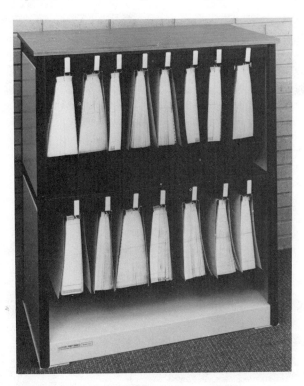

Illus. 13-3   Tabulator Printout File

media used. Information produced by EDP must be available immediately when needed.

EDP Storage Media. Although punched cards and printout forms are still important data storage media for electronic data processing systems, other forms, such as magnetic tapes and magnetic disks, are extremely popular.

The stored information is not visible on magnetic media (tapes and disks) since information is recorded in the form of magnetized spots that create electrical impulses which can be "read" only by special machines. The magnetic tapes are similar to those used in an ordinary tape recorder in a home or office. Many magnetic disks are similar to those used on home or office record players.

A large volume of data can be stored on magnetic media. Since information on these magnetic devices cannot be read without being printed out or displayed on a screen like a television screen, it is vital that the indexing and coding of information be carefully planned before the recording process begins.

Indexing and coding must be carefully planned before the recording process begins.

Certain terms are in common use when discussing microcomputers and word processing. An understanding of these terms will prove helpful. The location of information is commonly called its **address** when reference is made to the magnetic storage devices. The identifier (title) of the document is commonly referred to as its **filename**. A set of instructions prepared for a computer is called a **program**, and the person who prepares the instructions is called a **programmer**. Programs that can be used with a computer are called **software**. The programmer must be thoroughly familiar with all phases of the actual business application that must be processed as well as with the capabilities of the machine.

Payroll work is one type of business activity that lends itself to EDP. All the steps for preparing a payroll, including the preparation of the paychecks themselves, can become highly automated under this system. As a by-product, a considerable amount of information regarding an employee may be stored on magnetic media and supplied whenever needed. For example, if a directory or list of employees and their work locations is needed, it is easily obtained automatically from a printout of the tape or disk through the use of electronic data processing equipment.

Storing EDP Media. When magnetic tape is being stored, great care must be taken to see that no dust or dirt collects on the tape. In addition, the temperature and humidity in the storage area must be carefully controlled.

In order to make identification easy, a visible label must be placed on each tape as it is being prepared. This label serves the same purpose as the drawer label in regular files. Many companies employ a **tape librarian**, whose job is to maintain control over the magnetic tapes and to see that they are stored properly, correctly charged out, and returned.

Magnetic tapes are filed on end or hung by a hook in specially designed cabinets or on specially designed shelves. Illustration 13-4 shows one such large installation. Note the use of consecutive numeric indexing in this company. Other numeric systems and various alphabetic systems, including subject indexing, are also used.

The security of data processing files is vital.

The security of data processing files is a vital responsibility of the tape librarian. The theft or destruction of one reel of tape could possibly cause the company to spend many valuable hours reproducing lost information. Many security devices are designed to help safeguard this information. Among these devices are lead carrying and storage cases; locks to make the use of the reel of tape impossible without the proper key or combination; security guards at the entrance to the storage area; and the preparation of duplicate tapes, called **back-up tapes**, to be safely stored in another location. Illustration 13-5 shows one method of security storage of magnetic tapes in a specially built safe. The tapes are labeled with a band around the reel using alphabetic or numeric indexing for quick and easy retrieval.

As discussed earlier, computer printouts are placed in specially designed binders and are filed on shelves or in file drawers designed for that purpose. The binders are labeled on the outside cover, on the back, or on tabs in the same manner as correspondence folders (See Illustration 13-3).

Illus. 13-4   Computer Tape Storage File

Illus. 13-5   Security Storage of Magnetic Tapes

Filing of magnetic disks will be discussed later in this chapter. It should be remembered, however, that when handling disks it is necessary to avoid touching the recording surface or writing on the covers with firm or hard writing tools when the disks are inside the covers.

EDP systems eliminate a large amount of hand filing.

It is obvious, then, that a large amount of hand filing of certain types of materials is completely eliminated when an EDP system is installed. Nevertheless, the machine must be told how to do everything. The main difference in records control is *where the information is filed* and *through what means.* As long as information must be retrieved, a knowledge of filing procedures is necessary. Filing systems for EDP media must be as complete and efficient as systems used for index cards or for correspondence and other paper documents. The indexing systems used are the same as those used for other records—alphabetic, numeric, or a combination of the two.

Word Processing

In addition to the microcomputer, another recent mechanized system to affect information preparation, storage, and retrieval is word processing. The American National Standards Committee of Washington, D.C., defines word processing as " . . . the transformation of ideas and information into a readable form of communication through the management of procedures, equipment, and personnel." **Word processing (WP)**, therefore, is a combination of equipment, methods, and systems that converts ideas into the printed word. The machines used have made information *processing* (dictating, typing, and copying) easier, but in some respects they have made information *handling* (filing, storage, and retrieval) more difficult because documents are put on many different kinds of magnetic media as well as on paper.

Word processing is a combination of equipment, methods, and systems that converts ideas into the printed word.

Word processing is rapidly joining data processing so that numeric information processing, as well as words, are combined into one system. Microcomputers, minicomputers, and large (mainframe) computers have been connected to word processing equipment or have been programmed to produce, store, and recall information of many types.

Some data processing systems can transfer information from one machine to another machine automatically.

The goal of full office automation is a system of machine control based on the ability of certain office machines to transfer information to other machines automatically. Such a system follows this basic rule: *Do it only once.* This means that the exact information should be captured on some type of common language (machine-readable language) medium the first time the information is prepared. The next time this information is needed, it is automatically written from its common language form.

WP Storage Media. Many common language media are used with word processing. Understanding these media will help you understand how to file and retrieve the information when needed. We have already discussed computer tape and punched cards in the section on electronic data processing. The following storage media are also used in word processing.

Punched Paper Tapes. Punched paper tape is one type of common language medium. The tape can be prepared automatically by using a small attachment to a specially designed typewriter, adding machine, cash register, or other common business machine. As the operator types the original document, the paper tape is automatically punched. The next time the same information is needed, the tape is fed back into the device on the typewriter or other machine and an exact duplicate of the original is prepared automatically. Punched paper tapes are treated as unit records.

Magnetic Tapes. Some word processing machines use magnetic tapes to store information. These tapes are similar to computer tapes but are much shorter and narrower. Many are contained in cassettes exactly like those used on a home cassette tape recorder.

Diskettes. **Diskettes** are small, flexible sheets of magnetic material on which relatively large amounts of data can be stored in magnetic form. These are popularly referred to as **floppy disks** and are similar to those used with microcomputers. Like punched cards, diskettes are treated as unit records because generally only one topic or record series is on each disk. The identifier (title) of each document stored on a disk is called its *filename*.

Internal Storage Media. The term **internal storage media** refers to a variety of storage devices attached to or part of word processing equipment and many computers. Information can be recorded inside the equipment. This information can be retrieved instantly whenever the machine is keyed with the address (location) of the information. The machine is instructed to type or, if possible, to display the information on a video screen. The video screen is similar to that of a home television screen. The typewriter can type out the stored material requested on letterhead paper, invoices, ordinary blank sheets, or however instructed. Sometimes the information in internal storage is lost (erased) when the electric power is turned off. Therefore, a copy of the documents in internal storage is usually transferred to a tape, disk, or other machine readable medium for longer storage. This is referred to as **backup**.

Indexing and Storing Word Processing Information. Obviously information stored on magnetic media cannot be read by the person needing the information until it is either printed out on paper or displayed on a cathode-ray tube (CRT) such as a video screen. In order to be printed or otherwise displayed, the information must be located.

Punched paper tapes are usually kept in folders in a master file. The folders housing the tapes are constructed with small pockets into which the prepunched tapes are inserted—frequently with a printed paper copy of the contents of the tape. The operator simply removes the prepunched tape from its pocket and feeds it through the machine. The tape is then replaced in the pocket of the folder and filed until needed again. Similar machines also produce edge-punched cards as well as paper tape. Edge-punched cards perform the same function as paper tape. In addition, they are more convenient to file. Each tape must be placed in a special pocket, whereas cards are rigid and can be filed in a pocket or in a manner similar to that used for ordinary file cards. Illustration 13-6 shows a folder with pockets into which punched paper tapes have been inserted.

Folders with punched paper tape or edge-punched cards can be filed alphabetically or numerically, exactly like other paper records or cards.

Magnetic tapes are indexed alphabetically or numerically. Vertical drawer files or carrousels (either desktop or floor-stand models) are used for storing active magnetic cassette tapes. These devices are expandable as more storage space is needed.

Diskettes are becoming very popular for storing information since they are small, flexible (hence, called "floppy disks"), and easily stored. Illustration 13-7 shows the use of labels on floppy disks. The labels could be color coded if desired. Color coding of labels is popular for indexing all types of word processing media.

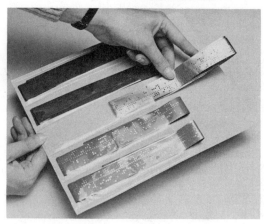

Illus. 13-6   Filing Punched Paper Tapes   **Illus. 13-7   Floppy Disk Label**

Illustration 13-8 shows various file storage methods for floppy disks: a desktop X file, hanging folders for a vertical file drawer, and a lateral file drawer with hanging folders that contain the printout material as well as the diskette. Notice that the guides in the drawer file are the same as those used for correspondence and other document files.

To aid in retrieving information on internal storage (storage of information within the machine), the address (storage location) is: (1) recorded on index cards, (2) typed on a standard sheet of paper, or (3) stored by the machine on another magnetic tape, disk or card for printout or video display when needed.

Diskettes in a Desktop X File

Diskettes in Hanging Folders

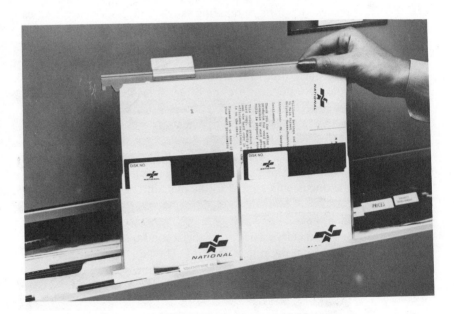

Diskettes in Hanging Folder with Printout

Illus. 13-8 **Storage Methods for Floppy Disks**

An auxiliary index is very important.

Since subject and numeric filing are used extensively both with word and data processing documents, an auxiliary index is very important. By first referring to the index for the proper address, retrieval is quick and accurate. In the index, material is listed by common titles and cross-referenced under other likely titles. Through this procedure, any one of many titles can be used to locate a specific document rapidly and accurately.

MICROGRAPHICS

Microfilming is a process of filming documents to reduce their size.

Microfilming is a process of photographing documents so as to reduce the size of the original to a very small (micro) size. These miniature pictures are generally taken on 16mm (millimeter) or 35mm film. For special types of work, 105mm or a variety of other sizes is used.

A broader term than microfilm is *micrographics*. It is more commonly used, it is preferred by specialists, and it is more descriptive by not limiting our thinking to just filming. **Micrographics**, then, is a total information system including filming, but also including the filing and retrieval of information.

Micrographics includes filming, filing, and retrieval of information.

Filming

The records control area involving micrographics is frequently part of the records management function. As a result, filers become involved in several important activities concerning micrographics. Most of these activities are similar to the filing responsibilities already discussed; for example, coding the records for filing, preparing labels and guides, selecting cabinets and shelves, filing the materials, and quickly retrieving what is needed. Once records are filmed in a particular order, they always remain in that order; therefore, the coding and arranging of documents before filming is of great importance.

The coding and arranging of documents before filming is important.

Many times filers are asked to help put records on film. They are frequently trained to use the cameras on the job. There are a variety of cameras designed for microfilming, but they fall into two basic kinds: planetary and rotary. The exact type selected depends on the nature of the material to be filmed and the uses to be made of the film after it is created.

Rotary cameras are used for many common types of business papers.

Rotary cameras are the most frequently used cameras. They are easy to operate, accept popular-sized documents, and photograph very rapidly when the documents are fed to the machine automatically. Rotary cameras are used for many common types of business papers such as correspondence, invoices, bank checks, and school transcripts (See Illustration 13-9).

Planetary cameras are used especially for filming large documents.

Planetary cameras are the second basic type and operate somewhat differently from the rotary cameras. The papers are usually hand fed one sheet at a time, but a greater variety of document sizes can be photographed and the picture shows details more clearly. Planetary cameras are popular, especially for filming large documents such as blueprints, engineering drawings, bound books, newspapers, and magazines. A smaller planetary camera is available for photographing smaller documents requiring the filming of fine detail (See Illustration 13-10).

Variations of the rotary and planetary cameras are used for photographing different information. For example, a type of planetary camera can create microfilm directly from computer tapes without producing a paper printout first. This is called **computer output microfilming (COM)**. Another is called a "step-and-repeat" camera for filming a series of images all on the same piece of film.

Cameras are now available to produce "updatable" microfilm. These cameras, using a special film, can update information by placing additional

Illus. 13-9   Rotary Camera

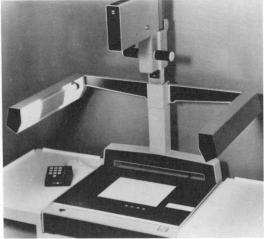

Illus. 13-10   Planetary Camera

images (records) on film that has already been developed. In addition, they can block out or place a word such as "void" on an image which is already on the developed film but is no longer needed.

Reading and Printing

Film is placed in a projector for viewing or reading.

After the film has been developed, it is placed in a projector for viewing or reading. This projector is called a **reader-viewer**, or just a **reader** (See Illustration 13-11). If the user wants to print out a copy of the picture, a **reader-printer** is used (See Illustration 13-12). After seeing which document is wanted, the operator obtains a print, called a hard copy, by merely pressing a button

Illus. 13-11   Reader-Viewer

Illus. 13-12   Reader-Printer

A hard copy is any copy that can be read without a viewer.

or switch on the reader-printer. The term **hard copy** refers to any copy that can be read without the use of a viewer or other magnifying device. A reader-printer can reproduce the document to any one of various sizes—smaller than the original documents, the same size as the original, or larger than the original. Some readers are small enough to be portable and are very inexpensive. They can be carried in a briefcase and can be used whenever and wherever necessary. Reader-printers are larger than readers and are not portable.

Microforms

Microfilm can be created and/or used in many formats. These formats include roll film, aperture cards, microfiche, and microfilm jackets. Although most of these formats begin as roll film, their end use may be different. It is in describing this end use that the term "microform" applies (See Illustration 13-13).

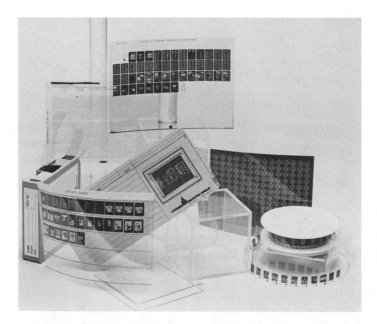

Illus. 13-13   Common Microforms

Roll microfilm is a length of microfilm on a reel or spool.

Roll Microfilm. The most popular, and least expensive, form in which microfilm is produced is roll microfilm. **Roll microfilm** is simply a length of microfilm on a reel or spool. It appears similar to motion picture films and is generally in rolls of 100 feet, although other lengths are used.

Large quantities of information are recorded on each roll microfilm. The information is recorded serially, in the exact order in which it is placed into the camera. It is suited to recording lengthy documents that do not need updating frequently. The recording of correspondence, bank checks, invoices, entire computer runs, and other daily transactions are popular roll film contents. In order to update a roll of film, the entire roll must be photographed again or the new transactions must be photographed and spliced (cut out and glued) into the existing roll. Splicing destroys the legal acceptability of microfilm in many cases.

Retrieval requires that documents be indexed, coded, and arranged before they are filmed.

Retrieval of specific documents or other information from all microforms requires that the documents be indexed, coded, and arranged in correct filing order before they are filmed. Guides, called **targets** or **flash targets**, in microfilm are prepared and filmed at the beginning of each group of records. The targets are prepared with print that is large enough to be read without magnification. Targets serve the same purpose as the guides and folder tabs of a regular filing system and contain alphabetic, numeric, date, or short subject titles. The targets are also readily seen as the film is moved rapidly across the screen of the reader. When information is coded and arranged correctly before filming, it is mostly self-indexing.

Other more sophisticated coding systems are available to index filmed materials for use with complicated searching equipment. For example, counting devices (counters) are used to measure the feet of film run through the reader. This counter is similar to an automobile's odometer, which measures the miles the car has traveled. By recording the counter reading, a particular document can be located rapidly.

In another indexing system, each document is automatically numbered as it is filmed. This number, now part of the microfilm frame, serves as the address of the document. In the same way, magnetic codes can be placed on the film and automatically "read" by a special attachment on the reader. By use of a keyboard, the code can be requested and the reader will move rapidly to that location.

Microfilm and regular filing are similar.

Microfilm filing and regular filing are very much alike. Roll film is placed in small individual boxes. A label (similar to that on a file folder) is prepared and glued to the cover of the box. The boxes are placed in drawers, on shelves in a cabinet, or on a carousel for active use. Drawers and shelves are also labeled in the same manner as in conventional filing systems.

Aperture cards contain holes in which frames of microfilm are placed.

Aperture Cards. An **aperture card** is a card containing an aperture, or hole, cut into the card that provides a place for one or more frames of microfilm. Aperture cards are unit records, like punched cards, and are referred to as **unitized microforms.** The microfilm frames are cut from roll microfilm after the roll is developed. Frames are then placed into the apertures provided in the card (See Illustration 13-14).

Aperture cards are usually the same size as the cards used in a card punch and sorter. Through the use of a card punch, holes are created for use in machine identification of the card and its microfilm image(s). Then the aperture cards can be filed and retrieved through the use of a mechanical sorter. When properly labeled, they may also be filed and retrieved manually. Aperture cards have been used extensively for engineering drawings but are also popular for X rays and some business records.

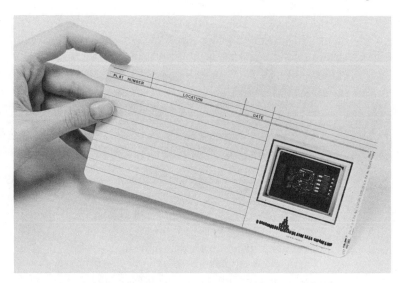

Illus. 13-14   Aperture Card

Indexing and coding of aperture cards follows the same procedures as for other cards. Aperture cards can be produced in color or contain color lines to aid in quick visual retrieval and refiling. They are generally housed vertically in boxes, on shelves, or in specially designed drawers. Guides and drawer labels aid in the same manner as for other paper files. Cards may also be filed in pockets of standard-sized folders containing related documents. Machine sorting is a common method of card retrieval. As more images are placed on the card, however, the room for the punched holes is reduced, making machine retrieval less effective.

Microfiche is a transparent rectangle of film on which images have been photographed.

Microfiche. Another unitized microform is the microfiche. A **microfiche** (pronounced *micro feesh*) is a transparent rectangle of film onto which 60 to 98 small images have been photographed. Illustration 13-15 shows a microfiche being read. The standard size of a microfiche is 6″ × 4″. Many advances have been made in microfiche. One is the development of what is called **ultrafiche**. One 6″ × 4″ ultrafiche film will hold images of thousands of papers. Microfiche is a common product of computer output microfilm (COM). Microfiche is the microform most frequently used for updatable microfilm systems described earlier in this chapter.

Next to roll microfilm, microfiche is the most popular type of microform and is growing in use rapidly. It is used for the storage of related documents, such as a pamphlet, a parts catalog, a customer mailing list, or patients' medical histories. The publishing of book reports, magazines, catalogs, and newspapers on microfiche is called **micropublishing** and is becoming common.

The "header" is used for identification of the fiche.

A filing code and other information usually is printed across the top or bottom margins of a microfiche film. This is called the **header** and is used for identification of the fiche without having to use a reader-viewer. Color coding

Illus. 13-15 Using a Microfiche Reader

can be used to aid in filing and retrieving microfiche. Color may be a horizontal band across the entire header, one or more vertical strips at the top of the fiche, or the entire fiche may be placed in a color-coded envelope. Color is usually used in conjunction with other coding systems.

All varieties of alphabetic and numeric indexing systems are used in filing microfiche.

Microfiche Jackets. Although not a microfiche in the strictest sense, another unitized record, a **microfiche jacket**, is frequently used instead of the actual microfiche. The jacket is made of two panels of very thin transparent film-like material. Lines of adhesive join the panels horizontally, dividing them into three or more strips into which microfilmed images are inserted (See Illustration 13-16). The images to be inserted are cut from roll microfilm and slid (either as individual images or as strips of images) into the channels of the jacket. The insertion is done either by hand or by using a specially designed machine. Images no longer needed may be removed from the channels of the jacket and, if desired, new images may be inserted to update the information already placed in the jacket. Illustration 13-17 shows a microfilm jacket reader-loader. Microfiche jackets are usually the standard 6″ × 4″ size but other sizes are available.

Jackets are frequently used instead of actual microfiche because the special "step-and-repeat" camera process needed for microfiche is expensive and takes up a lot of office space. The jacket process uses regular roll film and can

A microfiche jacket is frequently used instead of the actual microfiche.

Illus. 13-16   Microfilm Jacket

Illus. 13-17   Microfilm Jacket Reader-Loader

use the more compact rotary camera. Microfiche jackets and microfiche can be viewed in a special reader or in many readers made to accept a variety of microfilms. A hard copy of any image in the jacket can be obtained by using a reader-printer. Microfiche jackets are indexed in the same manner as microfiche.

Values of Microfilm

Microfilming techniques and forms have developed rapidly in recent years. As a result of these developments, many values are claimed. Duplicate copies can be made of rolls of film, microfiche, or aperture cards in less than one minute on small office-type copiers. Prints of microfilm images are made even faster, and prints can be made larger or smaller than the original document to make copies easier to read and handle.

As much as the contents of a five-drawer file can be recorded on two 100-foot rolls or one 200-foot roll of film. This amounts to approximately 20,000 $8\frac{1}{2}'' \times 11''$ documents on the rolls. Thousands of $8\frac{1}{2}'' \times 11''$ documents can be placed on one $6'' \times 4''$ ultrafiche. Frames for about 350 microfilmed documents can be mounted in a five-inch high stack of aperture cards. Microfilming makes possible the saving of enormous amounts of floor space and great numbers of filing cabinets. As much as 98 percent of the space can be saved.

Although documents reduced to microfilm save considerable storage space, microfilm cannot be economically used for space savings alone because the cost of the microfilm equipment may be greater than the cost of the space saved. In an active file, when the original filing arrangement is accurate, microfilm simplifies and speeds up the retrieval of information by making it impossible to refile an item incorrectly. It must be remembered that microfilm captures not only the records but all of their defects as well. Records must be carefully and correctly arranged before filming.

Microfilm, especially microfiche, can be mailed to other locations at a minimum cost. Microfilm systems can be adapted to both high- and low-volume offices. Microfilm also offers security for valuable records in that copies are sent rather than originals. Cross-references are easily handled by photographing extra copies whenever they are desired. Microfilm is durable in that, depending on the type of film used, it can be kept a long time and when used does not show as much wear and tear as the original document would.

Applications of Microfilm

Microfilm is useful as a method of processing and retrieving information on an active basis.

Specific uses of microfilm have been mentioned for the various microforms. Microfilming was once used exclusively as a method of protecting vital records or as a means of saving space. Today it is even more useful as a method of processing and retrieving information on an active basis.

Almost all types of businesses now use micrographics. The largest users include utilities (gas, electric, water), financial institutions (banks, investment companies, savings and loan associations), insurance companies, government agencies, military agencies, transportation companies, educational institutions, libraries, manufacturing firms, retail and wholesale distributors, and hospitals.

Questions for Discussion

1. Why have mechanical and electronic machines been developed to help with the creation, filing, and finding tasks? (1)

2. What has been the effect of these newer systems on the indexing and coding process of filing? (1)

3. What is the major impact of data processing tools and systems on filers? (1)

4. How has the use of microcomputers affected filing work? (1)

5. Why are punched cards known as unit records? (2)

6. How are punched cards stored? How are they retrieved? (2)

7. In what ways are tabulator printouts filed? (3)

8. What data storage media are used for EDP systems? (3)

9. Why must indexing and coding of information be carefully planned before the recording process on magnetic media is begun? (4)

10. What is the job of a tape librarian? (5)

11. Who is responsible for the security of data processing files? (5)

12. What is word processing? (6)

13. What storage media are used with word processing systems? (7)

14. How are the following items stored for retrieval? (7)
    a. Punched paper tape
    b. Magnetic tape cassettes
    c. Diskettes (floppy disks)

15. Why is an auxiliary index important in filing word processing and data processing documents? (8)

16. What is microfilming? What is micrographics? What are the advantages of using microfilm? (9)

17. In what typical filing activities might filers become involved when working with micrographics? (9)

18. What is a hard copy? (9)

19. What is roll microfilm? How is roll microfilm filed? What are targets? What purposes do targets serve? (9,10)

20. What is an aperture card? How are such cards filed? (10)

21. What is a microfiche? What is a microfiche jacket? How are they filed? (10)

22. What is a header? How is a header used? (10)

PART 6

Records Control

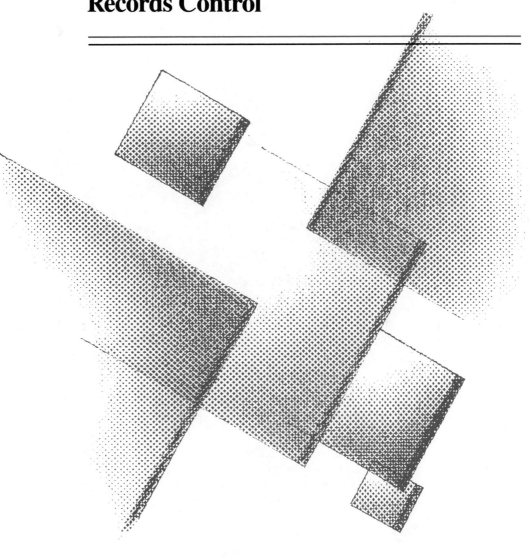

CHAPTER 14

Equipment Used in Records Control

Learning Objectives

After completing Chapter 14, you will be able to:

1. Defend the importance of evaluating equipment needs, availability, and costs when selecting filing equipment.
2. Define manual, mechanical retrieval, and computer-based filing equipment.
3. List distinguishing characteristics of manual filing equipment.
4. List advantages of mechanical retrieval equipment.
5. Explain why computer-based filing equipment is a reasonable alternative to manual filing equipment.
6. Define computer database equipment.
7. Define computer output microfilm (COM).
8. Define computer-assisted retrieval (CAR).
9. Define optical data disk (ODD) storage.
10. List advantages of optical data disk storage.

SELECTING FILING EQUIPMENT

The use of automated electronic equipment has not decreased the volume of paperwork as many people thought it would. Rather, computer technology has created a greater volume of paper, as well as a variety of magnetic media records, to be stored and controlled. The old, traditional files have taken on a new look to meet the increasing demands placed on them and to fit into the new open, or landscape, office designs. Needless to say, selecting the best style of filing equipment for controlling records today is a challenge. This chapter will help you to understand that challenge.

Variety of Equipment

Paper records, microforms, and magnetic media work harmoniously, not competitively, in the office and require new and different types of equipment to store and to protect them. In Chapters 1 and 13, you have already seen some storage equipment used for paper and paperless records.

Browse through magazines such as *Modern Office Technology, The Office, Administrative Management*, and numerous supply catalogs from computer supplies and accessories vendors. See for yourself the staggering volume of equipment and supplies for managing office records advertised in these publications. Equipment in a wide range of sizes, shapes, capacities, costs, and colors is available (1) to speed up information storage and retrieval processes, (2) to cut down on the number of misfiled records, (3) to reduce the amount of record storage space, and (4) to complement a new office design or layout.

Challenge of Selection

Selecting from a variety of filing equipment is like purchasing a pair of shoes. First, the shoes must be appropriate. Sneakers would not be appropriate to wear to the junior prom, nor would a pair of loafers or open-toed high heels serve well on a camping trip. After you have assessed your needs, determining how much you are willing to spend and selecting from what is available conclude the purchasing process.

Consider needs, availability, and cost.

Similarly, the selection of filing equipment requires consideration of these same three basic purchase factors: needs, availability, and costs. The success of the purchase depends on the knowledge, experience, and personal taste that accompany a full exploration and understanding of (1) the filing equipment needs of the organization, (2) the equipment that is available, and (3) the cost (or savings!) realized. Each organization has its own set of priorities, needs, and values. Often it is difficult to know what has been sacrificed or compromised when the ultimate decision to buy is reached. Look more closely at these purchase factors as they relate to the selection of filing equipment.

Equipment Needs. The selection of filing equipment begins with needs—future needs as well as present needs. Rarely are any two filing systems exactly alike. Every organization has individual and specific requirements concerning the kinds, the uses, and the anticipated growth of its records. Before filing equipment and supplies can be selected for any given office, it is necessary to know:

1. The kinds of records to be filed and controlled.
2. The frequency with which each kind of record will be handled during the day—constantly or infrequently.
3. The number of people working at the files at one time.
4. The volume of records to be handled in a given period of time—every six months or every year.
5. The method of filing best suited to handle the records—alphabetic, geographic, subject, numeric, or some combinations of these methods.
6. The type of charge-out and follow-up system used.
7. The transfer method used.
8. The security and retention requirements of the records.

9. The organization and distribution of records—centralized, decentralized, or a combination of these plans.

Concerns such as these help to identify equipment needs and, when matched to appropriate types of filing equipment, ensure a filing system that is properly planned and controlled.

Equipment Availability. The more knowledgeable you become about filing equipment, the better prepared you will be to make intelligent equipment selections. It is in the area of equipment availability that this chapter will be of most value to you. Although space prohibits the coverage of every piece of filing equipment, you will become familiar with the basic types of equipment found in the office. As you study the basic types of filing equipment, the selection of equipment alternatives becomes evident.

Cost extends beyond initial cost of equipment.

Equipment Costs. Cost is the factor that makes the ultimate equipment purchase a reality. Whether it is a $100 vertical filing cabinet or a $125,000 computer installation, cost plays an important part in the selection process. Because labor accounts for about 80 percent of total filing costs, the decision to purchase must extend beyond the initial cost of the equipment. Remember the benefits/cost ratio presented in Chapter 1. It is a timely reminder that a business expects a fair return on the dollars it invests. In addition to the cost of the equipment, look at any short- and long-term savings to be realized from the investment. If the additional cost of one piece of equipment over another is to be justified, then some savings must be realized eventually through more efficient office space utilization, higher productivity, and/or reduced time and labor costs.

GENERAL TYPES OF FILING EQUIPMENT

A mixture of hard copy, micrographics, and electronic storage is taking place.

Although paper continues to be the primary information-storage medium for most businesses, a transition from paper-intensive filing systems to a mixture of hard copy, micrographics, and electronic storage is taking place. This means that increasing skill will be required of filers in the future. Filers must be familiar not only with the kinds of record media used for information storage and retrieval but also with the filing principles and equipment needed to manage them.

Used harmoniously with one another, most filing equipment fits into one of three categories: *manual, mechanical retrieval,* or *computer-based* filing equipment. **Manual** filing equipment, stationary or mobile, requires manual (physical) energy to operate it—office records are stored and retrieved manually. **Mechanical retrieval** equipment provides fingertip records access—letters, cards, tapes, and other office records are mechanically delivered to the filer or workstation. **Computer-based** filing equipment generally stores information, rather than actual source documents. Information enters the computer by keyboard or scanning device, for example, and is stored in digit (numeric) form. This information must be changed to human readable language for displaying on a terminal or for printing.

Manual Filing Equipment

The most common filing equipment falls into the category of manual filing equipment. Designed to hold paper and paperless records, manual filing equipment includes (1) vertical cabinets, (2) open-shelf files, (3) lateral cabinets, (4) hanging folder equipment, (5) mobile files, (6) rotary files, (7) desktop and deskside files, and (8) specialized filing equipment.

Vertical Cabinets. Vertical cabinets are rectangular shells that hold a series of large, bin-like drawers. The drawers are constructed so that papers can be filed in an upright, vertical position with the writing facing forward (toward the filer). Illustration 14-1 shows two-, three-, four-, and five-drawer vertical cabinets.

Vertical cabinets are the most widely used pieces of filing equipment.

The vertical cabinet is the most widely used of all filing equipment. It has been updated and looks quite different from its traditional gray ancestor. The cabinets now come in a wide variety of colors and contemporary wood veneers to fit into most modern office designs. If you have ever pulled out too many drawers at a time and had the cabinet tip over, you will appreciate the vertical cabinet that is now equipped with an interlocking device that prevents the filer from pulling out more than one drawer at a time.

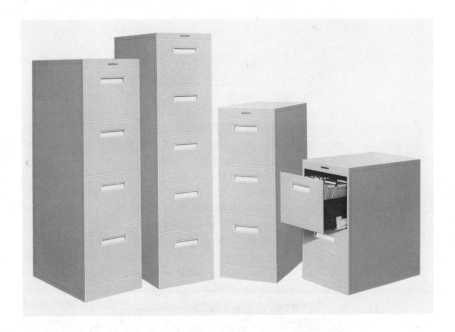

Illus. 14-1   Two-, Three-, Four- and Five-Drawer Vertical Cabinets

Because cabinets are available in various sizes, they can be adapted for use in a number of ways:

1. One- and two-drawer units may be used near desks to provide easy reference to very active papers.
2. Three-drawer cabinets may be used as work counters and as dividers between sections in an office.
3. Four- and five-drawer cabinets may be used as blocking partitions in an office area. Frequently units of these sizes are selected because active and semiactive materials can be handled in the same cabinets. (This procedure is described in Chapter 7.)

Some cabinets are made of very heavy metal, and the cabinet shells are insulated to provide some degree of fire protection for valuable papers and documents. Heavy cabinets are also made with combination locks and necessary reinforcement to permit their use as safes for the storage of vital and valuable documents and papers.

Vertical cabinets have the advantages of providing closed, convenient, and relatively compact storage space in drawers that can be organized under any of a variety of systems for guiding purposes. Vertical cabinets are most useful when individual papers are being handled rather than when entire folders are to be taken from the files.

The principal disadvantage of vertical cabinets is their bulk. They occupy a great deal of floor space; and, when very active files are in operation, they require wide aisles to allow for pulling out file drawers. As a result, much floor space is lost. Although the vertical cabinet is still the most popular piece of filing equipment in the office, other types of filing equipment are gaining in popularity.

Open-Shelf Files. In an effort to minimize some of the disadvantages of filing certain types of records in vertical cabinets, various forms of shelf filing equipment have been developed and are widely used. The equipment and supplies used with shelf filing differ from those used with vertical filing cabinets because folders are placed on open shelves with the visible portion of each folder along the side edge rather than across the top. Thus, tabs on both guides and folders must be cut so that their notations show vertically (down the side) rather than horizontally (across the top).

Folders are placed on open shelves with tabs positioned along the side edge.

Illustration 14-2 shows an open-shelf file with removable sections. Folder-supporting devices are usually included as part of an open-shelf filing system. The supporting devices pictured in the open-shelf file in Illustration 14-2 are small bin-like sections that can be removed by the operator. Such sections are used to hold guides and folders in an upright position as well as to serve as dividers and carriers of files materials.

Very active papers are usually not held in shelf files mainly because entire folders must be pulled off the shelf before papers can be filed or found. Furthermore, guide and folder notations are not as readable as are those on top-tabbed guides and folders in vertical cabinet filing systems. Therefore, semiac-

Illus. 14-2   Open-Shelf File with Removable Sections

tive materials are more apt to be held in shelf files. Some insurance papers, case histories in hospitals, legal papers, and contract job records can be held most efficiently in shelf files.

In general, the advantages of shelf filing over cabinet filing are these:

1. Floor space is saved because room for pulling out drawers is not needed; therefore, aisles between shelves can be narrower than aisles between vertical cabinets.
2. Direct access to folders is easier because these are held on open shelves and are always visible.
3. Costs for shelf filing equipment are much less than those for vertical cabinet filing because shelf equipment is relatively simple in construction.

The disadvantages of shelf filing over cabinet filing are these:

1. An entire folder must be withdrawn from a shelf before any action can be taken to find or file papers.
2. Open shelves do not provide adequate protection from dust.
3. Notations on folders and guides are not as readable as those on the top edges of guides and folders in vertical cabinets.
4. Open shelves are not always neat in appearance.

Lateral Cabinets. A lateral file is one in which folders and guides are held in pull-out drawers constructed to hold papers in a lateral direction. Lateral cabinets are constructed in either of two styles: (1) with drawer fronts

Lateral cabinets contain pull-out drawers that hold papers in a lateral position.

that can be opened to expose the contents of the drawer, as in a shelf file, or (2) with drawer fronts that are fixed parts of file drawers and thus move as the drawers are being pulled out of the cabinet area, as in a vertical file cabinet. This factor is important because the system of guides and folders varies with the type of drawer being used in a lateral cabinet. A lateral file with solid drawers (See Illustration 14-3) can use only top-tabbed guides and folders, while a lateral file drawer with a sliding front panel (See Illustration 14-4) can be equipped with either top-tabbed or side-tabbed guides and folders. The contents of the drawer with top- and side-tabbed guides and folders can be arranged so that the tabs can be read either from right to left or from left to right. This factor can be used to gain maximum working space when several lateral units are being placed in a filing area.

Illus. 14-3 Lateral Cabinets with Solid Drawers

The lateral cabinet shown in Illustration 14-4 shows four open panels and one closed panel. Closed drawers are opened by pulling the front panel up and sliding it back into the body of the cabinet shell. The two card file sections in the bottom open correspondence drawer are auxiliary parts that can be ordered and fitted into the space that usually would be occupied by a single correspondence drawer. Cabinets with exchangeable sections are advantageous when there is a need for storing mixed records in the office.

A comparison of lateral cabinets with vertical cabinets and shelf units shows that the laterals require less floor space than do the verticals because less aisle space is needed for opening and closing drawers. Since shelf units do not require any aisle space for drawer action, these are the most economical in terms of floor area required.

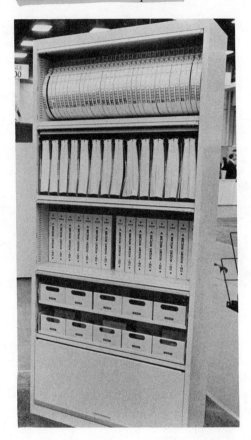

Illus. 14-4   Lateral Cabinet with Sliding Front Panels

Hanging Folder Equipment. The hanging folder (or suspended folder) method of holding records represents a very adaptable and widely used form of records control. Hanging folders are usually constructed with metal or plastic strips across the top edge of the front and back parts of the folders. The strips extend beyond the sides of the folders and fit over parallel rails that run along both sides of the file drawer. A drawer can be arranged so that the hanging folders are positioned in two sections facing the filer (See Illustration 14-5). The folders hang suspended over the rails. In this suspended position, folders are more easily moved and more readily accessible than are folders in standard vertical or lateral cabinets. Illustration 14-5 shows hanging folders in a lateral cabinet. This same kind of system can be used in vertical cabinets by adding parallel rails to the sides of a file drawer not originally equipped with them.

Hanging folder equipment suspends folders from rails or rods.

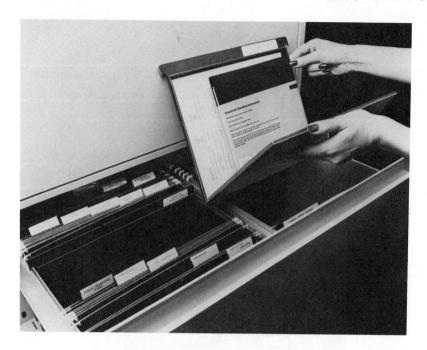

Illus. 14-5   Hanging Folder System in a Lateral Cabinet

There are many uses for hanging folders systems because (1) materials of different sizes can be held more efficiently in them than in the more stationary vertical folders; (2) folders are easily moved, opened, or replaced without disrupting other folders in the system; and (3) some types of hanging folders can be indexed more completely than is possible with other types of folders, making records more accessible in a hanging or suspended folder system.

Mobile Files. Mobile files are formed by having a series of file sections mounted on rollers. This makes it possible to move any section of the files along a fixed track. The theory behind the mobile file is to eliminate the conventional, nonproductive aisles between ranges of shelves. Illustration 14-6 shows a bird's-eye diagram of the conventional shelf arrangement with an aisle between each range of shelves. Illustration 14-7 shows how to double the number of shelf units in the same storage space by eliminating the aisles.

Mobile files eliminate the conventional aisle between ranges of shelves.

Both electric and manually operated mobile shelf systems enable a full bank of shelves to move easily and quietly along tracks on the floor so that one or more aisles are created only where they are needed at the moment. Illustration 14-8 shows such a mobile file unit. The operator easily moves the entire range of shelves until an aisle is created where the record is located.

Although it is a great space saver, the mobile file may be a poor choice for a system that is very active and used by many people. Much time could be lost waiting to create the aisle that you need to store or to retrieve a particular record.

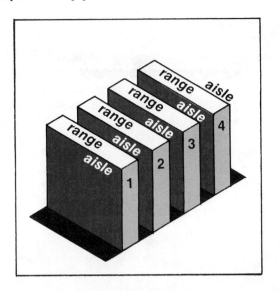

Illus. 14-6   Conventional Shelving Arrangement

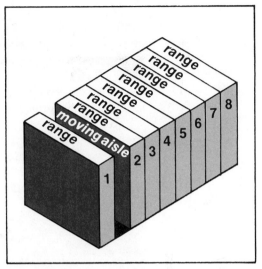

Illus. 14-7   Spacesaver Mobile File Arrangement

Illus. 14-8   Mobile File Unit

Rotary Files. The production of rotary files for holding correspondence and related materials is a developing phase of the office equipment manufacturing industry. In essence, rotary units are composed of a large outer shell within which a series of circular shelves are rotated in the manner of a lazy-Susan server. On the rotating shelves, guides and folders are set and carried as spokes are carried on a wheel; or folders and guides may be set into rectangular bin sections formed as separate units on the "floor" of the rotating shelves.

Rotary units contain a series of circular shelves that rotate.

Rotary files are available in a variety of styles. They can be from one to six tiers high. Some are available with casters so that they can be moved to various workstations around the office. If record security is a need, cabinet enclosures that can be locked are available. Illustration 14-9 shows a rotary file with five user positions.

Illus. 14-9   Rotary File

Some advantages of freestanding rotary files include:

1. Savings in floor space.
2. Flexibility of tiers to hold any size record from 5″ × 3″ cards to computer printouts.
3. Ability to add tiers or entire carousels as they are needed.
4. Easy access to files by several filers because the open tiers are highly visible and each moves independently.

Desktop and Deskside Files. Two of the more important work areas that require planning and equipment for records control are the desk and related workstations. In areas such as these, filing systems are limited to rather small, but compact, units. The equipment provides ready access to information that is frequently needed. In Chapter 12 you saw the popular wheel files used as desktop and deskside card filing units. Rotary files are also

Desktop files provide ready access to information.

used as desktop and deskside files. Illustration 12-11 shows a desktop rotary visible stand for holding single lines of information, such as names, telephone numbers, or product numbers. Illustration 12-12 shows a deskside rotary file.

Other types of useful auxiliary units are available in portable or stationary styles. One such unit is the sorter and temporary file shown in Illustration 14-10. This is designed as an auxiliary unit for holding current papers at a ready position for a period of time so that the retrieval of very active papers will not require a search of the general files.

Illus. 14-10   Sorter and Temporary File

Specialized Equipment. Up to this point, equipment and systems have been considered for correspondence, documents, cards, and microrecords. There are, however, many other types of records that must be held under control programs because they are vital to successful operations either in an entire organization or in a department.

Control programs are necessary for many types of specialized records.

Catalogs and Directories. Catalogs and directories are representative of a type of reference material used in many business, industrial, and service organizations. These records may be found in bound-book form or in loose-leaf binders, or they may be in transcribed form and written on cards that are filed in either visible or vertical card systems.

When records of the catalog type are in active use in their original form, rotary filing units are frequently used to hold and carry these bulky books. The rotary units are much easier to handle and are more easily accessed by a number of workers at the same time than would be the case if such materials were held in cabinets or on book shelves. Also, catalog-type material transcribed onto cards which are held in large visible books also may be used to greatest advantage when held in rotary units.

When catalog-type material is semiactive or when it is used occasionally by only a few workers, it may be kept in bookcases or in vertical filing cabinets. When held in these ways, catalogs may be marked and filed according to several plans: (1) by firm name—with a supplementary card index file listing alphabetically the items or subjects included in each catalog, (2) by number—with an alphabetic card file of firm names and the subjects included in each catalog, or (3) by subject—with an alphabetic card index listing of firm names. Cross-references may be made in the catalog card index, just as they are made in any other card system. The cross-reference for a catalog card is made by listing on one card the places where related material can be found.

Bulky Materials. Many of the important records that are kept by business and industrial organizations are not written on standard size cards or sheets of paper. Because of this, special indexing and filing problems are encountered. Among these types of records are X rays, maps, blueprints, tracings, duplicator plates and stencils, some types of forms, and computer printouts.

Many of these records are too large or too bulky to be held in standard filing equipment. Most of these records can be easily stored in hanging folders that are large enough and strong enough to hold large sheets or bulky objects. A system of this type frequently is used by hospitals to hold large items such as X-ray film and other related data. A numeric system of guiding is used so that hospital records are maintained by an indirect system and remain confidential. The records department keeps a master index which shows personal names in alphabetic order and lists the folder numbers assigned to those persons.

Mixed Media. When it is convenient to store a combination of media in one location, equipment such as that shown in Illustration 14-11 is used. Such mixed-media storage cabinets are available in a variety of colors, sizes, and configurations. The mixed-media cabinets shown in Illustration 14-11 are of a modular design with an adaptable interior to accommodate a variety of records media: letter- and legal-size folders, computer tapes, hanging printout binders, microfilm cartridges, cassette tapes, hanging folders, disk packs, and ring binders. Adjustable shelving holds filing and general office supplies. The cabinets easily adapt to changing and expanding storage requirements.

Mixed-media storage equipment adapts to changing storage needs.

Mechanical Retrieval Equipment

Mechanical retrieval filing equipment is electronically or power operated in some way. The equipment stores records on shelves or in metal trays or bins in the unit. Entering a pre-established code on the electronic keypad activates the system, delivering a record or batch of records to a walk-up or seated workstation in seconds. Two such units are described and illustrated here:

Illus. 14-11   Mixed-Media Storage Cabinets

The Minitrieve manufactured by Supreme Equipment & Systems Corp. and the Lektriever by Kardex Systems, Inc.

Minitrieve. The Minitrieve unit shown in Illustration 14-12 consists of (1) a console (workstation), which is located at the front of the unit and (2) a vault-like enclosure in which records are stored behind the console. The operator seated at the console is referring to a folder taken from a tub that has been delivered to the console by the process described below.

Illustration 14-12 shows the two sections of the Minitrieve electronic file in detail. Within the vault area there are two facing banks of metal file tubs separated by an area occupied by an electronically operated conveyor (center, rear in picture). Upon a code signal from the operator at the console, the conveyor moves to a desired tub, which is drawn onto the conveyor and then moved forward into reference position at the console. After the desired paper, document, or folder has been removed or reviewed, the operator presses a button labeled "Restore"; the tub then is moved back to its original place in the vault area.

For complete control of records held in any of the mechanical types of equipment, there must be guiding plans, identification of filed materials, charge-out of papers or folders borrowed, and transfer of semiactive and inactive materials.

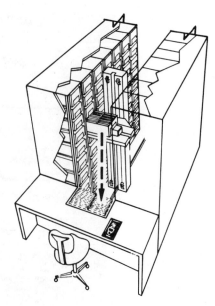

Illus. 14-12   Minitrieve—Console and Storage Sections in an Electronic File

Systems like the Minitrieve shown in Illustration 14-12 have the following advantages over manually operated systems:

1. Storage space utilization is increased considerably because units can use space from floor to ceiling in a storage area.
2. Push-button speed in retrieval is superior to any other mechanical or manual method.
3. Papers and documents can be kept in security control because of the completely enclosed area in which they are held and because they are accessed by a single operator.

Units the size of the one in the illustration and larger are being included in the construction plans of some of the newest office buildings in metropolitan areas.

Lektriever. The Lektriever shown in Illustration 14-13 is capable of storing letter- and legal-size documents, computer tapes, and trays of different sizes. Trays are available to hold a combination of mixed-media records such as cards, hanging folders, cassette tapes, and microforms. A pre-established index code entered on the electronic keypad activates the system, delivering records to either a walk-up or seated workstation. A computer interface (link) is a Lektriever option that provides instant access to records or file locations. This unit is similar to the Kardveyer illustrated in Chapter 12, except that the Lektriever stores a wider variety of media records.

Illus. 14-13   Lektriever

Computer-Based Filing Equipment

Since UNIVAC I, the first digital computer built for commercial use in 1951, computers have become more powerful, smaller, and affordable. This trend is continuing. The first computer filled an entire room. Today, even in the smallest offices, desktop computers are commonly performing word processing (typing and text-editing), spreadsheet analysis (numeric manipulation and calculation), and database (information storage, manipulation, and extraction) tasks. Will computers outmode the paper filing systems and equipment as we now know them? It is not likely for these reasons: (1) computers appear to have added to the "paperwork explosion" in the office. Most computer input functions originate from paper records of some sort, and tons of paper flow from computer printers in the form of correspondence, forms, reports, and statistical data; (2) the need for some business operations to work from hard copy or original source documents; and (3) the unwillingness of many organizations to destroy paper records that may have been saved for "future reference."

Computers have added to the paperwork explosion in the office.

Nonetheless, computers have become a reasonable alternative to many paper records storage and retrieval tasks. Computers are now user friendly (easy to operate). They are more powerful and less expensive. They can increase records control productivity and reduce filing time and labor costs. They are space efficient in terms of information storage. They are generally an essential and justifiable complement to most records control systems.

Computers are a reasonable alternative to paper records.

Traditional filing tasks have been enhanced by **computer database, computer output microfilm (COM), computer-assisted retrieval (CAR),** and **optical** data disk (ODD) systems. Developments in these technologies are rapidly taking place; therefore, whatever contributions these technologies can make to the records control effort require frequent and careful consideration. Study the brief descriptions of these technologies which follow.

Computer Database. Database refers to any data organized and stored so that it can be added to, deleted, changed, calculated, and then retrieved in a variety of formats. For example, information pertaining to every student in your school might be stored on 5″ × 3″ cards that look like Illustration 14-14.

```
NAME
  Kelly Nancy
GRADE
  11
HOMEROOM
  211
SEX
  F
DATE OF BIRTH
  01/15/--
COMMENTS
```

Illus. 14-14   **Student Information Card**

Once cards are prepared for each student, should they be arranged by name? By sex first and then by name? By grade and then alphabetically by name? By homeroom? Wait a minute! It is possible to sort manually the cards in only one arrangement at a time.

If the same information were stored as computer data, it is possible to sort the information in a variety of ways and to print many useful reports: an alphabetic list of all students in the school, a list of all men or all women, a list of students alphabetically by homeroom or by grade, a list of all 15-year-olds, or a list of all the girls in ninth grade! Any combination of variables is possible. The value of a computer database is not so much in the ability to store information, because the information can be stored more easily and economically on cards. It is the ability to manipulate (add, delete, change, and calculate) data and to generate different reports from a single input (information is entered only once) that makes the computer database equipment so useful.

Computers have the ability to manipulate and print data.

Computer Output Microfilm. As you have already studied in Chapter 13, **computer output microfilm (COM)** is a process of transferring information from the computer directly onto microfilm or microfiche, eliminating the paper (hard copy) printout. The Kodak Komstar Imaging System shown in Illustration 14-15 is completely automatic. Computer output is printed onto film by laser, dry processed, duplicated, and collated. The Kodak Komstar

Illus. 14-15 Kodak Komstar Imaging System

combines both imaging and processing functions for 16mm microfilm and 105mm microfiche. The processor requires little manual intervention. An internal minicomputer automatically controls the COM for each job, selects the appropriate lens, and determines the film spacing and retrieval indexing to be applied. Komstar is capable of producing and collating 2,000 microfiche duplicates an hour.

Film is easier to store, access, and distribute than paper.

Microimaging has become an increasingly popular alternative to hard copy storage because of space conservation and information retrieval and distribution—film is easier and less expensive to store, access, and distribute than reams of paper.

The decision to install microimaging equipment is based on many factors. Some of these factors include volume of records, anticipated growth, record use, records distribution and retention requirements, and installation and maintenance costs. A careful cost analysis of hard copy versus microimage systems will determine whether the conversion to microimage equipment is justified, or cost effective.

Computer-Assisted Retrieval (CAR). Computers can assist in the retrieval of all kinds of records. CAR programs can assist in locating a box of records held in a storage facility or in locating a single image on a roll of microfilm. The early computer-assisted microfilm retrieval systems were simply computer-generated reports that listed the address (location) of an image on a roll of microfilm. For example, someone looking for Order No. 34570 would look up the order number on a printout that cross-indexed the microfilm address. The filer would then insert the correct roll of film into a reader-printer and advance to that microfilm image address to view or print the document.

Today, CAR systems more commonly are connected to microimage retrieval terminals like the Kodak IMT-350 shown in Illustration 14-16. The IMT-350 microimage terminal is a high-speed, keyboard-request unit for automatically retrieving information recorded on microfilm and for printing dry, ready-to-use copies.

When the terminal is linked to a CAR computer, the computer database is used to store a file address for each specific image. For example, the filer, through the CAR computer, tells the IMT terminal to find and copy a given microimage file, including attachments and supporting documents. The terminal then provides the file number and image number within the file. The desired image quickly appears for screen viewing or printing up to 99 copies of the image.

Illus. 14-16   Kodak IMT-350

Optical Data Disk. The term **optical data disk storage** refers to data recorded on a disk by a laser (light amplification by stimulated emission of radiation). Laser technology, developed for use in areas of space technology, medicine, and manufacturing, has made optical data disk (ODD) storage possible.

ODD technology is the process of converting images into digital (numeric) data. Images (documents, pictures, signatures, and illustrations) normally stored only on microforms, can now be stored on an optical data disk in digit form with other electronic data—electronic data and microimage storage on a single storage medium! ODD appears to be a promising information storage and retrieval medium in the automated office.

ODD: a promising new storage medium.

The optical data disk shown in Illustration 14-17 is capable of storing images equivalent to 40,000 8½″ × 11″ pages. The disk, which looks much like a phonograph record, is 12″ in diameter, and is encased in a cartridge for protection when handled.

Optical data disk cartridges are used in a jukebox-type device called an Optical Storage and Retrieval library, or OSAR. Illustration 14-18 shows the interior storage of two racks of cartridges. The robotic mechanism, shown on the left, can retrieve a disk cartridge from either rack and insert it in the optical data disk drives located at the bottom of the picture. Illustration 14-19 is the FileNet Image Management System with an OSAR library (the large unit on the right side of the illustration). The OSAR library can contain from 1 to 64 disk cartridges for robotic insertion, and retrieval from, up to four ODD drives within the unit. The storage of the unit is equivalent to 2.5 million document-images—the contents of over 200 five-drawer filing cabinets!

The OSAR library = 200 five-drawer filing cabinets.

Illus. 14-17   Optical Data Disk

Illus. 14-18   Interior of Optical Data Disk Library

Illus. 14-19　FileNet Image Management System

Even more astonishing is that this FileNet system can accommodate up to eight OSAR libraries on a single document-image processor. The FileNet document-image processor with eight OSARs has the storage capacity of 1,024 billion characters or

1. 20 million pages of information,
2. 1,700 five-drawer filing cabinets,
3. 1,000,000 word processing diskettes,
4. 6,667 cubic feet of warehouse storage space,
5. 812 IBM 3380 high capacity magnetic disk drives, or
6. 2,800 rolls of microfilm.

Will optical data disk record storage equipment outmode the electronic digital and micrographic storage equipment? The technology is too new to make such a prediction. For now, however, it appears that optical data disk storage and retrieval may be limited to large-volume, permanent storage record systems because data is etched permanently on the disks, storage capacity is tremendous, and the equipment is expensive.

As you review what you have learned about manual, mechanized, and computerized records storage equipment, you are aware that there is no one type of equipment that satisfies all records storage and retrieval needs of an organization. What equipment is best? The best equipment is that which has been selected through a skillful analysis of what is needed and a thorough understanding of the alternatives to meet those needs.

Questions for Discussion

1. Of the three factors to consider when purchasing filing equipment, which do you think is the most important? Be prepared to defend your choice. (1)

2. Define manual, mechanical retrieval, and computer-based filing equipment. (2)

3. List two distinguishing characteristics of each type of manual filing equipment listed: (3)
   a. Vertical cabinets
   b. Open-shelf files
   c. Lateral cabinets
   d. Hanging folder equipment
   e. Mobile files
   f. Desktop and deskside files
   g. Mixed-media cabinets

4. List some advantages of using mechanical retrieval equipment. (4)

5. What makes computer-based filing equipment a reasonable alternative to manual filing equipment? (5)

6. Define computer database. (6)

7. Define computer output microfilm (COM). (7)

8. Define computer-assisted retrieval (CAR). (8)

9. Define optical data disk storage (ODD). (9)

10. List advantages of ODD storage and retrieval equipment. (10)

CHAPTER 15

Maintaining and Improving Records Control

Learning Objectives

After completing Chapter 15, you will be able to:

1. Identify two problems you may face on your first job.
2. Explain your first step if you are assigned the responsibility of a poor filing system.
3. List and describe the three levels of activity in a filing system, the equipment and supplies used with each level, and the average number of papers held in each folder according to each level of activity.
4. Explain why thickness measurements for guides and folders are important, what these measurements mean, and what thickness would be used for specific files.
5. Describe a records management manual, why it is necessary, and what information it should include.
6. List ways to avoid overcrowding files.
7. Explain the importance of free space in a filing system and the amount of space necessary in each drawer.

You will be involved in solving filing problems immediately.

You will be involved in solving filing problems from your first job on. Practically all office jobs, and most other jobs, include creating, using, storing, and retrieving information. Even if your job is only partly in the records area, there is a good chance that you will come face to face with the following problems: (1) You will be the user of a filing system that may be weak and inefficient and (2) you will be expected to file all documents and to find quickly the ones that are needed, when they are needed.

In many cases, it will be up to you to use an existing system; to improve that system; or, frequently, to develop a new, more effective system. Chapter 15 is designed to help you keep a filing system under control. It includes ideas and suggestions about methods that you can use to locate, correct, and prevent filing problems. These suggestions will help you reduce the cost, and work, in filing.

What can you do if on your first job you are assigned the sole responsibility of a poor filing system? Obviously not all situations are alike. Most businesses and offices are different. However, now that you have studied BUSINESS RECORDS CONTROL and completed a business-like practice set, you will know what is needed to use and control a records system.

Be sure to write down the problem and solution.

Your first step is to find out why things are not as they should be. Be sure to write down the details of what seems to be wrong. Think about what the problems are; then form a plan for solving them and write that down too. Talk with your supervisor and get your supervisor's approval. Then start on your plan of improvement. It may take a while, but it will be worth it.

You may be fortunate and begin working in an office where a good records control program has been developed. If so, learn all you can about the operations of that system. There will probably be a handbook, called a **records management manual** or *filing manual*, which describes the filing system and the procedures to be used in the system. Of course, you will study and follow this manual so that your job will be easier. Your supervisor will be a great help to you. Feel free to follow his or her advice completely.

An efficient filer is a valued worker.

When you know how to use the records system, you will be a valued worker. You should then be able to enjoy your job because it is interesting and because you are performing a service that is vital to the success of your company. The more proficient you become and the more you learn about records control, the more likely you are to be promoted to even higher jobs.

The remaining parts of this chapter are designed to give you ideas and show you procedures that can be used to make you an efficient and effective filer.

FILES ACTIVITY RATES

You must know how frequently the filing system and all its parts are used each day. Checking the activity of a system requires keeping information in the records department on the following activities: (1) how many papers are coded, sorted, placed in folders, and removed from folders each day and (2) if a perpetual transfer system is being used, how many papers and folders are weeded out or transferred each day.

Each of these activities takes time, involves paper handling, and is a part of the entire system of records processing. If you keep a tally on each of these items for about a month, you will know the amount of activity in your filing system.

There are three levels of files activity.

There is a very general way of measuring the activity of your files. In this general method, there are three levels of activity: active, semiactive, and inactive.

1. An *active* filing system is one where 5 percent or more of the total papers are acted on each day. "Acted on" means in any of these ways: coded, sorted, placed in folders, removed from folders, destroyed, or transferred. When 6 percent or more of the total numbers of papers in a file are acted on each day, the system would be considered a *very active* system.

2. A *semiactive* system involves processing from 2 percent to less than 5 percent of all papers.

3. An *inactive* system results from a less-than-2-percent action with papers in the system.

These ranges of files activity are subject to error because, once again, not all businesses are alike. However, the rates are useful as a very general indication. They can show how much and what types of equipment and supplies are needed to make a system operate at top efficiency. For instance, if records processing is in the less-than-2-percent range, the system should be in the storage or inactive area. There, guides are not needed and containers are boxes rather than the drawers or shelves that are much more costly. On the other hand, if daily records activity is between 2 and 5 percent, the records should be kept in drawer or shelf files located near the users.

RECORDS CONTROL SUPPLIES AND EQUIPMENT

Guides and folders vary in thickness, weight, and strength.

Guides and folders vary considerably in thickness, weight, and strength. They are usually made of *pressboard* or of a heavy paper called *manila*. The term used to describe the measure of the thickness of pressboard and manila is called **caliper**. The scale used to measure thickness is known as the **point system**. Under this system, one point equals one-thousandth of an inch (.001).

Why are these measurements important? Well, the thicker the guide or the folder, the more space it occupies in a file drawer or on a file shelf and the more expensive it is to purchase. On the other hand, the heavier the guide or folder, the more effective it is in keeping papers upright instead of allowing them to slide down or wrinkle.

Guides

Most guides are made of pressboard. They range in caliper measurement from 20 to 35 points. Guides are also made of 18-point manila stock. About 50 of the 20-point guides take up an inch of filing space, but about 28 of the 35-point guides take up an inch.

Durability is important in guides.

Durability is the primary factor to consider when buying guides. Guides used for active to very active files are generally 20- to 25-point pressboard. Eighteen-point manila guides are sometimes used in semiactive files because such guides are less expensive than others. Since they get less use in semiactive files, manila guides are acceptable if they are needed to assist in the finding and filing of papers.

The choice of guides of a particular thickness should be measured not only by durability but also by their relative cost. Guides are expensive. Money can be saved by not "overguiding" a filing system. Considerable savings can be made if the grade of guides selected is related to the activity of the system that is to be equipped. For example, to equip a semiactive file with an expensive guiding system would be a great waste of money. On the other hand, buying manila guides for an active system would be wasteful. Such guides would wear out quickly and would have to be replaced frequently.

Folders

The caliper of manila folders ranges from 8 to 18 points; that is, from 8 thousands (.008) of an inch to 18 thousandths (.018) of an inch. The difference between .008 and .018 does not seem very important, but if your system had only 10 five-drawer cabinets, the .018 folders would use 144 inches of file drawer space while the .008 folders would use only 64 inches—a difference of 80 inches. Eighty inches of space equals more than three file drawers 26 inches deep. This much space would be lost if you did not need the heavier folders. Lost space means more cost for filing services. Cost is vital and must be kept as low as possible.

Folders used for heavy-duty purposes, such as the carrier folders that were described in Chapter 6, page 73, are made of a heavy stock that ranges from 20 to 25 points. Some heavy folders are made with W-shaped bottoms to permit expansion for carrying or holding bulky items.

The caliper of manila folders in general use is either 9½ or 11 points. A paper stock called *kraft* is also used for file folders. Kraft and manila are comparable in quality and price. Kraft is the darker color of the two and is less apt to show soil.

Paper weight is measured by the pound. The usual weights for correspondence paper is either 20 pounds or 16 pounds. Before correspondence paper is cut to the standard size of 8½ by 11 inches, it measures 17 by 22 inches. Five hundred sheets of the 17 by 22 inch paper weigh approximately 20 pounds. This is then cut to four packages of 8½ by 11 inches each. For office use, paper is usually purchased in packages of 500 sheets. Each package of 20-pound paper would then actually weigh five pounds but is referred to as 20-pound paper. The thinner paper used to make carbon copies is usually 13-pound paper and is called copy paper.

Approximately 150 sheets of 20-pound paper will fit into a folder when the base of the folder is expanded to its maximum distance of three-quarters of an inch. If the weight of the paper is lower, much more can be stored in the same space—for example, 260 sheets of 13-pound paper in an expanded file folder.

Overfilled folders cause problems.

Obviously it would be difficult to find a document if the maximum number of sheets of paper that would fit were placed in a folder. The amount that should be considered as the maximum for efficiency and storage and retrieval is determined by the activity of the filing system. The more active the system, the fewer sheets of paper in a folder.

Supplies and Equipment for Varying Activity Rates

The activity rate of a filing system determines the equipment and supplies needed. The more active a file, the closer the filing equipment should be to the user and the more guides and folders that should be used.

Active Files. The active file is the "heart" of a records control program. It must be carefully planned and maintained in first-class order. It should have the best and most appropriate equipment and supplies.

When the files are very active, they must be housed as closely as possible to the filer or user of the information. The files can be held in the file drawer of a desk or in the drawers of a deskside unit (See Illustration 15-1). An A-Z set of primary guides is needed. Folders that are used in a manner similar to that of general folders can be added behind each primary guide. Individual folders can be started as required by an accumulation of papers for a person or a firm. These are easily moved to the active system when the need for them in the "hot" file has diminished. In very active files, papers are not held for a very long time, therefore, the number of papers in each folder is not a problem.

Illus. 15-1   Active Records Are Close to the User

A very active file can also be held to advantage in a sorter that is located near the filer. After being coded, incoming papers are filed in one of the many types of sorters available. The papers are held until the rate of demand for them has decreased, then they are placed in a file drawer, or they are transferred to the active files.

Active filing systems should not have too many nor too few guides in each file drawer or shelf. Having too many guides uses valuable space and can cause distractions in a searching operation. Also, guides are expensive—it is wasteful and costly to purchase too many. On the other hand, searching is more difficult if there are too few guides. This costs money in the form of salaries and wasted time.

How many guides should be used in an active system? Usually the amounts given in Illustration 15-2 are recommended.

Number of File Drawers	Number of Guides Needed
1	20-25 (Divisions of
2	40 the Alphabet)
3-4	80
5-6	120
7-8	160
9-12	240
13-16	320
17-24	480
25-36	720
37-50	1000

Illus. 15-2 Number of Guides Needed for Various Size Files

The number of folders that should be used behind each guide varies according to the types of materials that are being held in an active system. When there are many individual folders in a system, it usually is advisable to have not more than six folders behind each primary guide. Less active systems can take more than this number; eight to ten folders are frequently found behind primary guides as files activity is lowered. In active files, the folder capacity standard usually is a *maximum* of 50 sheets to each folder. This means that the *average* number of papers in folders will be about 25. The activity of the filing system is the most important consideration when determining folder capacity.

Semiactive Files. Semiactive filing systems are the "in-the-middle" ones—not "hot" but not "cold" either. They hold papers that have been transferred from the active system. You will recall that, depending on the way transfer is handled, semiactive files can either be in the same area as the active files or held in the storage files.

If the semiactive files are in the same cabinets as the active files, the semiactive files will be more usable if they are equipped with a set of primary guides. The guides do not have to be of the same quality as those used in an active system nor does the set need to have as many guides. For example, if the active system were held in the two upper drawers of a series of 12 four-drawer cabinets, it would need 480 primary guides (the number recommended for 24 drawers in Illustration 15-2). These guides would divide the alphabet into 480 parts. If the semiactive file were held in the two lower drawers of each of the 12 cabinets, it would need about five primary guides per file drawer, or a total of 120. This is only one-fourth of the number needed for the active system.

Semiactive materials frequently are held on shelf filing units rather than in cabinet drawers (See Illustration 15-3). If such a system is in the upper level of semiactivity, one primary guide for each six inches in horizontal space is recommended.

All of the folders in a semiactive file are used first in the active system and then are transferred to the semiactive or storage files. Therefore, the number of papers to be held in folders has been fixed by the rule used for the active system. However, during this process it is possible to combine several folders holding related material into one folder. Material in individual folders is especially adaptable to reductions of this kind. This reduces the number of folders that will be held and usually reduces the number of papers to be transferred because dead materials can be easily located and removed during the transfer process. The *average* number of papers per folder in semiactive files can be extended to about 50. Some folders will hold up to 100 sheets without harm to the filing and finding operations.

Illus. 15-3 Semiactive Files May Be On Open Shelves

Inactive Storage Files. Guides are not used in storage files because the number of times that stored records are requested for reference is relatively low. Because of this, the demand for papers is much less urgent than it is in an active system.

In this situation, general folders can be used as guides because their tabs show the same notations as do primary guides. Therefore, during the transfer process, when material is being placed in transfer boxes or cases, general folders can be moved from the back of alphabetic sections to the front position. There they will serve the same purpose as do the primary guides in the active files. Inactive storage files use the same folders and contents as the semiactive files. Consequently, the folder capacity for inactive storage files is the same as for the semiactive files.

RECORDS CONTROL PROCEDURES

A good records program does not "just happen." It must be carefully planned and then implemented. In order to have a successful operation, attention must be given to all procedures. A records management manual and a records control checklist can be used as aids when you are considering improvements in any phase of your filing system and its operating problems.

Records Management Manual

Regardless of how large or how small a records department may be, it is always advisable to have a records management manual to be used as a guide by all who work in the department. This is especially true because of two factors common to all records control work:

1. All records control work must be as closely related as possible to the unique practices and standards used in any particular company. Each company has certain routines and standards unique to its own type of operation. Workers must know these procedures if efficient operations are to result. As procedures are developed or improvements are made in departmental routines, they must be explained in permanent form. Unless all procedures are written, they will be lost, misunderstood, or misused as time passes and personnel changes occur.
2. A records management manual assembles in summary form a variety of technical information that is vital. Many of the rules and procedures that you have studied will be found in company manuals. However, it should be understood that some of the rules and routines given in this textbook may be adapted for use in a particular company. For example, the basic rules for indexing must be used consistently by all who keep records. Your company might operate in a specialized field that would require a change of one or more of the basic rules for indexing. In addition, it is possible that a company dealing with agencies or branch offices in foreign countries may require a more detailed statement of the basic indexing rule for processing foreign names. Such an extension of the rule would be explained in the company manual. Appendix B of this textbook contains some common alternatives to the basic indexing rules presented in Chapters 2, 3, and 4.

As a minimum, a records management manual should include technical material such as:

1. A general description of the records control system and its various parts or divisions.
2. A list of indexing rules to be used.
3. A description of the coding practice to be followed.
4. A description of charge and follow-up procedures.
5. A definition of procedures to be followed prior to and during transfer time.

In summary, records management manuals are prepared for the following reasons: (1) to formalize records control procedures used in a given company so that all personnel will be informed and will be able to proceed in a consistent manner; (2) to record technical information in order to guide and train departmental personnel; and (3) to relate general standards of performance to the specific needs of any given organization.

Records Control Checklist

A checklist helps you improve your filing system.

A checklist helps workers complete a task without missing necessary actions. A records control checklist will help you improve your filing system. The list should be reviewed frequently and a date or check mark placed after each point when it is completed.

1. Records control routines should be carefully planned and strictly followed. Even though filing is only a part of general office or secretarial work, a definite amount of time should be made available for it.

2. Papers should be indexed, coded, and processed in accordance with definite rules and routines.

3. All related papers filed in the same folder must be assigned a code. This code can be a name, an order number, a job number, a case number, a reference number, or a title.

4. Responsibility for directing filing and records control operations should be definite. One person should be given this duty.

Only trained personnel should file.

5. Only personnel trained to perform records work should be allowed to work with the filing system.

6. A records management manual (guide) should be available and should be kept up-to-date.

Files should not be overcrowded.

7. The files should not be overcrowded with papers and folders. Attention should be given to the following matters:
   a. Room for expansion should be provided in all file drawers and on all file shelves.
   b. Unneeded papers should be screened out during the scanning and coding phase of operations.

c. Material already in the files should be scanned on a continuous basis. Uncalled for papers should be removed whenever possible. Such a "weeding out" requires knowing which folders and/or papers are used for reference and which are not. One way to recognize unwanted material is to make a tally mark on the top edge of a paper or a folder each time it is requested. A lack of tally marks indicates a "dead" folder or letter.

d. File folder capacity needs to be checked regularly. The varying activity rates need to be considered when making these checks.

e. Papers should be transferred from active files into semiactive or storage files according to a carefully developed transfer program.

f. Papers should be eliminated according to the established records retention schedule.

Leave at least four inches of space in each drawer.

8. At least four inches of free space should be left in every 26-inch deep file drawer to allow for expansion and easy access. An appropriate amount of free space must also be left on shelves holding active or semiactive materials. If papers accumulate very rapidly in an active file, more than four inches should be left when starting the new file. For example, if business is increasing about 20 percent a year, at least five inches (20 percent of 26 inches available) should remain free.

   Storage boxes and transfer cases holding inactive materials can be filled but should not be crammed with folders and papers.

9. Equipment and supplies used in the control program should be selected after careful study has been made of the need for them and their probable uses.

10. A plan for charging and tracing borrowed materials should be in operation.

11. Order should be maintained in all phases of record control by using accepted practices such as the following:
    a. Notations on guide and folder tabs should be typed or printed in a uniform style.
    b. Worn folders should be replaced.
    c. When folders are returned to the files, they should be neatly aligned with those folders already in position. Follower blocks in file drawers are needed to keep folders from sagging. Boxes or blocks need to be used to hold papers in a neat, upright arrangement on shelves.
    d. Torn sheets need to be mended and "dog ears" straightened.
    e. Pins and clips should be taken off papers in files.
    f. Tops of filing cabinets or shelves should be kept clear of all materials.

12. General folders should be checked regularly, and individual folders should be started for active correspondents.

13. Individual folders should be inspected and additional folders with the same caption added when it is necessary.

14. Special subject, geographic, and date sections should be added as needed to make the system more efficient.

Extra copies should not be filed.
15. Extra copies of materials should not be made nor kept in the files. Photocopy control is an important part of records control. When copies are needed for distribution, only the exact number of copies should be made. The information contained on the records of an organization is critical to its operation and survival. Workers in records control have a very responsible job. They must see that all information is available when and where it is needed. By following the recommendations in the records control checklist, filers will be able to support their organization well. They will have the satisfaction of contributing a vital service.

Questions for Discussion

1. What two problems might you have to face on your first job? (1)

2. What should your first step be if you are assigned the responsibility of a poor filing system? (2)

3. What are three levels of activity in the filing system? What is the difference in activity of each of these levels? (3)

4. What equipment and supplies would be used with each of the three levels of activity described in No. 3? (3)

5. What is the *average* number of papers recommended to be held in file folders in each of the three levels of file activity described in No. 3? (3)

6. What is the measurement of the thickness of guides and folders? Why are these measurements important?   (4)

7. Would a 35-point pressboard guide be used in a semiactive file? (4)

8. Why are records management manuals prepared? (5)

9. What should a records management manual include? (5)

10. How can you avoid overcrowding files? (6)

11. Why is free space important in a filing system? How much space is recommended for every 26-inch file drawer? (7)

APPENDIX A
Computer Indexing Considerations

The alphabetic indexing rules in Chapters 2, 3, and 4 were developed to aid in both manual and computerized filing systems. Ease and consistency of use were primary considerations.

When planning for computer indexing, storage, and retrieval, many factors must be understood. Most computers (especially microcomputers) store each character (space, symbol, punctuation, number, letter) as a numeric code. This code is known as the American Standard Code for Information Interchange (ASCII). These code numbers are read by the computer character by character with the lowest number operated on first. Using the ASCII codes, the sequence begins with the space, then symbols, some punctuation marks, numerals, additional punctuation marks, capital letters, and lowercase letters in that order. Computers can be programmed to change this order of reading. A developer of commercial software (a program) for filing use determines the order in which the characters are to be read. The purchaser is told of this decision and chooses to buy the software based on this information. To change this program or to write one especially for the application could be costly. Many organizations accept the method designed into a purchased software program because of these cost considerations.

SOME POSSIBLE CHANGES

When using a computerized filing system, consider two assumptions: (1) names are to be entered into a computer according to the simplified indexing rules and (2) computers will process a name in the exact form it is entered. Some possible considerations when changing from manual indexing to computer indexing may include:

1. The computer may read, process, display, and print out names exactly as they are entered—spaces, symbols, punctuation, numbers, capital letters, and lowercase letters.
2. Computers consider words and numbers character by character instead of as complete indexing units (21 before 9).
3. If symbols are to be considered as spelled out, they must be entered into the computer in spelled-out form (& as *and*).
4. All punctuation must be disregarded when entering if names are to be considered in indexing order according to the indexing rules. Spaces, symbols, and punctuation are read and arranged by the computer before alphabetic characters.
5. Capital letters are considered before lowercase letters.
6. Hyphens are considered after spaces but before numerals or letters.
7. In computers, the field (space allotted to an entry) may be limited. Some nonessential words or units may have to be omitted in indexing.

COMPUTER LISTING OF EXAMPLES

To assist computer users in studying the indexing rules in Chapters 2, 3, and 4, the *examples* of each rule are given below in computer order if that order would differ from the listing in the chapters. In following the indexing rules when names are entered into a computer, some assumptions for each rule are indicated to clarify the order listed.

Rule 1: Order of Indexing Units

Assumptions: Names are entered in indexing order according to Rules 1A and 1B.

No changes in the order of examples.

Rule 2: Minor Words in Business Names

Assumptions: Symbols are spelled out when entered; when *The* is the first word, it is entered as the last unit. Example 2 follows 3 and example 5 follows 6 because lowercase *a* is considered after capitals *L* and *M*.

Examples of Rule 2

	Name	Key Unit	Unit 2	Unit 3	Unit 3
1.	The In Town Motel	In	Town	Motel	The
3.	The Inside Lounge	Inside	Lounge	The	
2.	Inside & Outside Painters	Inside	and	Outside	Painters
4.	Intown Auto Repair	Intown	Auto	Repair	
6.	The Matsumi Music Hall	Matsumi	Music	Hall	The
5.	Matsumi and Miranda Attorneys	Matsumi	and	Miranda	Attorneys
7.	Mechanics & Plumbers Shop	Mechanics	and	Plumbers	Shop
8.	Monica Torres Cosmetics	Monica	Torres	Cosmetics	
9.	Montana Bakeries	Montana	Bakeries		
10.	Montana $ Savers	Montana	Dollar	Savers	

Index Order of Units in Names

Rule 3: Punctuation and Possessives

Assumptions: Symbols are spelled out; apostrophes, hyphens, and other punctuation are omitted. Examples 1, 3, and 9 would be moved because of lowercase letters.

Examples of Rule 3

	Name	Key Unit	Unit 2	Unit 3	Unit 4
2.	Sarah A. Bank	Bank	Sarah	A	
1.	Bank of Atlanta	Bank	of	Atlanta	

Index Order of Units in Names

		Index Order of Units in Names		
Name	**Key Unit**	**Unit 2**	**Unit 3**	**Unit 4**
4. Arnold M. Banks	Banks	Arnold	M	
5. Bank's Dump Trucks	Banks	Dump	Trucks	
6. George R. Banks	Banks	George	R	
7. Bank's Portable Coaches	Banks	Portable	Coaches	
8. Banks' Window Washing	Banks	Window	Washing	
3. Banks & Georgi Foods	Banks	and	Georgi	Foods
10. Bank-Town Credit Association	BankTown	Credit	Association	
9. Banktown Apple Cider	Banktown	Apple	Cider	

Rule 4: Single Letters and Abbreviations

Assumptions: Personal names are entered under Rule 1A, and business names are entered as written with punctuation omitted and symbols spelled out. If the symbol (&) were used instead of *and*, example 3 would be moved ahead of 2.

No changes in the order of examples.

Rule 5: Titles

Assumptions: Both personal and business names are entered according to indexing rules, punctuation is not entered, and spaces are not substituted for punctuation.

No changes in the order of examples.

Rule 6: Married Women

Assumptions: Names are entered according to indexing rules, punctuation is not entered, and spaces are not substituted for punctuation.

No changes in the order of examples.

Rule 7: Articles and Particles

Assumptions: Names are entered according to indexing rules, punctuation (including apostrophes) is not entered, and spaces within prefixes are omitted. Capital letters being considered before lowercase letters changes order of examples 2, 8, 10, and 18.

Examples of Rule 7

		Index Order of Units in Names		
Name	**Key Unit**	**Unit 2**	**Unit 3**	**Unit 4**
2. Professor Maria D'Amico	DAmico	Maria	Professor	
1. Dr. August T. Damian	Damian	August	T	Dr
3. Damico Match Company	Damico	Match	Company	
4. Dana Maclean Art Supplies	Dana	Maclean	Art	Supplies
5. De La Camp Sports Wear	DeLaCamp	Sports	Wear	

Index Order of Units in Names

Name	Key Unit	Unit 2	Unit 3	Unit 4
6. Delano Meat Market	Delano	Meat	Market	
8. Brother Joseph E. Dell'Armi	DellArmi	Joseph	E	Brother
7. Miss Evelyn K. Della	Della	Evelyn	K	Miss
10. Rev. Loretta C. FitzGerald	FitzGerald	Loretta	C	Rev
9. Henry H. Fitzgerald	Fitzgerald	Henry	H	
11. LaSalle Interior Designers	LaSalle	Interior	Designers	
12. La Salle Mfg. Representatives	LaSalle	Mfg	Representatives	
13. Amanda D. Macks	Macks	Amanda	D	
14. Mack's Corner Market	Macks	Corner	Market	
15. Francis Q. Saint John	SaintJohn	Francis	Q	
16. San Francisco Cab Company	SanFrancisco	Cab	Company	
17. Gerald Q. Van Den Berg, Ph.D.	VanDenBerg	Gerald	Q	PhD
19. Vanden Berg Moving & Storage	VandenBerg	Moving	and	Storage
20. Van den Berg Office Supplies	VandenBerg	Office	Supplies	
18. Vandenberg Hospital Supplies	Vandenberg	Hospital	Supplies	

Rule 8: Identical Names

Assumptions: Names and addresses are entered according to indexing rules, and the computer is capable of considering street names before house numbers.

No changes in the order of examples. If the computer cannot read the street name before house numbers, examples 7 through 13 would be arranged in the order of 8, 12, 13, 9, 11, 7, and 10 because a computer would read the numbers digits by digit starting from the left.

Rule 9: Numbers in Business Names

Assumptions: Numbers and names are entered according to indexing rules; *th* is entered for clarity; numbers are considered digit by digit; hyphens are added for clarity; and capital letters are considered before lowercase letters. Examples 1, 2, 6, 7, 8, 9, and 13 would be moved.

Examples of Rule 9

Index Order of Units in Names

Name	Key Unit	Unit 2	Unit 3	Unit 4
9. The 18000 Apartments	18000	Apartments	The	
8. 1812 Records, Inc.	1812	Records	Inc	
3. 8 Dollar Motel	8	Dollar	Motel	
4. 8 Track Recording Co.	8	Track	Recording	Co
7. The 800 Daniels Shop	800	Daniels	Shop	The
6. 800-812 Daniels Court	800-812	Daniels	Court	
5. 8th Ward Headquarters	8th	Ward	Headquarters	
1. 8th & Indiana Exchange	8th	and	Indiana	Exchange
2. 8th and Western Garage	8th	and	Western	Garage

Index Order of Units in Names

Name	Key Unit	Unit 2	Unit 3	Unit 4
10. Eight Ball Restaurant	Eight	Ball	Restaurant	
11. The Eight Bells Room	Eight	Bells	Room	The
13. Eight-Thousand Club	Eight-Thousand	Club		
12. The Eighth Day, Inc.	Eighth	Day	Inc	The
14. Route 18 Motel	Route	18	Motel	
15. Route 21 Hotel	Route	21	Hotel	
16. Route By-Pass Diner	Route	By-Pass	Diner	

Rule 10: Organizations and Institutions

Assumptions: Names are entered according to indexing rules.
No changes in the order of examples.

Rule 11: Separated Single Words

Assumptions: Names are entered according to indexing rules.
No changes in the order of examples.

Rule 12: Hyphenated Names

Assumptions: Names are entered according to indexing rules, hyphens and apostrophes are not entered, and capital letters are considered before lower-case letters. Examples 2 and 12 would be moved. (If hyphens and apostrophes were entered, examples 2, 3, 10, and 12 would be moved.)

Examples of Rule 12

Index Order of Units in Names

Name	Key Unit	Unit 2	Unit 3	Unit 4
2. Anti-Cruelty Society	AntiCruelty	Society		
1. Dr. Rita F. Antic	Antic	Rita	F	Dr
3. Anti-Mite Termite Control	AntiMite	Termite	Control	
4. Antioch Insurance Agency	Antioch	Insurance	Agency	
5. Antonio's North-East Pizza	Antonios	NorthEast	Pizza	
6. Miss Mei-ling Niu	Niu	Meiling	Miss	
7. North Shore Boat Rentals	North	Shore	Boat	Rentals
8. North-East Tree Service	NorthEast	Tree	Service	
12. North-Shore Home Rentals	NorthShore	Home	Rentals	
9. Dr. Sandra Northey-West	NortheyWest	Sandra	Dr	
10. North's Service Station	Norths	Service	Station	
11. Northshore Grocery Store	Northshore	Grocery	Store	

Rule 13: Compound Names

Assumptions: Names are entered according to indexing rules, hyphens are not entered, and capital letters are considered before lowercase letters. Examples

10 and 12 would be moved. (If hyphens were entered, no additional changes would occur.)

Examples of Rule 13

	Name	Key Unit	Index Order of Units in Names		
			Unit 2	Unit 3	Unit 4
1.	Miss Mary Ann Mercado	Mercado	Mary	Ann	Miss
2.	Miss Maryann Mercado	Mercado	Maryann	Miss	
3.	Mid America Snow Blowers	Mid	America	Snow	Blowers
4.	Mid-America Computer Sales	MidAmerica	Computer	Sales	
5.	New Jersey Casualty Co.	New	Jersey	Casualty	Co
6.	Sandra Lee Newhouse	Newhouse	Sandra	Lee	
7.	Pan American Bus System	Pan	American	Bus	System
8.	Pan-American Life Ins. Co.	PanAmerican	Life	Ins	Co
10.	PanOhio Mortgage Co.	PanOhio	Mortgage	Co	
9.	Panel-Fab, Inc.	PanelFab	Inc		
12.	Barbara Saint John	SaintJohn	Barbara		
11.	Sainte Marie Park	SainteMarie	Park		
13.	San-Dee Chemical Products	SanDee	Chemical	Products	
14.	San Jose Luxury Apartments	SanJose	Luxury	Apartments	
15.	South Dakota Trucking Co.	South	Dakota	Trucking	Co

Rule 14: Government Names

Assumptions: Names are entered according to indexing rules, and the computer has a large enough field for long government names. If the field will not accommodate a lengthy name, it is recommended that as much of the name as possible be omitted while still entering a clear identification.

No changes in the order of examples. The following list provides illustrations of possible abbreviations of names for limited computer fields.

Examples of Rule 14

1. Alabama
   Commerce Dept
   Montgomery AL
2. Arkansas
   Public Welfare
   Little Rock AR
3. Canada
   State Secretary
   Hospitality and Conference
   State Protocol
   Ottawa ON
   CANADA
4. Hartford
   Public Works
   Hartford CT

5. Leon County
   Public Welfare
   Tallahassee FL
6. Tallahassee
   Safety Department
   Tallahassee FL
7. United States
   Agriculture
   Research Service
   Management Divisions
8. United States
   Commerce
   Patent Office
9. United States
   Food and Drug Admin
   Enforcement Bureau

APPENDIX B
Alternate Indexing Rules

The simplified indexing rules presented in Chapters 2, 3, and 4 may be modified occasionally by some organizations. The nature of the business or the uniqueness of the documents to be filed may make this advisable. In other cases, the volume of documents already stored may make a complete change to the new rules too costly and time-consuming to do immediately.

Whenever changes are made in the simplified rules, the changed rule must be stated clearly in writing and followed consistently by all filers.

Studies have shown that one or more of the following alternate rules have been adopted by some organizations. Many of these alternate rules are helpful for special applications. With each alternate rule given, the number(s) of the simplified rule(s) from Chapters 2, 3, or 4 is indicated in parentheses after each alternate rule.

1. A business name is filed as written unless it includes the full name of an individual. The full personal name in a business name is transposed. (1B,10)

2. The name of an association, a club, or a service organization is indexed according to the most descriptive unit in the name. For example, Fraternal Order of Eagles would be Eagles, Fraternal Order of; Miami Rotary Club would be Rotary Club, Miami. (1B,10)

3. Denominational names of religious institutions, if known, are used as the key indexing units followed by the name of the institution. Words such as *Church*, *Temple*, or *Cathedral* are not used as key indexing units even though they appear as the first words in the names of religious institutions. (1B,10)

4. The most distinctive word in the name of a college or university is used as the key indexing unit. If city names are not already part of the college or university name, they are added only if necessary to distinguish between institutions with identical names. (1B,10)

5. Locations are used as the key units in names of newspapers. If the location is not part of the name of the newspaper, it is written in as the key unit. (1B)

6. The names of hotels and motels are filed as written except that the words *Hotel* and *Motel* are never key units but are transposed to follow the other words in the name. (1B,10)

7. When an *apostrophe s* ('s) is added to a name, the *s* is not considered in indexing. When the ending is *s apostrophe* (s'), consider the *s* in indexing. (3)

8. Organization nicknames or acronyms are changed to the official organization name for indexing and filing. (4B)

9. Abbreviations used in company names are indexed as spelled out. (Sampson Co. would be indexed as Sampson Company even though Company actually appears on the letterhead as Co.) (4B)

10. Single letters in company names, including radio and television call letters, are each indexed as separate units even though they may be written together without spaces. (4B)

11. Family designations (seniority titles such as II, III, Jr., Sr.) are not considered filing units but only as aids to determine filing order when necessary. (5A)

12. All surnames which are pronounced *Mac*, such as M', Mac, or Mc, are filed as if they were spelled as spoken. For example, McArdle would be filed before Macbeth. (7)

13. When there are a significant number of names starting with a particular prefix, such as Mc or Van, the prefixes are filed as a separate letter group preceding the other names. For example, McArdle, McBeth, McGonigle would be filed ahead of other names beginning with M, such as Maas, Magonigle, and Mason. (7)

14. Numbers either at the beginning of or within a company name are considered as spelled out and filed in the appropriate alphabetic sequence. The entire number as spelled out is considered one unit. (9)

15. Compass terms in a name are considered as one unit regardless of whether they are written as one word, a hyphenated word, or separate words. For example, North East and Northeast are both one indexing unit. (11,13B)

16. The parts of a hyphenated surname of an individual are treated as separate indexing units. Hyphens are ignored. The last element of the hyphenated surname is the key unit, the first name or initial is the second indexing unit, and the first element of the hyphenated surname is the last indexing unit. For example, Mary Sutton-Jones would be indexed as Jones/Mary/Sutton. (12A)

17. When two or more initials, words, names, word substitutes, or coined words in a business name are joined by a hyphen, each part of the name is indexed as a separate unit and the hyphen is ignored. (12B)

18. Any word in a business name that may be written as one word is considered as one indexing unit, regardless of how the word is written. For example, Air Port, Airport, and Air-Port are all indexed as one unit even if they are hyphenated or separated by a space. (12B, 13B)

INDEX

A

Abbreviations, indexing, 22-23, 229
Accenting, color, 96
Accession book, 125, 126
Accu-Find, 103-104:
   color scheme, 103-104
   system design and guide arrangement, 103
Acronyms:
   cross-referencing, 22, 23
   defined, 22
   indexing, 22-23
Active files. *See* Active records
Active filing system, 217, 220-221
   See also Active records
Active records, 81-82:
   defined, 10
   See also Active filing system
Activity rates, files, 217-218
Address, 178
Address, filing identical names by, 28, 31-33
Albums, fan-styled, 7
Alphabetic, defined, 52
Alphabetic card filing systems, 12-16, 161-162:
   defined, 12
   organization of, 15-16
   uses of, 12-13
Alphabetic correspondence file, 52-65:
   defined, 52-53
   examination of, 53-59
   placing correspondence in file folders in, 65
   preparing correspondence for, 59-63
   sorting correspondence in, 64
   use of, 59-65
Alphabetic filing systems, 6:
   subject sections in, 118
   use of color in, 96-104
Alphabetic indexing, 3:
   personal and business names, 17-19
   process of, 17-18

rules, defined, 17
rules, need for, 17
rules, possible changes on computer, 17, 227-232
   specialized names, 37
   subjects as primary titles, 47
   See also Indexing rules
Alphabetizing, 18-19
Alphanumeric:
   coding, 59, 132-133
   defined, 59
Alpha-Z®, 98-100, 104:
   color scheme, 99-100
   system design and guide arrangement, 98-99
Alternate indexing rules, 233-234
American Standard Code for Information Interchange, 227
Aperture cards, 187-188
Arabic numerals, indexing, 33
ARMA. *See* Association of Records Managers and Administrators, Inc.
Arrangements in geographic files:
   dictionary, 144-145
   encyclopedia, 144, 145
Articles (foreign), indexing, 30-31, 229-230
ASCII code. *See* American Standard Code for Information Interchange
Association of Records Managers and Administrators, Inc. (ARMA), 5:
   rules adapted from, 17
Automated filing equipment, 164-166:
   advantages of, 165
   disadvantages of, 166
Automated shelves, 164-166
Auxiliary card guides. *See* Secondary card guides
Auxiliary file, 86
Auxiliary index, 182-183

B

Backup, 181
Back-up tapes, 178
Benefit/cost factor, 8-9
Binders:
   pocket, 7
   visible card file, 168
Bins, portable open, 164
Boxes, transfer, 89-90
Business names:
   compound, indexing, 41-42, 231-232
   hyphenated, indexing, 40-41, 231
   indexing units, order of, 20-21, 228
   minor words in, indexing, 21, 228
   numbers in, indexing, 33-34, 230
   single letters and abbreviations in, indexing,
     22-23, 229
   titles, indexing, 27-29, 229

C

Cabinets:
   data media, 4
   filing, 6
   lateral file, 199-201
   stationary, 164
   vertical file, 6, 7, 53, 197-198
   visible card file, 167-168
Caliper, 218
Cameras:
   planetary, 184, 185
   rotary, 184-185
Canceling, 73-74:
   defined, 68
Captions:
   defined, 14, 55
   on guide tabs, 55
CAR. *See* Computer-assisted retrieval.
Card files:
   posting, 160, 161, 163
   punched, 175-176
   reference, 160, 161, 162
   vertical, 160-167
   visible, 167-169
   wheel, 169-170, 171

Card record systems, 158-171:
   alphabetic, 12-13, 161-162
   factors affecting choice of system and
     equipment, 170-171
   punched card, 174-175
   subject, 162-163
   uses of, 159-160
   vertical, equipment for, 163-166
Cards:
   aperture, 187-188
   catalog. *See* Cards, record control
   characteristics of, 158-159
   cross-reference, 45
   index, characteristics of, 14
   index, organization of, 15
   index, typing, 23-24
   punched, 174-176
   record control, 90-91. *See also* Cards, record
     storage index and destruction control
   record storage index and destruction control,
     90-91. *See also* Cards, record control
   requisition, 68-69
   storage arrangements, 160
   transfer control. *See* Cards, record control
Careers, records control, 3, 5-6
Carrier folder, 73:
   advantages of, 73
   defined, 73
   method of charging, 73
Cartridges, optical data disk, 213
Cases, transfer, 89
Cassette tapes, 3
Catalog cards. *See* Record control cards
Centralized records department, 3:
   subject filing in, 110-111
Character, computer storage of, 227
Charge-out file, 92
Charging:
   defined, 68
   methods of, 69-73
Checklist, records control, 224-226
Codes:
   ASCII, 227
   numeric. *See* Numeric codes
Coding, 60, 115, 150:
   alphanumeric, 59, 132, 133
   color. *See* Color coding
   correspondence, 115
   decimal, 133